Inequality
In Classroom Learning

Edward P. Morgan

The Praeger Special Studies program—utilizing the most modern and efficient book production techniques and a selective worldwide distribution network—makes available to the academic, government, and business communities significant, timely research in U.S. and international economic, social, and political development.

Inequality
In Classroom Learning

Schooling and
Democratic Citizenship

PRAEGER SPECIAL STUDIES IN U.S. ECONOMIC, SOCIAL, AND POLITICAL ISSUES

Praeger Publishers   New York   London

Library of Congress Cataloging in Publication Data

Morgan, Edward P   1945-
    Inequality in classroom learning.

    (Praeger special studies in U.S. economic, social,
and political issues)
    Bibliography: p. 213
    Includes index.
    1. Educational equalization--United States.   I. Title.
LC213.2.M67   370.19   77-5577
ISBN 0-275-24510-1

PRAEGER PUBLISHERS
200 Park Avenue, New York, N.Y. 10017, U.S.A.

Published in the United States of America in 1977
by Praeger Publishers, Inc.

789   038   987654321

Printed in the United States of America

TO JOYCE

Much has been written and said about the failure of our educational institutions. It is quite possible that no other public institution has been subjected to as much criticism or scrutiny by so many people. During the 1960s, schools were seen as oppressive and discriminatory. Two distinct lines of criticism evolved from this era: one arguing that schooling is dehumanizing and impersonal and the other that schools violate their mandate to provide an equal educational opportunity for all. Common to both of these is the view that schools simply are not doing their job of educating the young.

For the most part, these two traditions have remained separate. Most systematic studies of schooling and most of the educational policy debate have focused on the issue of equal opportunity. Rarely has the consideration of educational policy drawn on systematic analysis of the socialization experience in schools. Although a richly detailed literature on "oppressive schooling" emerged from the 1960s, it generally lacked a systematic focus on measurable school traits. As a result, the policy debate has been largely colored by a dominant concern for equal opportunity, with unfortunate results for socialization experiences.

My own high school teaching experience gave me a concrete sense that much of the "libertarian" literature was sensitive to important learning concerns. While teaching in a school for emotionally disturbed adolescents, I gained insights into the socialization processes that enable individual students to function more effectively and independently in society. Simultaneously, I perceived a stark contrast between this learning environment (with its share of human faults) and the faceless, ineffectual educational institutions that were under attack in the late 1960s. Indirectly, my teaching experience spawned this study, as I set out to examine systematically the high school learning experience from a "political" perspective.

Since completing the original study, I have been more directly involved in the consideration of educational policy. In the process, I have found the traditional policy emphasis less than satisfactory, particularly as it relates to equal educational opportunity. In essence, policy makers have few guidelines for the evaluation of school programs and policies other than narrow, measurable "inputs" and "outcomes." My research and experience have led me to the view that educational evaluation ought to reflect broader, more inclusive concerns, including democratic political values. Most fundamentally, we need to examine the quality of the education that we seek to distribute equally. While far from definitive, this work considers the issue of "equal quality" in education, drawing on an empirical study of high school learning.

At the same time, this work supports those critics who argue that educational reform is systematically tied to social reform. In short, the quality of the classroom experience reflects, and perhaps contributes to, qualities of life in American society. The parallels are numerous. In this book, I approach systematic characteristics of public schooling from the bottom up, that is, I touch on social, political, and economic forces as these appear in the dynamic world of classroom learning.

With a degree of distance from these findings, I continue to be impressed by two noteworthy realizations: most of our young people find their schooling experience meaningful only as a social gathering place or a stepping-stone to later rewards, and most of the policy debate is carried on without regard for the socialization experience. In fact, preoccupation with equal opportunity concerns only promises to make schooling increasingly meaningless to its students. I do not feel we can afford to continue in this direction.

ACKNOWLEDGMENTS

A number of people have made invaluable contributions to my work, which culminates in this book. Three of my graduate readers at Brandeis University gave invaluable assistance during my dissertation study: George A. Kelly provided support and insightful comments throughout the project and Bruce I. Oppenheimer was especially helpful on methodological issues. I am particularly indebted to Martin A. Levin, whose careful reading of the manuscript and comments were extremely useful in the revision process and who duplicated this earlier effort with this manuscript. I am also grateful to Jerome T. Murphy for his comments on the completed dissertation. Finally, I owe a special word of thanks to Stephanie Marchak who typed most of the manuscript.

Additionally, this study would not have been possible without the willing participation and interest of the teachers, students, and school personnel at each of the three high schools studied. Although they must remain nameless, I thank them all. As noted, much of my original interest in this topic and many of the insights I have gained into the learning process stem from a gratifying four years of teaching at the Arlington School in Belmont, Massachusetts. The interest and financial support of the James Gordon Fellowship Program was instrumental in the completion of my graduate project.

On a more personal note, I am indebted to my parents, my family, and many friends for their interest, support, and tolerance at numerous times during the past several years. This is particularly true of my wife, Joyce. Throughout the project, she has shared highs and lows, typed portions of the manuscript, and has offered advice and encouragement when they were needed most. With appreciation, I dedicate this book to her.

CONTENTS

LIST OF TABLES AND FIGURES

INTRODUCTION: BEYOND EQUAL OPPORTUNITY

In a democratic society, such as ours purports to be, the functions of public education include at least two that are shaped by the principle of equality. In the first place, public schooling is assigned the task of socializing the young in ways appropriate to their conduct as democratic citizens. Knowledge of the political process and internalization of democratic values are part of this task. The principle of equality requires that democratic citizenship must be open to all; hence, education is universal and compulsory. No one is to be excluded from this socialization process or from access to adult citizenship.

Second, public education is assigned the function of providing all citizens with an opportunity to realize individual potential. From the social perspective, this function aims at a "fair" distribution of economic rewards, social standing, and political influence based on merit rather than such irrelevant criteria as skin color or inherited wealth. This function also applies universally. No one is to be excluded from the opportunities embedded in public education.

In many ways, however, we fall far short of both objectives. In terms of democratic citizenship, we are troubled by widespread political apathy and social alienation. Furthermore, existing political participation is dominated by a relatively small portion of the population, particularly those of high socioeconomic status.[1] Access to political influence is far from equally distributed. Despite the claims of critics, however, the role of public schooling in contributing to these conditions remains unclear.

Similarly, we hear of the failure of schools to provide all the young with an equal educational opportunity. Identifiable segments of society, particularly racial minorities and lower socioeconomic groups, have been discriminated against by the very educational system that is supposed to enhance their future chances. The agents and the extent of this discrimination have been the subject of considerable controversy. Yet the weight of available evidence suggests that schools fall far short of providing all with an equal educational opportunity. Even if some may gain through their schooling experience, there is precious little evidence of effectiveness in the schools' overall contribution to social and occupational mobility among society's have-nots. [2] We need only consider such policies as compensatory education, desegregation, community control of schools, and school finance reform to see how much agitation there has been to equalize educational opportunity and how little overall has been accomplished.

For ethical as well as political and economic reasons, the equal opportunity function of schools has dominated the public forum far more than the function of citizenship socialization. For the most part, the two topics have been considered separately. This work, however, takes a different approach; the two concerns can be perceived as critically interdependent.

Essentially, what follows is an empirical examination of forces in the learning process that are relevant to the concern of democratic citizenship. This empirical study of everyday life in the schools results in a critical view of the learning experience: schooling is fundamentally antidemocratic, yet it is unequally so. Some identifiable groups of students encounter learning environments that are significantly more democratic than those encountered by other groups.

These empirical findings, described in detail in subsequent chapters, lead to an analytic critique of the prevalent equal opportunity focus of educational policy. In the first place, it is argued that the pursuit of equal opportunity in society through the institution of public schooling reinforces pervasive antidemocratic traits of school learning. On the other hand, the systematic inequality in democratic socialization results in behavioral lessons that undermine our efforts to equalize educational opportunities. Put somewhat crudely, the failure to provide all students with even modestly democratic learning environments dooms efforts to achieve equal opportunity, while the effort to maximize equal opportunity dooms the chances for universal democratic learning.

Where does this view lead us? First, we need to clarify what we mean by equality. It is important to distinguish between a "democratic" concept of equal opportunity in education and the instrumental function of schools in supporting a "fair" socioeconomic hierarchy. The former describes an intrinsic function of schooling—maximizing learning and the development of individual abilities. The latter describes an extrinsic, instrumental function of schools—maximizing chances for subsequent occupational, social, and economic success.

In the process of pursuing the latter function, schools become an instrument of distributive justice in society. Simultaneously, they perform the function of social selection according to legitimate criteria that reflect society's needs.

Second, it will be argued that it is necessary to move beyond the instrumental concept of equal opportunity through schooling because of its built-in antidemocratic traits. As outlined in Chapter 6, we need to take a long, hard look at instrumental functions of public schooling, as well as the dysfunctions of income and status inequality in society.

Finally, we must move beyond a simplistic "input-outcome" view of equality in education to one that takes into account the socialization process. In short, we must examine the dynamics of the learning process itself. In order to pursue these objectives, we must develop democratically legitimate criteria for evaluating the quality of the learning experience as well as its noncognitive effects. And we must use these criteria to distinguish ways in which schooling is intrinsically unequal.

Such is the basic objective of this work. Starting from a democratic framework for evaluating the quality of the learning experience, an effort will be made to clarify the link between the antidemocratic traits of schooling and the instrumental function of social selection. Also to be demonstrated are ways in which the "democraticness" of learning, to the extent that it exists, is unevenly distributed among groups of students. This book concludes by analyzing the relationship between democratic learning and the broader context of educational and social reform. Before turning to this analysis, however, it is essential that we consider in greater depth the theoretical interdependence of the equal opportunity and democratic citizenship functions.

THE STUDY OF EQUAL OPPORTUNITY

For the most part, studies of equal educational opportunity have concentrated on the cognitive outcomes of school learning. Works like the massive Coleman Report,[3] which set the tone for most subsequent research, tried to uncover factors in the schooling experience that were significantly related to educational achievement. Essentially, the Coleman Report failed to discover any basic inequality in school resources that contributed significantly to student achievement. As a consequence, between-school inequality in school resources seemed less critical after publication of the findings. At the same time, public concern for equal opportunity became dominated by the input-outcome model of school effectiveness.

Critics of the Coleman Report have taken a number of tacks. [4] One line of criticism has been that the Coleman Report failed to measure and include intuitively obvious determinants of educational achievement, for example, dynamic characteristics of teaching "quality." Another line of criticism has argued that, for methodological reasons, the Coleman findings are unreliable. According to both critiques, significant inequalities exist in learning resources, and these have a bearing on how well students do in school.

The demonstration of this impact on learning, however, has proven difficult. As a result, some researchers have examined the underlying assumptions of the equal opportunity concern, namely, the overall effectiveness of schooling as a redistributive factor in the path to social and occupational mobility. The reassessment of family and school effects by Christopher Jencks and associates[5] extended the range of variables studied by Coleman to include occupational status and income inequality in adult society. The authors arrived at the startling and controversial conclusion that differences in school quality have little effect on test scores, educational attainment, occupational status, or income level.

Although the validity of the Jencks findings has not gone unchallenged,[6] the authors go on to argue that the traditional instrumental view of schooling should be revised. Speaking of the "factory" metaphor for schooling, Jencks writes: "Our research has convinced us that this is the wrong way to think about schools. The long-term effects of schooling seem much less significant to us than they did when we began our work, and the internal life of the schools seems correspondingly more important."[7]

The much-discussed message of Jencks's findings is that schools "don't make a difference" in subsequent adult standing. However, the authors qualify this conclusion on two accounts. In the first place, they are only speaking of a redistributive difference, not an additive difference, in the lives of students. They do not say that schools have no effect on the young or that students fail to learn anything worthwhile (or harmful) in schools. On the other hand, they are not able to say what schools do to young people. Evaluation of the quality of school learning clearly lies beyond the scope of their report.

In the second place, however, Jencks and associates suggest that precisely this kind of evaluation is needed. Specifically, they argue:

> The evidence reviewed in Chapters 6 and 7 suggests that noncognitive traits may play a larger role than cognitive skills in determining economic success or failure. The evidence of our senses tells us that noncognitive traits

also contribute far more than cognitive skills to the quality of human life and the extent of human happiness. We
therefore believe that the noncognitive effects of schooling
are likely to be more important than the cognitive effects.
But <u>we do not know what these noncognitive effects are</u>
<u>likely to be.</u> [8] (emphasis added)

One of the more compelling efforts to discern the noncognitive
effects of schools, <u>Schooling in Capitalist America</u>, [9] demonstrates
parallels between the personality traits rewarded by school grades
and those involved in hiring and promotion in the job market. Although
not an examination of the internal life of the school, this work suggests ways in which the schooling process has different noncognitive
effects on different groups of students.

Despite its strengths, the literature on equal educational opportunity is limited by the prevalent input-outcome approach to schooling.
For the most part, studies of school effectiveness focus on statistical
relationships between independent variables, such as test scores,
grade average, and years of schooling, and such dependent variables
as occupational status or income level. Studies of inequality in schooling focus on such inputs as student background, IQ, and measurable
school resources and on such outcomes as educational achievement
or attainment. By and large, they fail to study the dynamics of the
schooling process itself, leaving this instead to educational and social psychologists and the school critics. The literature concerned
with equal educational opportunity largely fails to get inside the schools
to examine diverse learning experiences and their variable impact
on students.

As a result, it is hardly surprising that this literature offers
no method of determining and evaluating the quality of learning experiences, other than by their cognitive outcomes or long-term redistributive effects (with at best limited success). This study takes
a different approach. Most fundamentally, it involves an effort to
examine the dynamics of the learning process to distinguish the noncognitive effects of the learning experience, and to evaluate both of
these in light of democratic principles. Its findings reveal patterns
of learning built into the schooling process that are contrary to the
norms of democratic citizenship and that undermine efforts to equalize educational opportunity.

This dynamic focus also results in a finding that is essentially
overlooked by input-outcome research—that a critical (perhaps the
most fundamental) inequality in the learning experience occurs within
rather than between schools. Regardless of which school they attend,
students in the higher or accelerated track levels encounter far more
democratic learning environments than their lower track counterparts

in the same school. At the very least, then, the schooling process
reinforces unequal behavioral lessons of consequence for social and
political participation among the adult citizenry. In addition, although
the empirical support is not definitive, one can say that the schooling
process "teaches" unequal behavioral lessons. This study not only
suggests that unequal lessons result from tracking; it also points to
learning dynamics that foster these lessons.

Finally, lessons associated with tracking are significant because they reflect the instrumental functions of schooling. Because
schools are functionally tied to employment opportunities, they must
sort students into categories of ability and behavior appropriate to
various types of employment demands. Because of the unequal lessons that result from this institutional separation of learning types,
one can argue that tracking, however legitimate or fair, closes as
many doors as public schooling purportedly opens.

This argument requires empirical amplification. For the present, it is argued that we need to move beyond a purely instrumental
view of schooling—even if our sole objective is equal opportunity. By
implication, we need to move beyond the traditional, instrumental
view of equal opportunity to construct a broader definition of equality
in education.

BEYOND EQUAL OPPORTUNITY

As noted, the principle of equal opportunity is a fundamental
precept of democratic ideology for two basic reasons: it stresses the
universal value of personal self-fulfillment and it provides a legitimate criterion for evaluating distributive justice in society. Differences in outcome—regardless of whether these are educational, political, social, or economic—are justifiable if the individuals involved
have full and free opportunity to prove their merit or to air their
claims.

Despite its obvious validity, one must question the equal opportunity principle as a guide to policy if and when it results in conditions
that are unjust or inhumane or that are socially dysfunctional. The
evidence gathered in this work suggests that precisely these conditions
prevail in the schools, due, at least in part, to the instrumental pursuit of equal opportunity through schooling.

Before considering the empirical evidence, it might be helpful
to clarify this argument by defining three flaws in our preoccupation
with equal opportunity as a standard for determining educational quality: theoretical flaws inherent in the principle of equal opportunity,
undemocratic outcomes of the institutionalization of equal opportunity,
and the cruel irony that affects the losers in the schooling race—that

they suffer the ill-effects of the equal opportunity incentive without
reaping its rewards.

Some Theoretical Considerations

The most fundamental criticism that can be made of equal opportunity as a political principle is that it contains the germ of its
own failure. A society in which public relationships are totally defined by the principle of equal opportunity is a society that constricts
the full development of individual personality in three vital ways:
equal opportunity reinforces the status quo in society by suppressing
imaginative challenges to social structures, it rigidifies an existing
class hierarchy in society, and it rewards antihumanitarian (or anticommunitarian) personality traits. All of these characteristics are
inextricably tied to the educational system and all can be discerned
in the schooling process.

Although equal opportunity is usually the rallying cry of progressive forces in society, it is a principle that is ultimately conservative. As a prescription for distributive justice, equal opportunity
draws its legitimacy from the liberal impulse to free individuals from
disabling social origins so that all may gain full membership in society. Violations of equal opportunity, or arbitrary obstacles to human advancement, seem to us inherently unfair. Over the years,
such criteria as birth, wealth, religion, race, and sex have come to
be seen as largely irrelevant criteria for social decisions made in
the public sphere.

A society based on equal opportunity is open to advancement
based on merit and motivation—presumably relevant individual characteristics. To use Michael Young's phrase, such a society is a
"meritocracy" (where "merit rules"). [10] In a meritocracy, the
achievement of elite status is comparable to a prize won in open contest by those who have earned it fairly—what Ralph Turner has called
"contest mobility." [11] A meritocracy is the antithesis of a closed society where existing elites select new recruits and grant elite status
to the "chosen"—a system of "sponsored mobility."

Historically, the movement of equal opportunity has been largely
progressive, opening doors in society to more groups of people. At
the same time, however, that movement has a constricting impact
on society. Because equal opportunity prescribes the manner in which
people should rise to social and occupational positions, it leaves the
ends or outcomes of those procedures unquestioned. More specifically,
as John Schaar has observed, the effort to equalize opportunity is an
effort to give everyone a chance within the existing order of "dominant
values, institutions, and goals." [12] In Turner's "contest mobility,"

the contestants are far more likely to assess and improve their
chances to win the contest than they are to question and evaluate the
ends of the contest.

So pervasive is this tendency that the bulk of social criticism
and political activity in such a society is concerned with who wins
rather than what is won. Most reform efforts, as can be seen in the
equal opportunity literature, aim to make the system work more effectively and equitably, not to evaluate and redirect systemic goals.
Emphasis on equal opportunity, in short, tends to draw attention
away from the objectives and side effects of the pursuit.

This conservative quality has a number of highly significant
implications. Most fundamentally, it assumes as inevitable the existing hierarchical structure in which everyone finds or is allocated a
notch. For every selection of a winner, there must be a loser. Although one cannot foresee an end to hierarchy in an imperfect world,
the acceptability of equal opportunity would seem to depend on whether
or not the existing hierarchy was just and functional. This study of
schooling suggests one way in which this is not the case.

A second major drawback of the equal opportunity principle is
that it tends to rigidify class differences. By widening the gaps among
class groups in society, equal opportunity contradicts its own norms
of morality and openness. This tendency is brilliantly portrayed in
Young's vision of the perfected meritocracy:[13] as society perfects
the mechanisms of equal opportunity, it achieves a "golden age of
equality," in which "all the advantages for the deserving" becomes
the guiding norm. Such a society remains hierarchical, and the hierarchy becomes more rigid. Those in the upper classes know that they
"deserve" their social standing; they know they are "better." Those
in the lower classes are resigned to their inferior position. They
know they deserve their low standing because they know they have had
a fair chance, a true test of their abilities. As interclass contact and
interclass marriage decline, intelligence becomes more and more
closely associated with social status. Interclass contacts gradually
approach a master-servant relationship.

It is not hard to see how such a society develops. The norm of
contest mobility requires that decisions affecting individuals' futures
be deferred as much as possible so as not to preclude late bloomers.
Ideally, there is no final success, but only relative successes. Turner
observes that contest mobility embodies a "fear of premature judgments" about people that may give to some a "special advantage."[14]
Because of the uncertainty of final attainment of success, the drive
to succeed and its consequences never subside.

In any society, the full pursuit of open contest mobility threatens
to become socially inefficient. At some point, for the sake of stability

and predictability, decisions affecting people's futures have to be made. Because of the contest ethic, society bases these decisions on predictions of human potential. In Young's meritocracy, society is able to predict with astounding accuracy the future potential and intelligence of tiny infants, even prenatal organisms. Because these testing mechanisms have been perfected, society can legitimately fit each infant with the "appropriate" kind of training and upbringing. The result, comparable to the system of tracking, contradicts the principles of openness and mobility. It is the antithesis of democratic universalism, which reflects, in Schaar's words: ". . . a way of thinking about the relations among men which stresses equality of being and which strives incessantly toward the widest possible sharing of responsibility and participation in the common life."[15]

A third by-product of equal opportunity is that it fosters and rewards essentially anticommunitarian personality and behavioral traits. The quest for the prize of elite status emphasizes a competitive ethic, as opposed to the norm of social cooperation. As Turner observes, contest mobility rewards the personality traits of the "deserving sportsman—namely, enterprise, initiative, perseverance, and craft."[16] All of these traits, however valuable, are colored by a quality of privatism, of "being in it for one's self," which undermines the value and denies the need for social interdependence.

Taken together, these three flaws inherent in the equal opportunity principle reinforce existing social and political control in a way that threatens to engulf the individual personality. Deviance is discouraged and conformity encouraged by the drive to win the race. Rigidity in the existing structure is fostered by the need to predict and separate future winners. Finally, participation in the social and political life in common is further undermined by the privatistic pursuit of self-interest. These qualities seem to be precisely the traits Alexis de Tocqueville had in mind in the 1830s when he expressed apprehension about the future of democracy in America. He envisioned:

> . . . an innumerable multitude of men, all equal and alike, incessantly endeavoring to procure the petty and paltry pleasures with which they glut their lives. Each of them, living apart, is as a stranger to the fate of all the rest. . . .
> Above this race of men stands an immense and tutelary power, which . . . seeks . . . to keep them in perpetual childhood. . . . For their happiness such a government willingness labors, but it chooses to be the sole agent and the only arbiter of that happiness. . . .
> The will of man is not shattered, but softened, bent, and guided; men are seldom forced by it to act, but they

are constantly restrained from acting. Such a power does
not tyrannize, but it compresses, enervates, extinguishes,
and stupefies a people, till each nation is reduced to nothing better than a flock of timid and industrious animals, of
which the government is the shepherd. [17]

Such a picture hardly conforms to our norms of democratic citizenship. It does, however, suggest characteristics of public schooling that derive ultimately from the instrumental pursuit of equal opportunity. These emerge in outline form as the principle of equal
opportunity in an institutional setting is considered.

The Institutional Impact

Nowhere are the destructive implications of equal opportunity
pursuits more visible than in the schooling process, particularly
when one scrutinizes this process from the perspective of democratic
citizenship. While empirical evidence of these antidemocratic implications will be examined in Chapter 2, ways in which the institution
of public schooling is shaped by the equal opportunity principle are
considered briefly here.

A society that emphasizes the social value of equal opportunity,
as ours does, looks to its system of public schooling as the central
institution responsible for freeing individuals from the accidents of
birth and wealth. In short, the schools are assigned the combined
tasks of teaching and testing the young. Built into these tasks are
both intrinsic, or purely educational, functions and those that are
extrinsic, or socially instrumental. Testing, for example, can be a
means of discerning specific educational needs of students in order
to teach them more effectively. At the same time, however, schools
are testing grounds on which individuals can further their future social and occupational standing. In their school performance record,
students see if they measure up to society's standards.

This instrumental function, like the principle of equal opportunity, has negative implications. As Turner has observed, "Under
contest mobility . . . , education is valued as a means of getting
ahead, but the contents of education are not highly valued in their own
right."[18] One might argue that the extrinsic instrumental functions
of schools are ultimately antieducational. As R. S. Peters has written of the English school examinations:

They act as tests of attainment and as incentives. But if
their main function is a selective one, then the teacher
may find himself caught in the logic of a situation where

he has to use his expertise in order to get children through
them rather than in the cause of education. A constant
complaint of secondary school teachers is that the examination system prevents them from doing what they regard
as educationally desirable. They have become agents of
a bureaucracy. Their task has become an instrumental
one. [19]

More relevant for our purposes here are the effects of these
functions on the equality of the schooling process and their implications for democratic citizenship. As noted in the previous section,
the pursuit of equal opportunity results in a kind of control that is
antidemocratic in three ways. Individual initiative and autonomy are
subverted by the pressure to conform in order to succeed. Active
social participation is undermined by the need to measure up to external standards while pursuing one's self-interest. Finally, mobility and open interaction are denied by the separation and specialized
training of different learning potential groups. As will be described
more fully in Chapter 2, each of these traits subverts a norm of democratic citizenship, and each can be perceived in the schooling process.

How do these characteristics reflect the instrumental pursuit
of equal opportunity in schooling? To start with, a school system
that is used as the testing ground for future citizens must be standardized if the principle of equal opportunity is to be served. If everyone is to get a fair chance, and if winners are to emerge, everyone
must be treated the same. Standardized, bureaucratic education
treats students as a mass, and separates learning into specialized
compartments and fixed, short time spans. Individual interests and
the varying pace of learning are submerged in an effort to construct
measurable, standardized lessons. In many ways, the institutionalization of equal opportunity translates the principle of equality into
one of identity or uniformity.

As will be described in Chapter 2, the school's function as a
testing ground compels students to learn by drawing on extrinsic motivations and externally imposed controls. Most pervasively, students
are compelled by the instrumental function of social selection—of getting ahead by doing well in school. A student is controlled not by the
intrinsic merits of the learning process, but by its outcome and the
instrumental importance of his or her performance. Where these incentives fail to engage the student, control takes on a more overt,
authoritarian nature, as can be seen in many inner-city schools.

These structural forces are encountered daily in the classroom.
Because of the instrumental functions of schooling, and the bureaucratic structure of schools, the classroom learning process is largely

established before the student encounters it. Learning topics and procedures are essentially determined by forces over which the student
has no control; in fact, teachers have remarkably little control over
these forces. As a consequence, classroom learning is fundamentally
shaped by forces that have little to do with learning, per se. Most
classroom activity is essentially passive rather than inquisitive—a
function of seeking and giving the "right" answers to the teacher or
to the book's questions. Work is both uniform and competitive; all
students spend most of their class time doing the same thing at the
same time, and doing it by and for themselves. As a result, the
teacher's primary task is not to develop and broaden the student's
interests or meet individual needs, but to interest the student in a
predetermined curriculum.

One can see in this learning structure two of the theoretical
equal opportunity by-products considered above. On the one hand,
students are compelled to suppress individual interests in order to
succeed in school; at the same time, they are engaged in a process
that rewards the pursuit of self-interest.

Finally, in a roundabout manner, the institutional pursuit of
equal opportunity results in the rigidification of class differences or
gaps between student groups. Schools simultaneously serve students'
future interests through the equal opportunity function and society's
interest through the social selection function. As a testing ground for
student performance, schools theoretically provide society with a reliable estimate of students' future performance. In a meritocracy,
schools are pressed by the ethical force of equal opportunity at the
same time that they must efficiently select and train the young according to observable potential.

Consequently, schools track children in ability groups almost
from the day they begin school. Slow learners are separated from
fast learners so that schools can better serve the learning needs of
all students. Simultaneously, this separation serves society's needs.
In the process, "types" of students become separated into increasingly
homogeneous groups, each experiencing a distinct type of learning
environment. By the time they reach high school age, students are
overtly assigned to specific tracks and these are highly associated
with students' social class origins. As described in Chapter 3, the
most significant variation in learning experiences corresponds to a
student's track assignment, not to the particular school he or she
happens to attend.

As a testing ground, then, schools rigidify interclass differences by separating class-related groups of learners. Furthermore,
the ensuing experiences teach different students different lessons that
have significant implications for future social and political behavior.

To generalize, one can say that students at the top—those destined to
be the winners in the educational world and beyond—learn a lesson of
independent acquiescence. They are likely to become the social and
political activists in society. Students in the middle learn a lesson of
dependent acquiescence. They are likely to become the hardworking
but relatively compliant middle level of society. Finally, students at
the bottom—the losers in the schooling context—learn the lesson of
alienated freedom. They will become society's losers, alienated
from involvement in public institutions but consequently "freed" to
be self-expressive.

    These lessons are described in greater depth in Chapter 4. For
the present, they are significant because they illustrate the final by-
product of equal opportunity as it is implemented in the institution of
public schooling. It is possible to see tracking as an institutional effort to organize learning experiences to fit the needs of identifiable
student types. No matter how "fairly" this selection takes place, however, it has the effect of closing more doors than it opens. Just as
Young's efficient meritocracy results in a more rigid class structure,
the system of tracking, and the functions it serves, isolates learners
into superior and inferior castes and provides educational experiences
that help to ensure that they will stay in these groups.

The Cruel Paradox of Equal Opportunity

    The lessons described above are derived from clearly identifi-
able patterns in the schooling experience that emerge from the empirical analysis undertaken in this work. It must be added, however,
that the existence of patterns does not entail a perfectly closed picture
of schooling. As will be discussed below, individual teachers have
an independent impact on the learning environments of their particular
classes regardless of track level. These teaching variations, described in Chapter 5, have significant implications for policy considerations. At the same time, however, the track-related patterns are
particularly sobering because they would exist in systems that had
perfected equal opportunity. And yet this is far from the case. What
results, whether intended or not, is a kind of deception whereby those
who need the schooling outcome most are most likely to be alienated
by the schooling experience. Let us examine this paradox.

    Ultimately, the perfection of equal opportunity, if it were pos-
sible, might well result in a redistribution of individuals among the
levels of schooling. However, it would leave intact the structure of
schooling itself. If one considers the variable lessons of tracking and
the overall lessons of schooling to be both humane and functional, they

can perhaps be justified. Given the kinds of antidemocratic implications of these lessons, however, the schooling structure and the functions it performs are vulnerable to criticism.

In fact, one can argue that the perfection of such a system would
only make the controlling structure more controlling and more rigid.
If schools truly selected according to some pure measure of merit,
there would be far less reason for losers to criticize them. Because
they would be performing their tasks legitimately, the tasks and their
behavioral by-products would be less susceptible to attack. The antidemocratic control of schooling would be reinforced, yet would appear
to be more democratic because it was more accepted. If anything,
students' lives would be more controlled by extrinsic forces.

If Jencks and others are right, however, we are far from such
a perfect world. Schools have not mastered the function of equalizing
opportunity; many are still disadvantaged in the race for educational
and occupational success. Yet school learning is shaped in antidemocratic ways by the instrumental functions as if equal opportunity were
available through schooling. The belief that school success is crucial
to subsequent occupational and economic success was widespread
among the students surveyed in this study, yet it was most pronounced
among students in the inner city and from lower socioeconomic backgrounds. In one sense, these students are right because without
school success they stand little chance of making it. Yet the bulk of
research to date suggests that, as a group, these students have little
reason to expect increased opportunities from their schooling experience. Still, they see this function as being performed, and they tend
to see the all-important grading function as one that is exercised
fairly.

In other words, to the extent that unequal opportunity exists,
students' lives are shaped not by the function of equal opportunity but
by the myth of equal opportunity. For those who internalize the functions of schooling in order to succeed, this would seem to be a cruel
hoax, for in the process, they are learning lessons that undermine
their full membership in a democratic society.

Ultimately, then, the schooling process would seem to be one
that controls students in antidemocratic ways without fulfilling effectively the legitimate function (equal opportunity) that requires that
control. This peculiar combination of forces has led some to see the
schooling process as the instrument of control used by those in power
to sustain their controlling position in society. Thus, for example,
Bowles and Gintis see in public schooling:

   . . . eloquent testimony to the ability of the well-to-do to
   perpetuate in the name of equality of opportunity an ar-
   rangement which consistently yields to themselves dispro-

portional advantages, while thwarting the aspirations and
needs of the working people of the United States.[20]

Regardless of who benefits or whether any conscious effort is
involved, the schooling process does seem to combine two antidemocratic traits. On the one hand, it seems to teach unequal lessons and
to close off opportunities at the same time that it purportedly creates
these. In this sense, it sustains a system of social mobility by as-
cription, hidden in the guise of merit and achievement. On the other
hand, it fulfills those characteristics of equal opportunity that suppress or undermine qualities of the human personality fundamental
to democratic citizenship. Schooling is both equal opportunity denied
and equal opportunity fulfilled. However, one can argue that the positive traits are largely denied, while the negative traits are fulfilled.

WHAT TO DO?

Clearly, the arguments against equal opportunity raise disturb-
ing questions for those concerned with educational policy. Before
turning to a discussion of policy implications in Chapter 6, it is necessary to consider the evidence against the instrumental equal opportunity function of public schools. Chapter 2 begins this process.

For the present, however, it would seem to be imperative that
we not leave our discussion of equal opportunity in its unhappy condition. Thus far, questions have been posed about the functions of
schooling in such a way that we are left in an either-or quandary. Do
we try to perfect institutional equal opportunity in the schools despite
the foreboding consequences for developing individual personality and
a participatory citizenry? Or do we accept the existence of schooling
handicaps and strive instead for a more humanistic, democratic
schooling process?

These questions seem more appropriate for a world of philoso-
sopher-kings than of educational policy makers. Later in this work
the feasibility of democratic schooling will be examined. For now,
however, we can consider the strengths and limitations of each type
of objective by examining two ultimately contradictory types of educational reform: the maximization of equal opportunity and the liberation of school learning. Given the imperfect world we live in, it is
unlikely that either objective can be fully and perfectly implemented.
However, it would seem imperative that decisions affecting educational policy be made with a full realization of their implications for
other democratic objectives.

Maximizing Opportunity Versus
Liberating the Schools

As the previous section suggests, we must question the total pursuit of equal opportunity through schooling. The pitfalls of this policy objective become even more distinct when we consider the full social implications. Nowhere do the authoritarian implications of equal opportunity become more apparent than in attempts to enhance equality by penetrating the earliest preschool years of childhood with programs designed to train "deprived" children in behavior that is conducive to school success. Actual practices in such preschool programs vary widely. [21] Some stress rigid drill learning in basic skills, while others follow behavior modification approaches; some use machines to individualize instruction, while some stress whole-child approaches to elicit the child's interest in learning.

Insofar as the objective of these programs is purely instrumental—training children to have reflex attitudes and behavior patterns that will enhance their progress along the schooling path to success—it is perfectly legitimate for the uniform hand of schooling to reach earlier and earlier into a child's life. The object is to mold, or mainstream, the child—to teach the child to accept and adopt conforming patterns of behavior—before the child can be disadvantaged by its deviant background or individual personality. The authoritarian, even totaliterian, implications of this effort are clear. As Peters has observed: "The obvious fact is that, descriptively speaking, there is no equality of opportunity and never can be unless equalitarians are prepared to control early upbringing, size of families, and breeding." [22]

Even with an emphasis on more democratic or humane methods, efforts to equalize opportunity through schooling use existing school procedures as the standard for acceptable behavior. The total pursuit of this objective only exposes its constricting, controlling traits. This is not to argue that there is no room, or even a need, for such preschool programs or for society's intervention in the preschool, even prenatal, world of children. Obviously there is a legitimate reason for safeguarding standards of health and nutrition at the earliest stages of life. There is also a social need for an element of socialization in common that applies universally to all the young. The issue remains, however: Are these objectives to be pursued in ways that frequently undermine the development of the individual personality or the interpersonal capacity for social participation?

Authoritarian characteristics of schooling have led to a libertarian critique of schools and an effort to liberate children from oppressive controls. [23] These libertarian critics cite the need for humanizing the schools, for enhancing personal creativity and meaningful individualized learning, and for removing the deadening hand of

centralized, bureaucratic authority. The effort to mold young children
to fit the schooling mainstream is anathema to these critics.

The libertarian movement has stimulated a variety of reforms
ranging from humanistic teaching techniques or materials, to open
classrooms, to alternative or "free schools. "[24] The libertarian approach to educational reform finds its ultimate expression in the call
to "deschool society." Its most provocative spokesman, Ivan Illich,
has argued that:

> . . . the inverse of schooling is possible; that we can de-
> pend on self-motivated learning instead of employing teach-
> ers to bribe or compel the student to find the time and the
> will to learn; that we can provide the learner with new
> links to the world instead of continuing to funnel all edu-
> cational programs through the teacher. [25]

In an effort to break away from the bureaucratic paternal authority
of schools, the libertarian argument implies, and in some cases ad-
vocates, the abolition of all external control in the educational setting.
Education consequently would become voluntary; it would grow freely
out of the interests and felt needs of each individual learner.

It has been argued that the equal opportunity impulse for reform is misdirected when it focuses exclusively on input-outcome
measures and ignores socialization patterns. One can also argue that
the libertarian impulse is frequently misdirected. Too often libertarianism strives to free the learner by getting rid of the teacher. Yet,
as data in Chapter 5 clearly demonstrate, the laissez-faire, or non-,
teacher is likely to have a negative impact on student involvement in
purposeful learning, while positive teacher control stimulates student
learning.

Another characteristic of overly simplistic libertarian reform
is the tendency to overlook systemic controls that underlie the authority of school personnel. The abolition of school controls would leave
intact the instrumental functions that schools perform in society, and
these are found to have a fundamentally antidemocratic effect on
learning. If compulsory schools were abolished, for example, we
might well find that new academies would spring up dedicated to help-
ing students get ahead. In the process, learning would be shaped almost exclusively by instrumental functions.

When taken to its logical conclusion, the most fundamental de-
fect of pure libertarianism becomes clear: It is ultimately antiegali-
tarian. In short, it reflects the same faith in voluntarism that marked
the laissez-faire philosophy of nineteenth-century liberalism—long
since discredited because of its implications for economic inequality
and exploitation. By concentrating exclusively on the objective of

school liberation, in other words, we relinquish other significant goals.

Put somewhat differently, there are important and legitimate reasons for public and compulsory, as opposed to private and voluntary, education. As long as we live in a world in which the state has not withered away, we need to ask, "Who will benefit from the abolition of school controls?" In all likelihood, the answer will be children who are raised in highly verbal, intellectual, or status-oriented homes, children who have greater opportunity to explore worlds far removed from their own.

Furthermore, the complete absence of educational compulsion would undermine the universality of democratic objectives. These legitimately include the skills, knowledge, and attitudinal orientation necessary for full participation in social and political life. Democratic participation is inclusive, not exclusive. Although schools presently reinforce the social isolation of different groups in society, this trait is not a necessary by-product of educational control, per se. Adoption of the laissez-faire approach would reduce the opportunities for social interaction, even if these are largely submerged at present.

These concerns underscore the degree to which the objectives of universality and equal opportunity remain important in our consideration of policy alternatives. Despite disputed evidence that schools don't make a difference, it does not follow that the absence of schools would be an improvement. Nor does it follow that schools cannot make a difference, particularly in light of evidence that will be presented in this work. Removal of the schooling path to success, even if its successes are infrequent, would be a bitter pill for egalitarians to swallow.

In short, we find ourselves in a policy dilemma. We can continue our quest for maximum equal opportunity through public schooling, all the while reinforcing systemic constraints on individual development. Or we can seek to liberate children from the grips of a frequently stifling socialization experience, while reinforcing private advantages and disadvantages.

The empirical evidence considered below suggests that in some respects we presently have the worst of both worlds. Systemic constraints effectively suppress the self-fulfillment and participatory capacity of many of the young at the same time that private advantages and disadvantages are rigidified and legitimized by the schooling experience. These findings underscore the critical need to reassess the instrumental functions of public schooling in light of democratic priorities. Such a task, in turn, directs our attention to systemic forces in our society that reinforce these functions and their impact on learning.

The final chapter argues that we can construct a balanced reform agenda that takes these contradictory impulses into account.
This does not mean we can resolve these reform conflicts in a neat,
internally consistent philosophy of educational and social reform. It
does require, however, a fundamental shift in our reform priorities.

At the same time, the empirical findings on secondary school
learning speak directly to the issue of reform. In short, the study of
high school classrooms uncovers teaching practices which are effective in making learning a relatively democratic experience. On the
other hand, this same study underscores the importance of the broader
context of classroom learning. Teacher effectiveness is constrained
by institutional characteristics of secondary schools, by the previous
inclinations and elementary school experiences of the students, and
by the incentive structure imposed by the instrumental functions which
schools are called upon to perform.

As a consequence, to maximize democratic objectives, we
must take into account the symbiotic relationship between classroom
learning and the broader environment of public schooling. The final
chapter discusses democratic reforms relevant to existing classrooms,
functional differences between elementary and secondary education,
and forces in society at large.

Back to First Principles

To lay the groundwork for the subsequent analysis, it is important to clarify the perspective taken in this work. At the outset,
the primary concern is the quality of school learning as a socialization process relevant to democratic citizenship. The objective is not
to accept the functions of schooling as a given, but to examine them
and their impact on school learning. This view sees life in the schools
as important in itself and as a significant experiential basis for learning citizenship orientation. Of particular concern are socialization
effects that have unequal implications for successful democratic
citizenship.

This approach requires that we step back and reassess the concept of equality as it applies to the schooling experience. As the
framework for empirical analysis and the discussion of reform, it is
suggested that equality in a democracy incorporates three educationally relevant concerns:

1. The need to safeguard the development of individual personality
   and a participatory capacity among all the young
2. The need for an element of socialization in common to provide a
   universal, nonexclusive basis for social participation

3. The need to maintain open access to the variety of social and occupational paths available after one's schooling is completed

In considering these objectives, it becomes clear that we confront a series of policy trade-offs. The single-minded pursuit of one
objective results in the denial of another. Thus, individualization of
learning moves us farther away from the pursuit of socialization in
common and from the standardization that advances the quest for
equal opportunity.

Chapter 2 begins the empirical analysis by proposing three
norms of democratic citizenship, each of which is reflected in the
policy objectives listed above. The resulting findings confirm that
schools fall far short of all three socialization objectives, but they
also point to successful democratic experiences in the schools. These
successes, in turn, suggest types of reforms directed to practices
in existing classrooms, to a restructuring of the schooling experience,
and to forces in society at large. In sum, we emerge with a picture
of educational reform that can be balanced against the traditional
equal opportunity view. The result is a redefinition of educational
equality.

NOTES

1. This pattern is documented by most of the literature on political participation. For interesting distinctions in the behavior of
the participating public, see Sidney Verba and Norman H. Nie, Participation in America: Political Democracy and Social Equality (New
York: Harper & Row, 1972).

2. Harvey A. Averch, Stephen J. Carroll, Theodore S. Donald-
son, Herbert J. Kiesling, and John Pincus, How Effective is School-
ing? A Critical Review and Synthesis of Research Findings (Santa
Monica, Calif.: Rand Corporation, 1972); and Christopher Jencks,
and Marshall Smith, Henry Acland, Mary Jo Bane, David Cohen,
Herbert Gintis, Barbara Heyns, Stephan Michelson, Inequality: A
Reassessment of the Effect of Family and Schooling in America (New
York: Basic Books, 1972).

3. James S. Coleman, E. Q. Campbell, C. J. Hobson, J.
McPartland, A. M. Mood, F. D. Weinfeld, and R. L. York, Equality
of Educational Opportunity (Washington, D. C.: U. S. Government
Printing Office, 1966).

4. For a general discussion of the Coleman Report, see
Frederick Mosteller and Daniel P. Moynihan, eds., On Equality of
Educational Opportunity (New York: Random House, 1972); see also

Christopher Jencks, "A Reappraisal of the Most Controversial Educational Document of Our Time," New York Times Magazine, August 10, 1969, pp. 12 ff.

5. Jencks et al., op. cit.

6. See, for example, the critiques collected in the Harvard Educational Review, "Perspectives on Inequality: A Reassessment of the Effect of Family and Schooling in America," 43, no. 1 (1973): 37–165; and Donald M. Levine and Mary Jo Bane, The "Inequality" Controversy: Schooling and Distributive Justice (New York: Basic Books, 1975).

7. Jencks et al., op. cit., p. 13.

8. Ibid., p. 134.

9. Samuel Bowles and Herbert Gintis, Schooling in Capitalist America (New York: Basic Books, 1976).

10. See Michael Young, The Rise of the Meritocracy (Baltimore: Penguin, 1971).

11. Ralph Turner, "Modes of Social Ascent Through Education: Sponsored and Contest Mobility," in Education, Economy, and Society, ed. A. H. Halsey, Jean Floud, and C. Arnold Anderson (New York: Free Press, 1961), pp. 121–39.

12. John H. Schaar, "Equality of Opportunity, and Beyond," in Nomos IX: Equality, ed. Roland Pennock and John W. Chapman (New York: Atherton Press, 1967), p. 231.

13. Young, op. cit.

14. Turner, op. cit., p. 124.

15. Schaar, op. cit., p. 241.

16. Turner, op. cit., p. 123.

17. Alexis de Tocqueville, Democracy in America, vol. 2 (New York: Vintage Books, 1945), pp. 336–37.

18. Turner, op. cit., p. 130.

19. R. S. Peters, Ethics and Education (London: Allen & Unwin, 1970), pp. 85–86.

20. Bowles and Gintis, op. cit., p. 30.

21. See, for example, Project Head Start: A Descriptive Report of Programs and Participants (Washington, D.C.: U.S. Government Printing Office, 1970).

22. R. S. Peters, op. cit., p. 140.

23. See, for example, such seminal works as A. S. Neill, Summerhill (New York: Hart, 1960); Paul Goodman, Compulsory Mid-Education and the Community of Scholars (New York: Vintage Books, 1964); John Holt, How Children Fail (New York: Dell, 1964); and Edgar X. Friedenberg, Coming of Age in America (New York: Vintage Books, 1965).

24. See, for example, Sidney B. Simon, Leland W. Howe, and Howard Kirschenbaum, Values Clarification: A Handbook of Practical Strategies for Teachers and Students (New York: Hart, 1972); Herbert Kohl, The Open Classroom (New York: Vintage Books, 1969); Charles E. Silberman, ed. , The Open Classroom Reader (New York: Vintage Books, 1973); George Dennison, The Lives of Children (New York: Vintage Books, 1969); and Jonathan Kozol, Free Schools (New York: Bantam Books, 1972).

25. Ivan Illich, Deschooling Society (New York: Harper & Row, 1971), p. 73.

2

THE ANTI DEMOCRATIC
STRUCTURE OF
SCHOOLING

In examining the nature of the learning process, our first task is to construct an overview of the general structure of schooling from the perspective of democratic socialization. In the process, it is possible to discern the effects of the instrumental functions of equal opportunity and social selection.

Before we turn to an empirical look at the schools, however, it is necessary to define what it is we are looking for and where we will look for it. What are the norms of democratic citizenship that are relevant to the schooling process? And where, in the school life of the young, do they apply? To begin this task, a normative framework for defining democratic citizenship has been constructed. Although the norms which are included may not be the only norms relevant to democratic citizenship, they incorporate fundamental principles of personal behavior and attitudes toward one's social milieu that have their ethical roots in democratic theory.

These guiding principles form a theoretical framework for discerning democratic and antidemocratic traits of schooling and for evaluating the schooling experience. In general, they prescribe the way people ought to be treated in any social context. Applied to school socialization, they suggest traits that the learning experience ought to encompass in a democratic society. Although it is relatively easy to test for cognitive elements in school learning, qualitative traits of the hidden curriculum are somewhat more difficult to distinguish. A brief discussion of the methodology used in this work will suggest ways in which democratic principles can be relevant to our consideration of schools and where and how we might look for them.

DEMOCRATIC PRINCIPLES OF LEARNING

In defining the norms of democratic citizenship, it is possible to distinguish three elements or types of norms, each with its roots in a particular democratic concern. First, we can speak of an individualist quality of democratic citizenship—most fundamentally, that a democratic society is one that considers its citizens as morally autonomous and intellectually independent personalities. Social situations where individuals are controlled ought to reflect a respect for the individual personality.

Second, we can also point to a social, or communitarian, element of democratic citizenship, growing out of the principle of self-government. This norm requires that formal political decisions reflect the will of the people; it aims at citizenry that participates in making decisions that affect their social lives and public environment. A society whose citizens do not possess attributes conducive to public participation is not really a self-governing, democratic society.

Finally, both the individualist and social elements of democratic citizenship are subject to a universal, or egalitarian, norm. All persons are to be treated in a way that respects individual personality, regardless of such characteristics as wealth, religion, race, sex, or age. This universal strain is also reflected in our concern that all persons have an equal opportunity to develop their full potential. Comparably, the social norm of citizenship is universal. All citizens ought to have access to political and social influence; no one is to be excluded from participation in public life. In other words, all persons ought to have an equal opportunity for full membership in society.

The Individualist Norm

Perhaps the starting point of liberal democratic theory is respect for the intrinsic value of the individual human personality. Essentially, we think in terms of individuals when we think of society. Political procedures and outcomes are justified on the basis of their impact on individual persons, not by some higher end or cause. Inherent in this view of citizenship, then, are the concepts of moral autonomy and intellectual independence. Instead of mindless conformity or submission to outside controls, we value the individual's independent ability to decide. Democratic citizens act not because they are told to or because of who tells them, but because there is a discernibly valuable reason for acting.

This individualist strain emerges most clearly in our concern for human freedom—in the fact that we consider that all persons have certain "inalienable rights." In a negative sense,[1] freedom serves as a check on control from without, particularly that control which violates fundamental attributes of the human personality. We usually refer to a series of rights, including the right of belief and opinion, and, more expansively, the right of privacy, free expression, and free association.

These rights become ends in themselves because of their relationship to the individual personality. As such, they define and prescribe qualities of legitimate control in the social setting. Thus, in specific instances, we weigh these rights against other ends, such as social needs or the equal rights of others. Control that impinges on the individual person is obviously necessary in a society. To be legitimate, however, it must be based on reasons that are justifiable in themselves and that reflect a respect for persons; it cannot be arbitrary or willful.

Within the educational context, the individualist element of democratic citizenship is one criterion for evaluating the legitimacy of control in schooling. Moral autonomy and intellectual independence are significant for learning in two ways. In the first place, as in society, they stand as checks on the exercise of control. A legitimate educational control structure respects the individual personality.

Second, an educational context is critically different from society in that it deals with young people, with a special category of developing personalities. As such, the qualities of legitimate control in learning reflect the end of educational needs as opposed to the social needs of the adult world. Control would seem necessary in an educational environment to accomplish collective educational aims, as well as to protect the equal educational rights of all learners.

Consideration of educational aims, however, imposes a second constraint on control in learning, namely, the objective of developing individual personalities capable of democratic citizenship. From the individualist perspective, this aspect of control places an additional burden on the way children are treated in learning contexts. One requirement of schooling, then, is that it develop children in such a way that they become fully free adults capable of rational decision making and effective pursuit of their interests and needs.

As in a democratic society, it is not a question of whether control is necessary in education, but what kind and how much control are legitimate. As John Dewey has observed: " . . . it is one thing to use adult accomplishments as a context in which to place and survey the doings of childhood and youth; it is quite another to set them up as a fixed aim without regard to the concrete activities of those educated. "[2] The development of moral autonomy and intellectual independence suggests the need for intellectual experience, for development of critical reasoning. To this end, a legitimate learning context cannot be rigidly imposed from without. At the same time, to

be socially meaningful, learning cannot derive solely from the personal orientations of the individual. Instead, learning requires an
environment based on the interaction between external and internal
forces and both are prerequisites to socially meaningful learning.

Dewey's concern for democracy in education led him to espouse
a concept of "interest" in learning. He wrote,

> . . . the value of recognizing the dynamic place of inter-
> est in educational development is that it leads to consid-
> ering individual children in their specific capabilities,
> needs, and preferences. . . .
> The problem of instruction is thus that of finding
> material which will engage a person in specific activities
> having an aim or purpose of moment or interest to him.
> . . . This means that the act of learning or studying is
> artificial and ineffective in the degree in which pupils
> are merely presented with a lesson to be learned. [3]

The principle of moral autonomy thereby requires the consideration
of pupils' interests in the learning process. One can also argue, as
Dewey does, that consideration of interests is a prerequisite for
meaningful education.

If we pursue the concept of "interest" in learning, we end up
with a teacher's dilemma that reflects a deeper democratic paradox:
What does an instructor do when it is in his or her pupils' "interests"
to pursue one activity, while they are "interested" in doing something
quite different? (In a democratic society, which ultimately relies on
the democratic inclinations of its citizens, how do we treat citizens
who do not play by the democratic ground rules?)

In both cases, we are confronted by the question of whether or
not control ought to be imposed. The use of control in both cases is
legitimate only insofar as it furthers democratically legitimate ends.
To some extent, resolution of the teacher's dilemma in the classroom
depends on qualities that we generally refer to as good teaching. In
the process, students become interested in an activity that promotes
their future well-being and their intellectual growth.

Applying the concept of interest to the learning context, we can
distinguish an intrinsic, democratic control from two alternatives—
an extrinsic, imposed form of control or the complete absence of
control. Intrinsic control draws on the interests of the young. It involves motivations that grow out of the meaning discovered in the
student's interactions with others and with learning tasks. And it allows room for intellectual independence. Extrinsic control, on the
other hand, is unilaterally imposed upon the learner. It rests on in-

centives that are fundamentally external to the learning process itself. Finally, the complete absence of control implies the absence
of an educating function. It suggests that, in terms of social outcomes,
the learning environment is meaningless or lacking in purpose.

Citizenship and Participation

The second norm of democratic citizenship focuses on the social
side of individual behavior. Like the individualist norm it derives
from ethical principles of democratic theory. Whereas the individualist concern reflects the concept of negative liberty, the social concern grows out of the concept of positive liberty, or the "freedom to."
Instead of placing a constraint on how much control, it prescribes
answers to the question "Who controls?"

In its most overtly political form, the principle of positive liberty is aligned with the concept of self-government. The democratic
answer to "Who controls?" is that the people ought to control their
own destinies. Although the decision-making process may vary, it
is democratic to the extent that it is responsive to the priorities of
the population it serves. The concept of consent of the governed requires that political and social outcomes reflect the will of the people,
however it is expressed. It suggests that those seeking decision-
making authority or those proposing specific policies compete for the
allegiance and approval of the population at large—a kind of competition at the top that reinforces control from the bottom up. This concept is reflected in Justice Oliver Wendell Holmes's faith that "the
best test of truth is the power of the thought to get itself accepted in
the competition of the market."[4]

Implementation of this principle suggests two ingredients of
citizenship that have implications for education. First, to be fully
democratic, a decision-making process requires some expression of
the public will. Thus, we seek to implement public participation by
such means as universal suffrage, frequent elections, and the concept of majority rule. In short, democratic citizenship stresses the
importance of open access to authority, measured in part by the distribution of participation throughout society.

Translated into educational terms, this principle would seem
to require that students gain a participatory capacity through their
educational activity. Among other things, this capacity requires a
cognitive awareness of the procedures of participation in society. At
the same time, it would seem to require a behavioral and attitudinal
orientation toward participation—not just internalization of the plati-
tude "It's good to get involved" but an experiential basis for active

participation in shaping one's environment. In a Deweyan sense, this would require that students perceive the meaning of participation by experiencing its fruits and frustrations in their learning experience.

A second implication of this democratic principle is that the young ought to learn the norm of social interdependence. In their learning experience, the young ought to acquire what R. S. Peters calls the "emotional underpinning" of a democracy, namely, the "feeling of fraternity for others as persons."[5] Among the aims of such an experience would be tolerance for views other than one's own, the need to compromise with others in order to reach common objectives, the need to form coalitions to pursue one's ends, and a public spiritedness or willingness to join in cooperative effort at some point in social interaction.

The principle of social interdependence is of ultimate importance in a democracy, for it provides the wherewithal to resolve competing interests in society. It is the oil that makes the machinery of government work. As Justice Felix Frankfurter declared:

> The ultimate reliance for the deepest needs of civilization must be found outside their vindication in courts of law. . . . A persistent, positive translation of the liberating faith into the feelings and thoughts and actions of men and women is the real protection against attempts to strait-jacket the human mind. [6]

In the view of participatory theorists like John Stuart Mill and Jean-Jacques Rousseau,[7] the process of political participation is itself educational. Through public participation, a citizenry gains the information, skills, and psychological orientations that best ensure active and informed self-government. In short, if participation is educational, education ought to be participatory. To maximize the participatory capacity of a citizenry, an educational system ought to encourage active student input into learning experiences. Through the learning process, students ought to come to feel that they have an input into their social and institutional environment. They ought to gain a sense of fate control, of being able to shape meaningful learning experiences on their own.

At the same time, because so much student learning takes place in a social context, students should also engage in work that teaches the lessons of social interdependence. They should gain a sense of cooperating in common tasks that pool the interests and abilities of each participant.

These elements of democratic learning suggest that the social aims of citizenship ought to be a part of the formal, or official, purposes of school learning, not simply benefits derived accidentally

(and unequally) outside official activities. They also suggest that
students ought to have at least some active role in shaping their individual and collective learning experiences.

The Principle of Universality

Both the individual and social elements of democratic citizenship are subject to the principle of universality, which has its ethical
roots in democratic equality. Individual autonomy and the inviolate
personality are principles that apply to all human beings equally; thus,
we adhere in theory to the principle of equal rights. Similarly, political participation knows no bounds; every person has an equal claim
on the political process.

Distinctions are made that constrict the universality of moral
autonomy and public participation are legitimate, yet they must be
based on other legitimate and socially relevant reasons. Thus, for
example, those who are too young to vote are a category of persons
who may be legitimately deprived of full participatory rights. In
terms of democratic citizenship, however, the principle of universality places an inclusive rather than exclusive emphasis on social and
political activity. It calls for society to be open rather than closed,
or, as Dewey has written, "a society which makes provision for participation in its good of all its members on equal terms," as opposed
to a society that "internally and externally sets up barriers to free
intercourse and communication of experience."[8]

Such a society requires certain traits in its educational system.
Most fundamentally, no one should be denied the fruits of the educational process. In terms of the learning experience itself, however,
the principle of universality also applies to the previously mentioned
characteristics of democratic socialization. No one should receive
a totally extrinsic, imposed learning experience. If intrinsic control
is to be the norm, the interests of all students, and of each one individually, need to be tapped in the learning experience. Furthermore,
no one should feel the brunt of arbitrary, willful authority; instead,
treatment of students should be based on legitimate reasons that apply to all in similar circumstances.

On the social side, all students should be the recipients of
learning experiences that enhance their participatory capacity. This
does not mean that all have to participate equally. However, no one
should be excluded from social interdependence; all should gain a
sense of efficacy over their immediate environment and a capacity
for participation.

The standards of democratic citizenship suggest a shift in our
definition of universal education. Treating students the same does

not mean treating them as if they were identical. It means allocating to all an educational experience that not only enhances their cognitive abilities but also their full membership in a democratic society.

THE STUDY OF DEMOCRATIC SOCIALIZATION:
AIMS AND ASSUMPTIONS

As normative principles, the components of democratic citizenship provide guidelines for what ought to be in a fully democratic educational system. They provide a framework for testing and evaluating the democratic quality of school learning. Our judgments, or the conclusions we draw, depend on a variety of factors, including the emphasis we place on these as opposed to other objectives and our view of the feasibility of accomplishing these ends. The view taken here is that these objectives are critical because of their relationship to the equal opportunity debate; their feasibility, in turn, depends on revisions being made in the traditional equal opportunity focus of educational reform.

Before turning to the empirical examination of school learning, we first need to consider the scope of this particular study. By outlining the basic methodological aims, we can discern one view, admittedly one of several, of where and how schooling is relevant to the concerns for democratic citizenship outlined above.

Most generally, these democratic prescriptions focus our attention on the nature of control in the school learning process. In particular, we need to ask such questions as; Is the control experienced by students conducive to the growth of the individual personality? Does it reflect a respect for persons? Does it in some sense emanate from the interests of the young, drawing on intrinsic motivations? Does it involve the learner in a kind of partnership of interests? Do school personnel exercise control fairly and impartially? Does learning control reflect the natural requirements of interdependent relations?

These questions direct our attention to two methodological concerns. First, what are the sources or agents of control in schooling? And, second, what is the impact of the control that students encounter? These questions have been addressed in two ways. First, we may examine the structural constants of control in the schooling experience—those characteristics of school control that one can attribute to schools in general. In distinguishing these, we can perceive ways in which the institutional structure and the social functions of public schooling control the learning environment.

Second, we may examine recognizable patterns of variation in the control structure of schooling. In particular, this concern focuses our attention on the way school personnel, especially teachers, exercise control. In the process, we can distinguish two types of variations, both of which have consequences for educational reform. We can distinguish patterns of control that correspond to structural characteristics of schools, for example, variations that are a function of a student's school, track, or grade level. Through these we can distinguish unequal lessons of schooling of consequence for democratic citizenship.

These structural patterns of control will be examined in depth in the next two chapters. At the same time, however, it is possible to discern variations in the exercise of control that are the result of particular priorities and approaches of school personnel. In particular, we can distinguish ways in which teachers affect the learning environment independent of track level or school structure. Through these, we can perceive a teacher impact that either enhances or diminishes the democratic quality of learning. By identifying certain teaching practices as democratic, we can draw inferences for educational reform. This effect of teachers is considered in Chapter 5.

In pursuing these objectives, it seems natural to concentrate on the classroom. Although a student may gain more from extracurricular or even "noncurricular" activities in school, the classroom is the focal point of his or her major contact with the school's primary educational and socializing functions. As a result, much of this work examines interaction within the classroom. In effect, it considers the classroom as a microcosmic political society, embodying certain forms of citizenship training.

In considering classroom learning, an effort is made to be as inclusive as possible. Teachers and students are the most obvious focal points. For example, we can examine teacher behavior and instructional approaches, as well as the quality and level of student participation. Additionally, however, it is important to consider the nature of curricular constraints and objectives by observing work procedures. In sum, we can discern a control structure in learning that encompasses roles, procedures, expectations, and reward systems.

Still it is vitally important to consider factors external to the classroom itself, factors that shape and constrain the nature of student learning. Clearly, classroom learning reflects the impact of such factors as school atmosphere, administrative rules and procedures, parental and community pressures, government regulations, and the prevalent orientations of the student body as a whole. These are ultimately critical in considering the limits and potential for reform. However, they are considered here only as they appear to influence the contained world of the classroom. More important in this chapter is the effort to distinguish social, political, and economic functions that are being performed through classroom processes themselves.

This perspective of the social functions of schooling suggests one reason why the high school level has been chosen for empirical examination. In many ways, the high school can be seen as an introduction to adult society, whereas the elementary school is more of an introduction to society in general (a kind of weaning away from the family). In this sense, one can expect the high school to embody more of the expectations and priorities found in adult society, with less adaptation to the particular needs of young children. Furthermore, such instrumental functions as social selection become more overt during high school, as the young confront decisions about their futures.

The high school years are also critical because they would seem to have a more direct impact on the citizenship orientations of the young. Whereas earlier childhood appears to be the time when children absorb and internalize their first cognitive and attitudinal political lessons (for example, "Our country is good," "The President is a good man," etc.), adolescence seems to be a time more suited to drawing direct social and political lessons from one's institutional environment. Much of the literature on learning and psychological and moral development points to the adolescent years as a time of significant selfdefinition in relation to a social and ethical environment.[9] As such, the high school years are a crucial time frame for what James Barber has called the development of a "world view." Writing from a political perspective, Barber observes that the increasingly future-oriented adolescent has "thoughts about the way the world works and how one might work in it, about what people are like and how one might be like them or not, and about the values people share and how one might share in them too. . . . "[10]

A Note on Methodology

In order to determine the degree of standardization and diversity in the learning structure, the empirical study is based on an in-depth, comparative analysis of three high schools. The empirical data obviously do not answer all theoretical questions raised in the book. Consequently, care is taken to phrase conclusions cautiously where either the data or the statistical techniques have clear limitations. However, methodological steps were taken to maximize the reliability of the findings and to ensure an authoritative foundation for the consideration of educational policy issues.

Although the empirical base is necessarily limited, a careful effort was made to select a representative sample of schools, teachers, and classes within a metropolitan area of over 2 million people. The field study consisted of two phases. An initial three month phase, during which classes were observed and a pilot questionnaire was administered, led to the final selection of teachers, observation techniques, and questionnaire items. A three month phase during the following school year was used to study the sample of fifteen classes.

In addition, no method by itself served as the basis for study conclusions. Instead, the findings were drawn from a combination of direct classroom observations, teacher interviews, and a student questionnaire, and the results of one approach were weighed against those of the other two. All aspects of the study were carried out by the author.

Located in a major eastern metropolitan area, each of the schools represents a carefully selected community-school type. Northdate High is an upper-middle-class suburban school. Middletown High is a working-and middle-class, small-city school. Central High is a racially mixed, working- and lower-class, inner-city school.

As will be described more thoroughly in Chapter 3, each school is distinguished by an identifiable school atmosphere. Northdale High has a flexible open campus, enjoys a high academic reputation in the area, and is marked by widespread student initiative in school activities. A large proportion of its students go on to attend four-year liberal arts colleges. Middletown High is housed in a massive new structure and exudes an air of bureaucratic efficiency in day-to-day activities. Its students are generally compliant in their behavior; a sizable proportion go on to attend public universities or two-year colleges. Central High is a fairly typical inner-city school, housed in an old red-brick building with worn-out facilities and exhibiting boisterous student behavior and something of a prison atmosphere. The majority of Central High graduates seek immediate employment, forgoing higher education.

Rather than covering a cross section of all high school classes in these schools, the study focused on a range of social studies classes. Although there is probably a fair degree of standardization in the structure of all high school classes, each discipline poses certain structural requirements. Because of their direct bearing on citizenship concerns, social studies classes seemed the obvious focal point for examination.

The sample of social studies classes included a cross section of age levels (sophomore through senior), ability levels, subjects, and teaching styles. Although the sample of teachers was positively biased by self-selection (all teachers volunteered or were selected by their department head, thus no "embarrassments" were likely to participate), teaching approaches ranged from classic laissez faire to strict authoritarian styles. Although the sample bias probably colored

empirical generalizations in a positive light, sufficient diversity was
present to elicit those characteristics of learning which are essentially
universal, those which differ systematically among various student
groups, and those which are the product of independent teacher input.
In short, the sample range is sufficient to support generalizations
about the structural constants of secondary schooling, the structure
of inequality in high school learning, and the independent impact of
effective teachers.

ANTIDEMOCRATIC CONTROL: THE ARGUMENT

Pursuit of universal public education has resulted in an institution that controls students in largely antidemocratic ways. The structure of control endemic to the institution of schooling grows out of
and serves social, political, and economic functions that schools perform in our society. In the most fundamental sense, control in schooling is undemocratic to the extent that the school's "clients" are not
the students it purportedly "serves," but rather its "true clients" in
society. If our high schools disappeared overnight, we might ask,
who would clamor most urgently for new ones? Probably not the students. More likely we would hear from members of the community,
parents with ambitions for their children, the police, and, ultimately,
potential employers in society at large.

In part, this speculation illustrates the extent to which schooling
is an experience society imposes on its young. To the extent that it
remains an imposition, or that the young themselves would not re-
quest new schools, we can discern one fundamentally antidemocratic
quality of schooling. It involves control from without that fails to engage the interests of the learner, and thus fails to reflect control
from within.

In considering democratic socialization, however, we need to
go beyond this speculative inquiry. Even if the young wanted to go to
school, this would not mean that schooling was essentially democratic.
We would need to clarify students' motivations for attending school.
Do students want to go because of the instrumental functions of schooling or because of attractions inherent in the school experience itself?
Do they want to go because their interests are engaged or because
their long-term interest is served? Finally, when they go, what kind
of political experience do they have?

Consideration of these questions leads to a descriptive analysis
of learning processes and the consideration of student motivations.
The remainder of this chapter offers evidence that student motivations
are largely extrinsic, and that the instrumental functions of schooling

reach into the classroom to shape learning in antidemocratic ways.
In describing these structural constants of the schooling experience,
we construct the boundaries of variable behavior within schools and,
by implication, the limitations of reform aimed solely at this behavior. We can begin by considering the general qualities of control in
the school as an institution—as a backdrop for subsequent examination of classroom learning.

INSTITUTIONAL CONTROL

Control as an institutional quality of schooling takes two forms.
It can be seen in the institutional functions of schools in the broader
social context and it can be seen in the structural manner in which
schools are organized to pursue those functions. We first consider
the way in which schooling is controlled by forces inherent in its social functions.

School Compulsion

Any discussion of control in the schooling experience must begin with the basic fact of compulsion in school life. Regardless of
the setting, one ultimately confronts the fact that students are compelled to go to school. School compulsion acts as a control on students
in three ways: it is legal, or based on compulsory school laws and
backed up by public enforcement; it is perceived by students as a
practical necessity of going to school and doing well; and it is made
effective by the essentially autocratic control of school officials.
    All three aspects of compulsion reflect the social, political,
and economic functions of public schooling as these have evolved in
America. Compulsory school laws reflect efforts to eliminate child
labor and to Americanize or acculturate immigrant children. Schooling is necessary because it serves such instrumental functions as
occupational opportunity and social certification. Finally, students
are ultimately controlled autocratically because schooling is an imposed process; overt autocratic control emerges where the other
controls have little effect.
    The most pervasive and universal characteristic of school com-
pulsion as it affects life in the classroom is the school's total control
of the path to later success, symbolized by the grading system. Students' awareness and internalization of this function is fairly universal, as data from the student questionnaire illustrate. Not surprisingly, 83 percent of all students responded "Yes" when asked, "Do you

feel it's very important to do well in school?" Only 4 percent responded negatively.

The reasons students give for the importance of "doing well"
underscore the extrinsic motivations at work in the schooling experience. Only 4 percent of all students volunteered that "doing well" was
important because it showed they were learning something. Thirty-
seven percent gave as a reason "It makes me feel like I've accomplished something." Strictly utilitarian or extrinsic reasons were far
more common: 36 percent felt "It makes things easier all around";
30 percent felt "It helps me get a good job"; 21 percent felt "It makes
my parents happy"; and 10 percent wrote "It helps me get into college."

The tendency to see school success as extrinsically important
is borne out by student responses to the attitude statement "Grades
are important because they have a lot to do with what kind of job you
end up getting." Students agreed with the statement by a 2:1 ratio.
Obviously, when grades and academic performance are perceived as
critical for the enjoyment of tangible future rewards, few would consciously want to do poorly. Still, the pervasiveness of the grading
control can be seen in student responses to the statement "The grades
I get have a lot to do with how I feel about school." Fifty-seven percent of all students agreed with the statement (half of these agreed
"strongly"), while only 25 percent disagreed. A greater proportion
of students in the more middle-class Northdale and Middletown schools
agreed than in the more overtly policed, inner-city Central High
School—supporting the contention that the more students internalize
extrinsic incentives, the less they need to be overtly controlled.

The fact that the extrinsic force of grading interferes with intrinsic qualities of learning, at least for a good number of students,
can be seen in responses to the statement "If it weren't for grades,
school could be really interesting." Forty percent of all students
agreed with the statement. On the other hand, 41 percent disagreed,
although nearly half of these tended to be alienated from school any-
way. ("When I'm in school, all I can think of is other places I'd
rather be.")

Although the pervasiveness of extrinsic control in schooling has
antidemocratic implications, the exercise of grading control comes
closer to fulfilling democratic requirements of impartiality. Fifty-
three percent of all students agreed with the statement "No matter
what people say about grades, you usually get what you deserve,"
while 30 percent disagreed. Lower-level students were somewhat
more critical of grading practices than the norm, yet these general
sentiments were fairly consistent. Like the principle of equal opportunity, however, fairness, is a two-sided coin. On the one hand, it

fulfills democratic requirements for the nonarbitrary exercise of authority. On the other, a pervasive sense of fairness legitimizes whatever control prevails. In the case of the extrinsic grading function, student perceptions of being treated fairly reinforce the constraining quality of that control. As will be seen below, this characteristic was mirrored in observed classroom practices.

Autocratic Structure: The School as Total Institution

In addition to legal and functional qualities of school compulsion, some discussion of the structural nature of school control is necessary if we are fully to understand the institutional context of classroom learning. In his classic study of schools, Willard Waller described the school as autocratic:

> Typically the school is organized on some variant of the autocratic principle. . . . The generalization that the schools have a despotic political structure seems to hold true for nearly all types of schools. . . . The manifestations of the authority principle vary somewhat, . . . but the basic fact of authority, of dominance and subordination, remains a fact. . . . [11]

Speaking of schools in general, but perhaps more tellingly of an urban school like Central High, Waller notes, ". . . the school is continually threatened because it is autocratic, and it has to be autocratic because it is threatened. The antagonistic forces are balanced in that ever-fickle equilibrium which is discipline."[12]

Waller's picture conforms to general impressions of Central High School, where an uneasy equilibrium and a policing atmosphere prevailed. In the other two schools, where the large majority of students conform to the necessity of school functions or of bureaucratic order, the autocratic structure is either less rigid or less obvious.

Further insights into this autocratic structure can be gained by an appraisal of the public school as a total institution—defined by Erving Goffman as "a place of residence and work where a large number of like-situated individuals, cut-off from the wider society for an appreciable period of time, together lead an enclosed, formally administered round of life."[13] Prisons and mental hospitals are cited as models of total institutions. It is not surprising, then, that some students were heard to complain of their school, "This place is a prison." Also, some teachers, notably in Central High, made comments similar to those made by prison guards.[14] For example, one

stated that it was necessary to be flexible in enforcing institutional
policies or "we'd have a riot on our hands."

This is not to argue that schools are prisons. Nor, for that
matter, is the comparison with total institutions in itself a criticism
of schools. Instead, it is part of an effort to understand institutional
forces that affect classroom learning. We can perhaps gain some insight into schooling from functional similarities shared by public
schools, mental hospitals, and prisons—regardless of differences between these institutions. Goffman's analysis of life in total institutions suggests structural parallels with school life:

> First, all aspects of life are conducted in the same place
> and under the same single authority. Second, each phase
> of the member's daily activity is carried on in the imme-
> diate company of a large batch of others, all of whom are
> treated alike and required to do the same thing together.
> Third, all phases of the day's activities are tightly sched-
> uled, with one activity leading at a pre-arranged time into
> the next, the whole sequence of activities being imposed
> from above by a system of explicit formal rulings and a
> body of officials. Finally, the various enforced activities
> are brought together into a single rational plan purport-
> edly designed to fulfill the official aims of the institution.[15]

Further parallels exist in the sense that all three institutions—
schools, prisons, and mental hospitals—have one function in common.
In each case, the aim is to fit, or refit, the individual into the prevailing social order. We must ask, however, if the manner in which
students are "fit" to prevailing standards is conducive to such traits
as rational and independent decision making, a sense of engagement
in and efficacy toward one's environment, and a feeling of social interdependence.

At first glance, this seems to be far from the case. School is
essentially a separate world that takes on characteristics of total institutions when in session. Thus, for example, students need official
permission for most activities that they could freely pursue outside
of school. The movement of students is largely fixed in time and location. Uniform procedures prevail. Exceptions to the total institution model occur in the form of flexible scheduling or the open campus adopted in schools like Northdale High, where total control is
limited to those times when students have scheduled activities.

To some degree, the school experience is shaped by order and
control simply because schools and classrooms are collective enter-
prises; schools and teachers have to deal with crowds. In terms of
democratic learning, however, we must ask what meaning can be

derived from this environment? Does the meaning of the control reflect intrinsic qualities of learning? Does it represent the path to successful accomplishment of a learning task? Does it connect the learner and his or her experience with a broader vision of experience? Does it derive from the social necessity of listening to others' views and joining in cooperative effort? Does it reflect the interrelatedness of learning, or, as Dewey put it, "such a network of interconnections that any past experience would offer a point of advantage from which to get at the problem presented in a new experience"?[16]

It would seem, for the most part, that the control embedded in the structure of schooling is diametrically opposed to this list of intrinsic considerations, that it reflects instead extrinsic, utilitarian meanings. In part, control is purely custodial, existing solely for the purpose of controlling the young until they are "ready" to fit adult roles. Experientially, this control suggests that social life is governed by control for its own sake. A second meaning of this control reflects the social selection function of schooling. Schools and classrooms are like controlled laboratories where student performance is observed and categorized according to presumed social needs. Standardization is necessary to distinguish levels of student achievement.

Finally, the fundamental meaning of the control structure is that learning tasks with their own built-in ends are superseded by external forces that range from the interruption of bells and constricting schedules to segmented, specialized subjects. These are external and arbitrary in the sense that their meaning has little basis in the learning experience, per se. Through these interruptions, the control structure essentially tells the learner that his or her interests and needs are relatively meaningless. The meanings of school control are imposed from without; they do not derive from the individual person's interaction with an external environment.

From the democratic perspective, this functional control is critical because it is all-pervasive and because it fosters and is reinforced by an ideology that defines students' needs in terms of institutional objectives. In large part, society tacitly condones this total control as part of the legitimate function of schools. Yet exceptions do exist. In some schools, students are able to exercise choice over which contained environments or classrooms they will enter. More generally, state legislatures and the courts have placed constraints on the absolute quality of control exercised over students' lives in school. The Supreme Court, for example, has granted constitutional protections to high school students in the Tinker[17] and Goss[18] cases. Speaking for the Court in the Tinker decision, Justice Abe Fortas noted:

> In our system, state-operated schools may not be enclaves of totalitarianism. School officials do not possess

absolute authority over their students. . . . In our system,
students may not be regarded as close-circuited recipients
of only that which the state chooses to communicate. [19]

Limitations based on free expression or due process do not contradict the total institution comparison; they merely qualify the exercise of control in some areas according to society's standards of
what is permissible. One can see similar tendencies in the public
concern for regulating excesses in prisons and mental hospitals.
Fortas's sentiments may derive from a view of high school students
that embraces concepts like individual personality and self-determi-
nation as democratic prerequisites. Yet the vast weight of institutional control that students encounter suppresses these aims—so much
so, in fact, that letting students wear black arm bands to protest the
Vietnam War or granting due process rights to suspended students
seems at most a superficial check on the control structure. As in
society in general, one can argue that such constitutional protections
are relatively meaningless unless the principles of respect for personality are embedded in the fabric of everyday life in the school.
And, as documented in these pages, this is clearly not the case.
     Despite the pervasiveness of institutional control in schooling,
the exercise of control varies from institution to institution. Schools
like Northdale High are more benevolent than schools like Middletown
or Central High in that students are allowed more curricular choice
and freedom of movement. It is curious, then, that students in the
flexible Northdale and the bureaucratically efficient Middletown are
more aware of being controlled by school officials. In response to
the statement "To get along in school, you have to do what people
say," 49 percent of all students agreed, while 30 percent disagreed.
Yet 56 percent of all Northdale students and 61 percent of all Middletown students agreed as opposed to only 25 percent of their counterparts in Central High.
     Again, one can discern the more effective and pervasive con-
trolling quality of the legitimate functions of schools. "To get along
in school" would seem to mean "to succeed" to the more achievement-
oriented Northdale and Middletown students. On the other hand, many
in Central High might read the statement as "to survive with minimal
interference," and they might accurately perceive channels of individual expression in a policing environment that are less accessible to
students in the more achievement-oriented schools.
     These student sentiments reflect the circularity of control in
schooling and, by implication, the pervasiveness of functional control. Where students internalize the compulsion in schooling, they
encounter less overt control. In fact, they are allowed greater choice
in their own school programs. Yet they are, at least potentially,

more totally controlled. Northdale students clearly encounter the
least autocratic environment; Middletown and Central High students
encounter institutions that are fairly equally autocratic—the difference being that Central High takes on a more defensive, policing pos-
ture toward its disruptive students, while Middletown controls its
compliant students more bureaucratically. Overt police control is
less evident in Middletown because it is less necessary, given the
internalization of schooling functions among the students.

In generalizing about the institutional setting of school learning,
one can say that the school is an institution in which the students'
learning experience is pervasively shaped and constrained by forces
that are external to the prerequisites of learning itself. This external or autocratic control is reinforced by extrinsic motivations that
are at the root of the social meaning of the schooling experience. So
pervasive is this control and students' reactions to it that it is surprising to find that teachers have much effect at all in fostering democratic learning. Yet, as we shall see in subsequent chapters, identifiable teaching approaches increase the democratic quality of the
learning experience, thus suggesting the potentially democratic role
of teaching authority.

Still, this teaching potential is greatly limited by the nondemocratic structure of schooling. In turning to an examination of classrooms, we can see how the same dynamics of control that pervade
the school are mirrored in the classroom. While teachers may succeed in overcoming some institutional constraints on democratic education, they do so by contradicting or downplaying role requirements
that fulfill and reinforce those nondemocratic traits. After all, theirs
is the role of making the functions of schooling work. In effect, teachers are caught between antidemocratic, institutional forces and the
more democratic forces of instructional and personal interaction with
students.

CONTROL IN THE CLASSROOM

The forces of school compulsion and control are brought directly to bear on students in the classroom through the person of the
teacher and the structure of classroom work. The classroom is the
place where students spend the bulk of their school hours, and where
the official educating functions of schooling are concentrated.

Not surprisingly, control in the classroom follows the pattern
of school control in general. The teacher, as the focal point of classroom control, possesses unilateral, absolute authority over classroom activities. Regardless of varying teacher practices, the only
effective input students have into classroom activities and decisions

is that permitted or delegated to them by the teacher. All 15 teachers involved in the study fulfilled this controlling function, even the one who took a consciously laissez-faire approach to her class. (In one instance, her students were told that they "controlled power" in the class, and thus were responsible for constraining one domineering student. The students protested en masse, saying, "He's not running the class, you're running the class. You have the power if you choose to let him have power. ")

At the same time, the exercise of teacher control varies significantly, depending on the personal policy preferences of individual teachers and the prevalent type of student encountered. If the teacher's authority is absolute in formal terms, it is a qualified absolute in practice. To generalize, two environmental forces, in addition to personal teaching preferences, constrain the absolute quality of teacher control. External forces include a range of invisible participants, such as school personnel, parents, various levels of government, and vested interests in the community.

Internal constraints on the absolute nature of teacher control reflect informal qualities of leadership that make for effective teaching. One can say that there is a quality of student "power" or input implicit in the "freedom" to accept or reject the teacher's authority—although individual rejection comes at considerable personal cost and collective rejection is constrained by the controlling ends of classroom learning. To some degree, students have an informal and collective role in participating in classroom decision making, a role that teachers must take into account.

A critical ingredient in this collective student input is the concept of legitimacy, deriving from two sources: student acceptance of the norms and functions of schooling and perceptions of the teacher as "fair" in the exercise of authority. As will be seen below, the latter perception is fairly universal, while the former varies according to track level.

As in the case of school in general, this perception of legitimacy reinforces the existence and effectiveness of control. Insofar as students perceive the teacher's exercise of control as legitimate, their classroom input is deflected into atomistic learning tasks. In the process, active student participation is undermined or controlled. The degree of informal student input that remains is minimal, providing little experience in democratic participation. As will be argued below, it is not the existence of teacher control, per se, that is non-democratic, but the nature of the control implicit in the learning process. Unilateral teacher control is pervasive, but it is made autocratic by the extrinsic structure of student work.

Students universally pursue uniform tasks in their learning, and compete for successful grades against both external standards and their peers. Together, uniform and competitive work structures make classroom learning a process in which extrinsic forces are dominant, regardless of teachers' efforts to the contrary. As a result, the extrinsic motivations and the imposed controls of schooling in general are introduced and reinforced in the classroom process. Closer examination of the two principals of classroom control, the teacher and the structure of work, sheds light on the nature of control in learning.

The Teacher

To distinguish between the structural control that is part of the teacher's role and actual, observed classroom practices, it is helpful to focus on three functions of teacher control in the classroom setting: the teacher as judge, or evaluator, of student performance; the teacher as director, or major decision maker, in curricular matters; and the teacher as regulator, in charge of maintaining classroom order. Each of the three focuses on particular qualities of classroom control relevant to democratic learning. In political terms, we might speak of judicial, legislative, and executive powers concentrated in the hands of the teacher.

Each function controls students in a particular way. The teacher-as-judge controls student access to school rewards (grades and recommendations), the teacher-as-director controls the structure of academic learning, and the teacher-as-regulator controls student behavior in the classroom in order to carry out the first two functions. This concentration of controls has led some to characterize the teacher as a kind of benevolent dictator, a description that would be highly accurate if applied to a comparable political leader. As Jacob Getzels and Herbert Thelen have observed of the classroom:

> If one thinks of authority, control, and leadership in political terms, it is clear that the classroom group, at
> least in its formal aspects, is about as far from democracy as one can get. Not only do the students have no
> control over the selection of their leader, they normally
> also have no recourse from his leadership, no influence
> on his method of leadership beyond that granted by him
> and no power over the tenure of his leadership. There
> are very few working groups in our society in which
> these essentially despotic conditions are legitimately so
> much the role. [20] (emphasis added)

Experientially, such a learning environment would seem to add little to the democratic capacities of the young. In part, the concentration of control functions reveals the complex and competing demands of classroom teaching. At the same time, these simultaneous functions underscore the pervasiveness of control in the classroom. External control over student activities is a fundamental trait of what we mean by classroom learning.

To determine the critically antidemocratic traits of teacher control, however, it is important that we move beyond formal characteristics to examine the way control is exercised by various teachers. In short, the simultaneous functions of teaching control open the way for variations in practice. Some teachers emphasize the more extrinsic control of the grading function or the more autocratic control of behavioral regulation. Others may accent intrinsic controls in the instructional process. Despite teacher variations, however, all three functions are present to some degree in the classroom, reinforcing each other.

The Teacher-as-Judge

In all observed classes and in schools generally, the teacher is clearly defined as the controller of access to good grades, the official measure of school success. Teachers involved in the study placed varying degrees of emphasis on grades, but all clearly functioned as the unilateral evaluator of student performance. Some teachers informally reminded students of grading concerns (for instance, one joked to students before a unit test, "Don't slump now; your work at the end is freshest in my mind when I grade you"). Most teachers frequently reminded students of work that was due or of the need for improvement in their grades. All but the one laissez-faire teacher in the study gave regular tests to students. In the one exception, the teacher graded on somewhat different criteria, but she, too, graded unilaterally. In general, students who complained about or questioned their grades were given some explanation by the teacher.

Several characteristics of teacher grading emerge from the evidence gathered in the three schools. In the first place, the teacher is the final arbiter when it comes to student grades. There is no appeal process comparable to that found in a judicial system, and it is not clear that anyone (including most students) feels there is a need for such a process. More significantly, the student's sense of accomplishment in learning plays no role in the evaluation of successful work, as might be the case in a context that draws on intrinsic motivations. In fact, the opposite is the rule; not only are the criteria for success totally external to the individual student but feelings of accomplishment are largely dependent on the external grades received.

On the other hand, grading is far from purely arbitrary. Teacher grading practices are limited by both external standards and the informal system of classroom legitimacy. Teachers clearly must and do provide students with reasons for grades. Still, norms that limit the operation of teacher grading are usually collective and unspoken. Dissatisfied individuals are left to their own devices; their plight is of little concern to their peers. Except in rare cases of extreme teacher behavior (none was witnessed), individual student self-interest prevails, and collective interest is submerged.

Furthermore, student input is limited by the substance of student expectations in the classroom. And these are, at the high school level, the result of years of classroom experience (if anything, student input is more submerged during the elementary years). These student expectations take a number of forms. In the first place, students are well aware of the control exercised through the grading function. Fifty-eight percent of all students agreed with the statement "You have to do things the way the teacher wants if you want to get a good grade," while only 24 percent disagreed. Observed student behavior revealed widespread compliance with this control, for understandable reasons.

A more precise picture of grading control is revealed by student perceptions of how teachers use grades. One fifth of all students felt that grades were used for overtly extrinsic purposes: 12 percent perceived their teachers using grades to "compare students for jobs and college" and 8 percent felt they were used to "punish and reward." A roughly equal number of students (19 percent) felt grades were used for intrinsic purposes: to "help students learn." A sizable majority of the students (59 percent) perceived a more subtle extrinsic use of grades, noting that they were used to "judge students' progress."

In other words, students tend not to perceive an overt social selection function in their teachers' grading practices, although they perceive this function in the overall use of grades and their school record. Still, they see grades being used to measure their progress according to what are essentially external criteria; in the process, classroom grading reinforces extrinsic learning incentives.

When asked what they perceive to be the most and least important criteria for school success, student responses reveal both democratic and nondemocratic traits. The four "most important factors in getting good grades" are "knowing facts" (22 percent), "understanding the subject," "careful, thorough work" (both 19 percent), and "hard work" (18 percent). The three "least important" factors are "being considerate of others" (37 percent), "teacher liking me" (23 percent), and "coming up with original ideas" (14 percent). Furthermore, students tend to see existing grading criteria as legitimate. Except for "knowing facts," the three criteria students perceived to be most important were the same criteria they felt ought to be most important. On the other hand, more than a third of all students felt "knowing facts" was either the most or second most important factor in school success.

Student acceptance of and compliance with the grading function are no doubt aided by the fact that the vast majority perceived their teachers as grading them impartially. When asked, "Do you feel that your teacher grades you on the same basis as everyone else in your class?" 71 percent of all students responded "always" or "usually," while only 11 percent selected "rarely" or "never." In addition, students felt the classroom grading system fairly reflected performance and student effort. In response to the statement "You really can't make excuses in this class because you get out of it what you put in," 66 percent agreed, while only 12 percent disagreed. Finally, these student perceptions paralleled direct observations of teaching practices; for the most part, all teachers involved in the study adhered in both theory and practice to the principles of fairness; only a few cases of subtle or overt favoritism were observed.

What do these observations and student views suggest? Taking into account the positive bias in the teaching sample, we can say that most or at least many teachers grade their students "fairly" and use legitimate criteria for evaluating student performance. As a result, students tend to encounter an environment in which grading control is perceived as legitimately exercised. The (nondemocratic) exceptions are the voices of a discontented minority, and the fact that the most frequently cited criterion for school success is "knowing facts."

What results is a kind of bureaucratic justice in which students are subjected to treatment that, for the most part, does not violate basic standards of impartiality. At the same time, however, as we will see in the next section, the nature of student work to which these standards are applied reflects forces that undermine democratic participation. It is not surprising to find that "knowing facts" is an important criterion of success in a bureaucratic structure that compartmentalizes learning in order to measure student performance. Nor is it surprising to find that the "teacher liking me" or "being considerate of others" are not perceived as important criteria for success.

The Teacher-as-Director

Closely related to teacher control through grading is the teacher's curricular function of directing learning activities in the classroom. Clearly, we would expect to find some element of teacher direction in an environment defined as instructional. However, teaching approaches vary significantly. In different proportions and with varying amounts of energy, teachers disseminate information, ask probing questions, construct skill-development exercises, and provide resource material for student learning. Each activity involves different qualities and degrees of curricular control.

Nonetheless, some teaching traits are fairly universal. As with the grading function, the teacher is the focal point of curricular control in the classroom. In all classes, teachers controlled official activities as the source of sanctions for student work. Student activity is made legitimate by virtue of the teacher's approval. In all classes, even the laissez-faire section, the teacher was ultimately the unilateral decision maker about curricular matters. All teachers formally began and ended the official class and all determined the basic schedule and nature of curricular activities, even where considerable student initiative was allowed. (The only observed instance in which students actively affected the teacher's decisions occurred in the laissez-faire unit, where the burden of initiation was placed largely on the students. On one relaxed spring morning, the teacher asked the class, "Well, what shall we do today?" After about 20 minutes of listless, scattered activity, the class responded favorably to a suggestion made by the teacher. On most days, students sat and chatted together or with the teacher, or responded to a suggested activity that was then pursued sporadically for several days.)

Despite the essentially unilateral quality of curricular control, teachers again functioned under two constraints. In the first place, all teachers work within external constraints. Most directly, these include implicit and explicit curricular expectations on the part of department heads or other governing offices. More pervasively, these constraints have their roots in the organizational prerequisites of bureaucratic scheduling, which chops the learning experience into finite periods of time and designated locations and requires considerable standardization in the learning process.

Additionally, teacher control is limited by the informal system of classroom legitimacy. Two elements of teacher activity seem particularly critical, one having to do with personal interaction with students and the other with academic work. Without exception all teachers cited the need to develop a "good rapport" with students. Furthermore, in completing the phrase "A good teacher is one who . . . , " students most frequently volunteered responses that reflect this personal element. Thirty-three percent felt that the good teacher "understands their problems"; 18 percent, "respects students, can communicate with them"; 16 percent, "cares about students, is friendly"; and 13 percent, "is open, flexible; listens."

The second, more academic factor of classroom legitimacy reflects teacher expertise. Twenty-six percent of all students felt a good teacher "helps students understand"; 18 percent, "makes class interesting"; and 18 percent, "is competent, knows subject." (Significantly less important were such traits as "is lenient, relaxed," 5 percent; "enjoys his or her work," 4 percent; and "doesn't overwork students," 4 percent.) In their perceptions of the specific teachers included in the study, 66 percent of all students agreed with the statement "Listening to the teacher is important because he (she) knows what he's (she's) talking about," while only 9 percent disagreed.

Student diffidence toward teacher expertise has been cited by critics concerned about teachers brainwashing their students. At the high school level, at least, this concern seems largely unmerited. The only instance of observed teacher moralizing occurred in sophomore classes, and only one of these teachers propagandized students with lessons drawn from subject material. Generally, teachers espoused the importance of objectivity. Most felt that expressing their opinions in class was good, especially to arouse student interest, but that these opinions should be clearly labeled as such.

Despite the general support for objectivity, however, teacher behavior varied widely. Some teachers openly expressed their views and challenged students to express theirs. In other cases, despite stated policies of objectivity, teachers established their opinions through more subtle word usage or even sarcastic ridicule. Student behavior also varied; in some cases when teachers expressed opinions, students sat quietly and continued to take notes as they did with factual information, while in others students openly challenged and disagreed with their teachers. Interestingly, in contrast to the concerns about teacher propagandizing, in three classes where teachers expressed their views freely and openly, students tended to disagree far more than the norm with the statement that it is "important to listen to the teacher." Students also seemed less repressed in these classes.

At least at the high school level, the degree of teacher domination built into classroom learning would appear to be a far more critical element of curricular control. Not only is the curriculum preestablished when students enter the learning environment but student interaction with the teacher and the subject matter is largely a matter of reaction and response rather than questioning and initiative. Teacher commentary dominated all classes regardless of the type of activity pursued, except for rare small-group or team projects. Overall, more than 80 percent of all classroom commentary was initiated by the teacher. Furthermore, 57 percent of all teacher questions across the spectrum of classes were right-answer questions, requiring that the student provide the single answer sought by the teacher.

Given this degree of teacher and subject domination, it is hardly surprising to find that students learn to feel they have little input into their classroom learning environment. Student feelings of classroom efficacy were universally low in the study. Only 19 percent of all students agreed with the statement "I feel I have a real influence on the way this class is run," while 46 percent disagreed (35 percent were neutral). Furthermore, these general sentiments were consistent throughout the various classes and schools studied. The only variation, and an interesting one, occurred among the lower track and Central High students, who tended to feel more influence over their classes. Twenty-five percent of the general track students agreed with the efficacy statement as opposed to 17 percent of all college and honors track students, while only 36 percent disagreed as opposed to 55 percent of the upper-level students.

Analysis of the student efficacy measure reveals two interesting findings. Higher student efficacy in low-track classes suggests that students feel they have more influence on classes that tend to be more disruptive. In part, that influence may itself take a negative, disruptive form (and consequently teach a negative lesson of participation). At the same time, student responses on the efficacy measure correlate significantly with only three other measures on the entire student questionnaire: two class-specific measures—the student's perception of having "plenty of chances to learn about things I am really interested in" and feeling "free to be myself" in class—and one schoolwide measure—"Most of my teachers are people I can talk to about things that are important to me." (All three measures exhibited a correlation coefficient of 0.27). In other words, students who feel they have a real influence on their classes tend to be those who perceive that their feelings and interests are of significance in teacher and subject-related aspects of school. Regardless of the setting, though, low student efficacy is the norm.

Finally, although teacher domination is the rule in all classrooms, the quality and degree of that domination are the variables that most clearly distinguish one teacher from another. As will be considered in the next three chapters, the variation in instructional approaches is of fundamental importance for two basic reasons. In the first place, it follows a pattern that tends to correspond most closely to student track level. Inequality, in short, is built into the learning experiences of different groups of students. Second, the variation in teaching approaches is causally tied to the level of student involvement in classroom learning. In other words, student learning varies according to track assignment in the degree to which it is extrinsically controlled (see Chapter 3), yet teachers are able to enhance the intrinsic qualities of learning through their own independent efforts (see Chapter 5).

As is suggested below, however, the degree to which teachers can vary the nature of their classroom domination is sharply con-

strained by forces built into the institutional structure of schooling.
Essentially systemic forces, like the instrumental functions of schooling and the bureaucratic requisites of large school structures, are
reinforced by school personnel, including teachers themselves. In a
work structure that is both uniform and competitive and in an environment that draws on and accentuates extrinsic motivations, curricular
domination by the teacher results in a tightly constricted, passive
learning experience that runs directly counter to the norms of democratic citizenship. Of all classroom factors, these most closely reflect the major antidemocratic traits of schooling in general.

The Teacher-as-Regulator

As in the case of grading and curricular direction, the teacher's
control of student behavior reflects an essentially autocratic structure
that is tempered by the input of student opinion and a range of variation in practice. Teachers are not only charged with the responsibility for curricular activities but also perform functions of policing,
crowd management, and group psychology.

Generally, to the extent that students were uninvolved in formal
curricular activities, teachers emphasized classroom discipline. Students were assigned specific seats in about half the classes (one of
the several means of control at the teacher's disposal). In almost all
areas of physical movement students were entirely subject to the
teacher's discretion.

As with curriculum direction, the exercise of behavior control
varies from teacher to teacher. Variations in student freedom were
due largely to differences in teachers' objectives and their perceptions
of student needs—subject to such external constraints as school or
departmental policies or the need for quiet in an adjoining room. In
many cases, however, the teacher's control of student behavior was
indistinguishable from curricular control. One teacher, for instance,
consciously used the curriculum as a means of maintaining classroom
order. By touching base with the lives and interests of individual students, he increased student involvement in the intrinsically controlling
process of learning. (At the same time, he was able to exercise the
option of excluding from class any "extremely unfit" student.)

On the other hand, teachers who imposed tight curricular constraints varied in their control of student behavior. The most authoritarian teacher continually reinforced class rules, for example, by
requiring late students to make up after school 3 minutes missed at
the beginning of class. Another teacher, whose curriculum direction
was equally constricting, allowed small groups of students to talk
among themselves, quieting them with regularity when they got out
of hand.

It one looks at classroom learning from the perspective of democratic concepts of individual freedom, it is clear that student behavior is highly controlled in the classroom. For two fundamental reasons, however, behavioral control is not the critical factor in making classroom learning an undemocratic experience. In the first place, as with many comparable group functions, classroom life requires a degree of quiet, orderly behavior, and restrictions of movement. In fact, one essential aspect of a class is that it is a controlled period of time, devoted to a particular activity, during which participants are closely observed and evaluated. In the process, they must be controlled so these functions can be performed.

From the democratic perspective, one can criticize the fact that almost the entire school learning experience takes place in these controlled settings. However, this control is essentially instrumental to another kind of control—that embodied in the curriculum. To the degree that the curriculum fails to control students, overt behavioral control becomes necessary. To the extent that curriculum control denies human individuality and undermines social participation, it is antidemocratic because it is engaging (or controlling) students for essentially extrinsic reasons. Only when the curriculum controls students through its intrinsic merits can we say that it is fully democratic.

A second and empirical reason for downplaying the importance of behavioral control is that variations in teacher regulation were not found to be demonstrably related to the democratic nature of learning. Teacher variation in behavioral control, per se, exhibited no significant relationship with such measures of intrinsic motivation as student involvement or interest in classroom learning. Where the curricular focus was narrowly constricted, students exhibited low levels of involvement regardless of whether or not the teacher was a disciplinarian.

Still, authoritarian behavior control can be criticized on the grounds that it provides an experiential basis for authoritarian or nondemocratic behavior. As we will see in Chapter 3, student behavior tends to be more overtly controlled among the lower-track groups; thus, authoritarian behavioral patterns are fostered and reinforced among these students. Additionally, these behavioral lessons are antidemocratic because of what authoritarian control means. Essentially, strict behavioral control means the curriculum itself is failing to engage the students—both extrinsic and intrinsic incentives are not sufficient to involve the student in the classroom process. Ultimately, this authoritarian control means control for its own sake.

Finally, as with grading practices, behavior control was perceived as "fair" by nearly all students. Fifty-seven percent considered discipline in their class to be "relaxed" and 25 percent cited "strict, but fair." Only 5 percent felt classroom discipline was "too harsh" and 7 percent "too easy."

The Structure of Classroom Work

Perhaps the single most important ingredient of antidemocratic control in schooling is the structure of classroom work. As a reinforcement of the external nature of school control, a direct reflection of the instrumental functions of schooling, and a limitation on the degree to which individual teachers are able to enhance democratic qualities of learning, the nature of the work process itself is a critical determinant of the "democraticness" of school learning. The most basic characteristics of the classroom work process are that it is uniform and competitive.

The vast majority of a student's class time is spent performing the same functions as all other students in the class—doing the same work at the same time in the same place. All 15 teachers across the spectrum of teaching styles estimated that students were working uniformly from 70 to 100 percent of class time. Whether the uniform work consisted of teacher lectures, whole-group discussions, or silent reading and note-taking, all students worked on identical projects during assigned blocks of time. Roughly half of the teachers actively incorporated diversified interests in formal portions of their curriculum—through small-group projects, individual topics within a common theme, and diverse presentations of common material. Most of the remaining teachers made allowances for varied student interests during discussions. Overall, however, student work rarely followed diverse paths. The classroom experience came far closer to fitting Robert Dreeben's description: "Within the classroom, all pupils very close in age and in capacities related to age, occupy a single position, are given similar work assignments, confront the same teacher, and are treated very much alike in instructional and disciplinary matters."[21]

An even greater proportion of student work is competitive or atomistic rather than cooperative. Only four teachers assigned work that required small groups of students to pool their resources and ideas in a common enterprise, and these cooperative projects were rare in these classes. In general, student work is comparative, or competitive, in the sense that students are evaluated on their individual performances against an external standard and their peers; everyone is in it for himself. Learning is not competitive in the sense of athletic team competition, but requires isolated individual effort that essentially competes against a common interest. As many have observed, cheating or unfairness is defined as cooperative or collaborative work in a setting where individual efforts are required.

If anything characterizes the universal classroom, it is the pervasive emphasis on individual effort and performance. Although a collective experience in one sense, the classroom is critically related to students' futures when it requires isolated individual effort. The structure of classroom work is such that it makes it necessary for individuals to stand out in some manner if they are to succeed. This is particularly so, for example, in competing with other students for the teacher's attention during class.

Although classroom work is essentially competitive, the degree of competitiveness, or student feelings of being in competition, is tempered by a number of forces. Only a small proportion (20 percent) of all students labeled their classes "competitive," and these were predominantly higher-level students. At the same time, however, classroom work is essentially a process that separates students. Forty-six percent of all students agreed with the statement "Grades make me feel like I'm always being told I'm better or worse than somebody else," while 32 percent disagreed.

Within the classroom, however, the impact of the competitive work structure is softened by student and teacher interaction. Thus, students establish informal norms against "curve raisers," and less involved students can influence the level of academic attentiveness in a given class. Additionally, a teacher can include cooperative learning projects, can contribute to a sense of classroom belongingness by communicating personal interest in individual students, and can convey an overall relaxed feeling to the class.

Furthermore, some types of whole-group activities involve greater sanctioned student interaction than others. In fact, the three types of classroom procedures that involve a degree of student interaction were cited by students as the "most interesting" kinds of class activity. Thirty-six percent of all students singled out "discussions" as most interesting; 19 percent, "student group projects"; and 18 percent, "combined lecture-discussion." On the other hand, the two activities that involve the least student interaction were viewed as the "least interesting" by students: 40 percent felt "reading and taking notes" was least interesting, and 25 percent had a comparable view of "lectures by the teacher."

Much has been written about the functional quality of the achievement motivation learned through the classroom process. Talcott Parsons, for example, describes the school's emphasis on achievement as the means through which "individual personalities are trained to be motivationally and technically adequate to the performance of adult roles."[22] Dreeben has noted that achievement "usually denotes activity and mastery, making an impact on the environment rather than fatalistically accepting it, and competing against some standard of excellence."[23]

In a more negative vein, however, the brand of individualism implicit in the classroom work structure is a far cry from the normative individualism that lies at the humanistic core of democratic principles. The institutional individualism of classroom learning submerges personal interests in identical tasks assigned to relatively homogeneous groups. Obviously, the purpose of this work structure is to make it possible to distinguish among individual performances. Yet, in the process, the individual personality is suppressed. Clearly, the structure of classroom work embodies little "respect for persons," that is, little concern about individual tastes, interests, and abilities and little opportunity for students to internalize these values by working cooperatively with their peers. As a critic of Dreeben observes, the stress on individual performance tends to "define others as outsiders," resulting in a society in which others are respected for "what they do" rather than "what they are as human beings."[24] Classroom work is fundamentally a group experience that is not really a group process.

From the democratic perspective, two basic critiques can be made of the uniform and competitive work structure. In individualist terms, classroom work undermines personal self-definition by standing the concept of democratic competition on its head. Instead of those at the top (that is, leaders, policies, or social objectives) competing for endorsement by those at the bottom, the reverse is true. In the process, democratic, or bottom-up, control becomes autocratic, or top-down, control. Students compete with each other for favorable evaluations according to standards that are essentially imposed from above. In the process, they become controlled by those external standards, for to deviate is to forfeit chances for advancement. The effort to do well in the learning structure—indeed, to do well in school—rests on incentives that draw on extrinsic motivations and that must remain largely unquestioned and unchallenged if one's self-interest is to be served.

At the same time that the external, competitive work structure is antidemocratic in an individualist sense, it is also antidemocratic in a social sense. School learning is a group experience. Yet, in participatory terms, there is little experiential basis for learning such values as tolerance, cooperation, compromise, or public spiritedness in classroom learning. Although collected in relatively homogeneous groups and performing similar tasks, students have very little chance to learn the value of interdependence because their work is essentially isolated and competitive. There is little collective identity or "in-commonness" fostered by the learning process itself.

According to the literature on cooperative interaction, a number of significant lessons are lost in the process. Morton Deutsch, for example, found that "cooperative social situations" resulted in higher "we-feeling," higher coordination of activities, fewer communication difficulties, greater "orientation awareness," higher productivity (qualitatively, though not necessarily quantitatively), and friendlier relations. [25] Seymour Spilerman found among the advantages of cooperative learning structures greater group solidarity, higher student interest in the group tasks and the attainment of individual group members, and greater ease in coping with failure. [26]

Finally, Getzels and Thelen suggest that the critical test for a teacher is posed by the need to create a sense of belongingness in a structure that is essentially hostile to this end. They write:

> The greater the belongingness, the greater the ease of
> significant communication between the teacher and the
> pupils and among the pupils themselves, and the greater
> the shared pride in the achievement of both institutional
> and individual goals. What was an "accidental" and com-
> pulsory group becomes a planful and voluntary group.
> The rigidity of the platoon or the instability of the crowd
> is changed into the flexibility of the team. They "know"
> what to expect, what to give, what to take. They find
> emotional support for their risk-taking, and the conse-
> quent increased individual security encourages "open"
> transactions between personality and role. . . . There
> is, at once, both greater autonomy and heteronomy for
> the individual. The depth of the person's involvement
> in the classroom is increased, and, in this sense, learn-
> ing becomes more meaningful. [27] (emphasis in original)

Put somewhat differently, we might say that a learning environment that fosters student belongingness is intrinsically controlled. To be successful, it requires a democratic input on the part of teachers. Yet we can also see in the Getzels and Thelen description a basic conflict between this democratic impact and the antidemocratic structure of school learning. Fundamentally, the personalized, affective input of teachers conflicts with the depersonalized, competitive structure of classroom work required by institutional traits of schools.

In order to create intrinsic learning incentives in an extrinsically controlling environment, the teacher has to engage the interests of individual learners. As we shall see when we consider the impact of individual teachers, this objective requires an element of active teacher direction, of contact with each individual learner in a learning task, and group interaction among the students. For the most part, students in the survey perceived their teachers as caring about and respecting students. Sixty-nine percent of all students disagreed with the statement "I don't feel the teacher cares very much about what I think," while only 12 percent agreed. And 64 percent agreed that "Even if I don't do well in class, I feel the teacher respects me as a person" as opposed to 13 percent who disagreed.

In a sense, then, teachers have to draw on a personalizing element in the classroom, and apparently most exude a basic respect for their students. Yet this requirement of learning encounters a structure that is fundamentally hostile to the development of these intrinsic learning traits. As a judge of student performance, the teacher acts as an agent of others who use the grade and credit measures of student worth. Consequently, teachers must grade all students on their individual performance, and thus must structure classroom work in ways that stress student differences. Learning must be standardized or uniform rather than individually meaningful to students. Where uniform activity fails to engage students, students are defined as problems; functional pressures weigh on the side of employing behavioral discipline rather than taking time to engage those students in meaningful learning. Since classroom work must also yield easily identifiable student differences, there is considerable pressure to rely on quantifiable measures of learning, in particular, the number of "right" answers to factual questions.

These external prerequisites of classroom learning conflict with the kinds of objectives teachers themselves espouse, although not all teachers articulated this conflict. The teachers involved in the study almost universally downplayed "giving information" as a classroom objective and emphasized instead "creating new interests," "broadening minds and horizons," and "sharpening skills." Yet classroom work predominantly consisted of the dissemination and reporting of factual information, to be temporarily absorbed by students. Some teachers bemoaned the effects of previous years of receptive learning on the part of students, noting how difficult it was to get students to take some initiative in class. By and large, the essential classroom function of most students was, as critics have remarked, coming up with the right answer.

The discrepancies between teacher objectives and teacher behavior, while not universal, underscore the pervasive controls implicit in the instrumental functions of schooling. Within these imposed functions, teachers pursue what they perceive as legitimate learning objectives, and these largely conform to democratic aims. At best, however, these objectives only manage to temper the extrinsic controls of learning. Not only do the instrumental functions of schooling control students but they control teachers. They also apparently so-

cialize teachers in such a way that they believe they are fulfilling democratic learning objectives far more than they are.

On the other hand, many teachers are aware and critical of
these external constraints. One experienced teacher in Central High
commented:

> It's unfortunate that we have to give grades. I'd rather we
> didn't have to, because in the ideal situation people are
> here to learn, not to get a mark. The whole system is
> based on points—getting points, adding points, you must
> take this, you must take that. . . . I think that's unfortu-
> nate. It's not ideal. It's not intellectual. It's not educa-
> tional. Also, it's based on failure. For every A, you're
> going to have a certain number of failures. Right off the
> bat you know that certain people are going to go down the
> drain, and there's not a damn thing you can do about it.
> The whole system accepts this, that's why I'm opposed
> to it. But I function in the system, so I try to make the
> best of it.

Extrinsic controls do not originate with the teacher. Yet they
result in a learning experience where students are fundamentally controlled by forces external to learning. In the process, the social environment of learning becomes largely incidental to the critical functions of the classroom. Ironically, a majority of all students agreed
with the general perception of schooling that "School is most interesting as a place to see friends" (56 percent agreed, 20 percent disagreed). Yet this intrinsic aspect of learning has little to do with the
formal functions of the school. As one teacher commented:

> This is a cliquey school. In most of the classes you go
> half a year without the students knowing each other's
> names. Students go to classes with their friends if pos-
> sible; otherwise they meet their friends after class.
> Class is just a kind of place they have to go in between
> social meetings. . . .

Exacerbated by such structural separations as tracking, the
classroom is essentially a missed opportunity for the kind of social
interdependence and participatory activity embodied in the norms of
democratic citizenship. The fact that students are most interested
in school as a "place to see friends" also suggests that school learning fails to draw on a fundamental intrinsic source of control. To the
degree that classroom work fails to incorporate social interdepend-

ence, it misses an opportunity to be other than imposed and extrinsically controlling.

In sum, we can perceive the most critical nondemocratic traits of school control in the structure of classroom work. Reflecting such instrumental functions as social selection and equal opportunity, schooling objectives require unilateral teacher evaluation, teacher domination of curricular activities, passive learning, and, where all else fails, tight behavioral constraints. While this structure is legitimized by the instrumental functions of schooling, its pervasiveness carries with it considerable democratic costs.

OVERVIEW: ANTIDEMOCRATIC CONTROL

Taken together, the various elements of classroom and school control form a structure that would seem highly dysfunctional, if not simply intolerable, in an open, democratic society. Two of the three norms of democratic citizenship outlined at the beginning of the chapter are fundamentally contradicted by this structure. The norm of intellectual independence and the inviolate personality is undermined by a structure that is basically imposed, that makes the student almost totally dependent on external meanings (despite the best efforts of teachers). The social and participatory element of democratic citizenship is undermined by an essentially passive learning experience in which students work in self-interested isolation.

As we shall see in subsequent chapters, however, this structure is not entirely monolithic. Instead, we can detect patterns of variation that result in more and less democratic experiences. These, however, raise the specter of inequality in school learning, the major focus of this work. For the moment, we can review the basic antidemocratic traits of learning and trace their functional sources.

1. In the first place, the formal characteristics of school control are essentially autocratic, reflecting the norm of dominance and subordination. Imposed unilateral decisions affect students' lives without involving explicit or implicit student input into those decisions. Regardless of whether or not these decisions serve the students' "best interests," they provide precious little experiential basis for learning and internalizing the norms of democratic citizenship.

2. Although this control structure varies in practice, it does so largely as students internalize the extrinsic incentives inherent in schooling. It is "safe" to consult students or to allow them some choice if they are sufficiently controlled by the need to succeed in school. The most pervasive motivating force in student learning is derived from the pressure to get good grades to ensure future success.

As a result critical independence is undermined; students are motivated to play the game because the stakes are high.

3. Work activities that students pursue in the classroom are
largely external to their interests. Most work activities are uniform
in subject and process, despite the diverse personal traits of individual students in the class. As a result, the work itself is fundamentally
imposed and becomes largely teacher dominated. Although the purpose of this work in common is in part to enlarge student horizons,
there is at best limited evidence of this taking place. Much of the
learning process fails to engage and involve a large number of students. Overall, students come to feel they have little input into their
learning environment.

4. This imposed work process becomes more totally controlling
through the competitive work process. The pursuit of individual self-
interest requires conformity to external standards and requirements.
The pervasiveness of atomistic learning undermines the formation of
collective interest and interdependence. Although competition is an
important element of democratic control, the direction of that control
is reversed in the learning process.

5. Finally, the existence and pervasiveness of these controls
are reinforced by a preoccupation with the manner in which control is
exercised by school personnel. By and large, most teachers and most
students felt that considerations of fairness were being met in their
classes and in school generally. Grading control was largely perceived as fair, as was classroom and school discipline. This positive
sentiment may be over represented in this sample, and the concerns
of fairness are by no means unimportant. An exclusive preoccupation
with fairness and equal opportunity, however, diverts attention from
the critical ends and by-products of the control structure itself. Students who perceive control in their environment as fair are more
likely to be students who comply with that control and all it entails.

These five characteristics of antidemocratic control are enumer-
ated to draw attention to systematic features of schooling. As will be
illustrated in subsequent chapters, the reader should not infer that
schools are uniformly antidemocratic or that institutional traits have
uniform effects on all students. The five antidemocratic characteristics are relevant to present concerns because all reflect the instrumental functions of schooling.

Autocratic control grows out of the fundamental imposition of a
testing ground on all our young people; the institution that teaches the
young also tests the young. This imposition becomes autocratic by
virtue of the fact that it is the only testing ground; in this sense it is
monolithic. As such, schooling becomes critical to future success
and thus appeals to extrinsic incentives instead of those that emanate

from individual interests. The overall imposition of schooling is mirrored in the classroom, where work is standardized. As such, work is external to student interests. To be successful, teachers must dominate the learning process; they must try to engage all students' interests in a process that has its origins outside the students' interests.

Efforts to draw on social interests of the young are stymied by the functional need to measure and evaluate individual student performance according to uniform criteria that apply to all. Evaluation is required by the testing-ground function of school learning. To be legitimate, the testing ground must maximize equal opportunity for all students; all controls—grades, classification of student performance, and behavioral discipline—must be exercised fairly.

The testing-ground analogy reflects the instrumental function of schooling. Although grounded in the ethical norm of providing all with an equal opportunity for social, political, and occupational success, the testing-ground function essentially serves a clientele in society instead of the clientele in the schools. The basic aim of the testing ground is social selection—distinguishing the various talents, motivations, and behaviors of students that are deemed useful by the controlling elements in society.

Although these functions would seem to be necessary and ethically legitimate in our society, we can ask whether the shape they take and their pervasive hold on school learning are necessary. Before examining the variable impact of schooling, we can perceive ways in which the instrumental functions of schooling redefine democratic principles in antidemocratic ways. In the process, we gain insight into the potential cost of institutionalizing these functions in the schools.

In the first place, the kind of freedom that is considered fundamental to human personality is constrained by an essentially imposed structure. Within this structure, to use Ivan Illich's phrase, "Freedom is reduced to a selection among packaged commodities."[28] Freedom is passive and reactive, and because of the way the success drive shapes student choice, it is in some senses nonexistent. About the only evidence of students acting or feeling free in school was in the inner-city school and lower tracks, where students protected their own domain by separating themselves from formal (and success-oriented) school activities.

Second, community does not mean the interdependence, the give and take, of a social group. Instead, it is translated by the learning process to mean simply the grouping of individual persons who resemble each other in such school-important ways as age and performance record. The concept of individualism, as mentioned above, is deprived of its humanistic thrust and instead takes on the traits of atomism.

Finally, as we shall see, equality does not mean treating all human personalities as if they were of equal worth, nor does it mean the implied universalizing of experiences conducive to democratic citizenship. Instead, equality comes to mean sameness or identity. The ethical prescription of equality becomes institutionally satisfied when all students are subjected to the same learning experiences. Where distinctions are made among students, as in the fateful tracking decision, they are based on "legitimate" reasons, namely, those that derive from the instrumental functions of the schools.

NOTES

1. For a full discussion of the concepts of negative and positive liberty, see Isaiah Berlin, Four Essays on Liberty (London: Oxford University Press, 1969).

2. John Dewey, Democracy and Education (New York: Free Press, 1966), p. 128.

3. Ibid. , pp. 130-32.

4. Justice Oliver Wendell Holmes, dissenting opinion in Abrams v. United States, 250 U.S. 616 (1919).

5. R. S. Peters, Ethics and Education (London: Allen & Unwin, 1970), p. 319.

6. Justice Felix Frankfurter, concurring opinion in Dennis v. United States, 341 U.S. 494 (1951).

7. See the excellent discussion of these and other theorists in Carole Pateman, Participation and Democratic Theory (Cambridge: Cambridge University Press, 1970), Ch. 2.

8. Dewey, op. cit. , p. 99.

9. See, for example, David Elkind, Children and Adolescents (New York: Oxford University Press, 1970), p. 70; Erik H. Erikson, Identity: Youth and Crisis (New York: Norton, 1968), p. 165; and Lawrence Kohlberg and Alan Lockwood, "Cognitive Developmental Psychology and Political Education—Progress in the Sixties" (Cambridge, Mass. : Harvard University).

10. James D. Barber, The Presidential Character: Predicting Performance in the White House (Englewood Cliffs, N.J. : Prentice-Hall, 1972), p. 10.

11. Willard Waller, The Sociology of Teaching (New York: Wiley, 1932), p. 10.

12. Ibid. , p. 11.

13. Erving Goffman, Asylums (Garden City, N.Y. : Anchor Books, 1961), p. xiii.

14. See, for example, Gresham M. Sykes, A Society of Captives: A Study of Maximum Security Prisons (Princeton, N.J. : Princeton University Press, 1958).

15. Goffman, op. cit., p. 6.

16. Dewey, op. cit., p. 340.

17. Tinker v. Des Moines Independent School District, 393 U.S. 503 (1969).

18. Goss v. Lopez, 42 LEd 2d 725 (1975).

19. Tinker, op. cit.

20. Jacob W. Getzels and Herbert A. Thelen, "The Classroom Group as a Unique Social System," in Dynamics of Instructional Groups: Socio-Psychological Aspects of Teaching and Learning, ed. Nelson B. Henry (Chicago: University of Chicago Press, 1960), pp. 79-80.

21. Robert Dreeben, On What Is Learned in School (Reading, Mass.: Addison-Wesley, 1968), p. 22.

22. Talcott Parsons, "The School Class as a Social System: Some of Its Functions in American Society," in Socialization and Schools, compiled from the Harvard Educational Review, Harvard College, 1968, p. 69.

23. Dreeben, op. cit., pp. 70-71.

24. Jan J. Loubsen, "Review Symposium of On What Is Learned in School (Dreeben), Sociology of Education 43, no. 2 (Spring 1970): 205-27.

25. Morton Deutsch, "The Effects of Cooperation and Competition Upon Group Process," in Group Dynamics: Research and Theory, ed. Dorwin Cartwright and Alvin Zander (Evanston, Ill.: Row, Peterson, 1953), pp. 319-53.

26. Seymour Spilerman, "Raising Academic Motivation in Lower Class Adolescents: A Convergence of Two Research Traditions," Sociology of Education 44, no. 1 (Winter 1971): 103-18.

27. Getzels and Thelen, op. cit., pp. 79-80.

28. Ivan Illich, Deschooling Society (New York: Harper & Row, 1971), p. 70.

3

PATTERNS OF
INEQUALITY IN
CLASSROOM LEARNING

In the previous chapter, we saw how the schooling process is shaped by structural characteristics common to diverse school types. These structural constants derive ultimately from instrumental functions that schools as institutions perform in our society. Although the functions themselves are democratically legitimate, they shape the schooling experience in essentially antidemocratic ways.

At the same time, however, there is considerable variation in the schooling experience. To some extent, this is simply due to chance characteristics of a local population or of particular school personnel. On the one hand, this variation is legitimate and desirable, for it reflects a diversity of local practices. Yet, when this variation reveals patterns in the learning environment that affect different groups in different ways, the issue of equality becomes relevant. To satisfy ethical prescriptions, identifiable patterns of variation must be based upon legitimate reasons for distinguishing among groups of individual students. Furthermore, the varying outcomes of these patterns must also be justifiable. When either the reasons or outcomes violate democratic norms, they become the focus for democratic reform.

Two kinds of patterns can be discerned in the learning experience. First, we can speak of structural variations rooted in the way schools as institutions define and treat different groups of students. These patterns result in an inequality that is embedded in the school as institution, and will be our primary concern in this and the following chapter. Second, however, we can detect patterns in the way school personnel, in this case teachers, behave, regardless of institutional traits. These teacher variations will be considered in Chapter

5. Both aspects of variation are relevant to policy concerns. The structural sources of inequality point to a need for institutional reform, while the effects of different teaching approaches suggest reforms directed at schools as they currently exist.

In examining the structural variations of school learning, we will again focus on the classroom where the institutional functions of schooling most directly affect the lives of young people. Additionally, this focus allows us to scrutinize variations within as well as between schools. At the same time, however, the three types of high schools involved in this study are very different institutions. On entering these schools, one is immediately struck by differences in tangible school facilities and intangible school atmosphere. These schoolwide differences will be considered at the outset—as a framework within which classroom learning takes place.

Some school characteristics, such as physical facilities and material resources, can be independently affected by political policies. Many school characteristics, however, reflect the type of student population served by a given school, as defined by schooling functions. These functional definitions of student types are based on the way schools distinguish among and classify student performance.

The most striking and consistent pattern of classroom learning corresponds to a student's track assignment, not to the particular school a student attends, or the student's grade level, or the particular teacher a student encounters. In effect, then, many of the differences among schools are a function of the differences within schools. In other words, observable between-school learning patterns are a reflection of the particular track emphasis in a given school. In short, the track makeup of the student population goes a long way toward explaining many of the observable differences from one school to another.

Because this track difference is the most systematic variation uncovered, and it is associated with a student's socioeconomic background, the principle of equality requires that we examine the functional reasons for tracking. Furthermore, because the tracking experience results in identifiable types of citizenship lessons or outcomes, we must question the cost of pursuing these functions to the extent that we do. Before considering the patterns of inequality in the classroom, however, we can consider the variations in schooling that are most readily apparent to the observer's eye.

SYMPTOMS OF INEQUALITY

As noted in the introduction, the three high schools selected for empirical study were chosen to represent three basic school types. Each represents a type of community relevant to policy considerations.

A fourth type, the rural school, would be an important addition for policy considerations that focus on such concerns as economic resources or local political participation. Because of the focus here on the internal dynamics of schooling, particularly those having to do with the institutional functions of schools, we can concentrate on a range of diversity represented by these three types.

Community Background

In many ways the roots of between-school differences are embedded in the communities served by the particular school. In sociological terms, each of the three communities and schools reflects a fairly classic type. Central High School is an aging structure located in the inner-city area of the core city under focus. Like many such urban areas, its population is largely nonwhite and predominantly lower class. Middletown High School, on the other hand, is the newest of the three schools, and is located in a self-contained, small city approximately 15 miles from the core city. The Middletown population, as the name suggests, is largely middle and working class and is almost entirely white; many families are upward mobile. Northdale High School is a relatively modern school in an upper-middle-class suburban town outside the core city. It is part of what is reputed to be one of the area's best school systems.

1970 census data included in Table 3.1 bear out these distinctions among the three communities. Easton, the inner-city area where Central High is located, is the most densely populated and the poorest of the three. Median family income is less than half of that in Northdale, and fully 18.7 percent of all families have incomes

TABLE 3.1

Community Income Level

Community Traits	Easton	Middletown	Northdale
Population	85,030	61,582	31,890
Median family income (dollars)	7,469	11,523	17,558
Percent below poverty	18.7	4.3	2.1

Source: U.S. Department of Commerce, Bureau of the Census, Census of Population, 1960 (Washington, D.C.: U.S. Government Printing Office).

below the federal poverty level. Furthermore, these income measures closely parallel differences in the occupational makeup of each community. Fifty-one percent of the working population in Northdale are classified as professional or managerial as opposed to 23 percent in Middletown and 12.7 percent in Easton. On the other hand, only 15 percent in Northdale are lower working class (operatives, laborers, or service workers), while Middletown has twice that proportion and Easton almost three times.

Finally, the educational attainment of adults in the respective communities reflects similar patterns. Eighty-three percent of the Northdale population have at least a high school diploma, while only 55 percent in Middletown and 41 percent in Easton are high school graduates. The median number of years of schooling for each population is comparable: 13.5 years in Northdale, 12.1 in Middletown, and 11.2 in Easton.

The Schools

In tangible terms, each of the three high schools reflects its community. Systemwide expenditure figures (1971) reveal that Northdale spends $935 per pupil, while the average local expenditure for the core city is $747 per pupil and that of Middletown is $713 per pupil. In terms of teachers' salaries, the unionized core city teachers have a somewhat higher starting salary than their counterparts. Northdale, however, has the highest median salary ($13,672), while core city ($12,084) and Middletown ($11,900) are considerably lower. In part, these median figures reflect the years of teaching experience of each population.

Turning to the high schools themselves, the most tangible differences are those that reflect the ability level and educational attainment of the students. Each school population, in effect, is dominated by a type of student, defined by track level and postgraduate pursuits. Northdale High has 17 percent of its students in identifiable honors or accelerated units, and 55 percent of its graduates go on to four-year colleges. Seventy percent of all Middletown students are in the basic college preparatory track, and graduates are evenly divided among those who attend four-year colleges, two-year colleges, and those who work. Four percent of the Middletown students are in an honors track. In Central High, there is no accelerated honors track comparable to that in the other two schools; instead, 59 percent of all students are in the general track and 41 percent are in the college track. Thirty-five percent of Central's graduates attend two-year colleges, 31 percent seek employment, and 25 percent attend four-year colleges.

These school data reflect the basic community types served by each school. Further data are included in the appendix. To discern the more qualitative differences among schools, especially those having to do with the environment of control, we can briefly consider the atmosphere or climate of each school.

Central High School

Located in the racially mixed inner city, Central High possesses many of those characteristics we have come to associate with the inner-city school. A first and lasting impression one gets of the school is of an old, dusty, red-brick building, patched and repaired to make it function as effectively as possible under far from ideal circumstances. From the outside, one notices an occasional broken window, usually where the heavy protective screening is missing. Inside the school, some of the doors between classrooms lack windowpanes, classroom floors are worn unevenly by the tread of countless student generations, and heavy classroom doors equipped with fortified wireglass windows frequently fail to close properly. One teacher complained that he had been "trying to get a missing window between classes replaced for two years without any luck."

At the same time, efforts to modernize the aged structure are noticeable. Corridors are well illuminated, although painted an ageless tan color. New tables, about the size of three card tables placed end to end, have replaced the old, fixed chair-desk combinations in the classrooms, although the original fixture marks remain on the floors.

Two qualities of school life in Central High strike the uninitiated visitor: constant supervision of the school buildings, especially the exits, and a high noise level when classes are not in session. The main (and only legitimate) entrance to the school is locked and all latecomers and visitors are monitored by school officials. Throughout the day, teacher-monitors are stationed at all the exits and patrol the corridors. Between class periods, the long central corridors resound with the loud shrieks and calls of students; the noise level requires simple conversations to be shouted. This kind of uninhibited student behavior contrasts sharply with the relatively controlled quiet that prevails in Middletown's and Northdale's corridors.

In essence, the policing quality of Central High reflects the concern for security, a concern that in turn reflects the basic antagonism between the prevailing student street culture and the culture of the school. Some school personnel expressed concern for their own safety. As one teacher put it, "I don't feel unsafe teaching here, or I wouldn't do it. But things like being held up at knife-point do happen, so you

never know. " As a result of security concerns, students' time in
school is completely filled with scheduled classes and a lunch period
(the scene of occasional disruptive incidents), and the administration
has established a detailed set of rules and regulations governing both
academic and nonacademic conduct.

In the implementation of school policies, the school personnel
are divided along faculty and administration lines, although the latter
group is supported by several teachers. In many respects, the administration of school life is similar to that found in many prisons—a
largely detached, policy-making administration, which dictates rules
to the teachers who (like prison guards) have to deal directly with the
students. Not surprisingly, teachers vary widely in adapting rules to
their own classrooms, with the result that several overlook requirements that interfere with their teaching. One teacher commented,
"If we enforced all the rules, we'd have a riot here. We really would.
We're the ones who deal with the kids every day, and some of the
rules are absurd—like suspending students for cutting class. " Another
observed, "I have to adapt school policies to my own objectives—for
survival. If I were to try to carry out the administration's rules to
the letter, I think life in the classroom would be unbearable. " Working against teacher flexibility is what one teacher termed "the good
soldier principle, " whereby teachers who adhere closely to school
policies and the emphasis on discipline are rewarded by promotion
to higher paying administrative positions.

The two most common teacher remarks about students focused
on their extremely poor reading skills and their passivity in learning—
problems compounded by growing numbers of French- and Spanish-
speaking students unable to become involved in the English curriculum.
One teacher observed of the indigenous students, "A lot of the kids
have been brought up in the city school system and are very restrained
and restricted. " At the same time, however, he noted, "For some
of these kids, school is like a second home. Their home life is so
bad, they really lean on you. The teacher is like a surrogate father—
sometimes the only rational adult they have to talk with. "

The teachers involved in the study seemed both resigned to the
obstacles in their path and determined to fulfill at least some of their
teaching objectives. The major frustrations encountered by teachers
are poignantly summarized by the response of one experienced teacher
to a question about "something missing" in his job. He said:

> Yes, a lot of things. I don't even know where to start.
> Let's start with the most obvious. First of all, the fa-
> cilities. In this school, the physical plant works against
> you rather than for you. The windows between class-
> rooms are broken, so sound carries from one room to

another. Doors either slam or don't close properly.
Sounds carry in from outside. The acoustics are ter-
rible. Those are the most obvious things . . . the
shortages of materials.

Other things that work against you are the pressures from the administration. The demands, the flood
of paper they throw upon you. . . . If you were to carry
these things out diligently, it would detract from your
teaching time. The administration's attitude, frankly—
and this is a fairly common one—is that the smart teacher is the one who wants to get out of the classroom and
be a supervisor. . . . They're more impressed by the
person who does outside things—who runs candy drives
or takes care of discipline. If you're a hard disciplinarian, this puts you in a good light with the administration.
. . . This sort of binds you in. I'd like to bring people
in here but can't, except on the sly, and then I expose
myself to a major hassle.

Middletown High School

In contrast to Easton, Middletown has a large new high school;
construction was completed six years before this study was undertaken, and the school exhibits few signs of wear either inside or out.
The school building is a three-story, light-red-brick structure that
covers about twice the area of Central High. On the outside, its im-
posing dimensions are lightened by vast expanses of plate-glass windows on all three floors. The inside of the building also reflects modern equipment; corridors are clean and brightly illuminated by fluo-
rescent lighting, pastel walls are spotless, and lockers lining the
halls are virtually unmarked. Office space is ample compared to that
in Central High, and facilities like the library are lushly equipped
with books, audiovisual material, and furniture. Unlike their counterparts in Central, teachers in Middletown registered no complaints
about shortage of teaching materials.

Compared to the agitation of Central High, Middletown functions
much like a well-oiled machine. During class time, the corridors are
almost completely still and patrolled by an occasional monitor. One
rarely sees a student outside the classroom when classes are in session, except for special missions legitimized by a written pass. Between classes—a time span of 3 minutes—hallway traffic is swift and
largely uninterrupted by other than hurried chatter and quick stops
at lockers.

At the same time, student behavior is far more closely super-
vised and controlled than in the more informal Northdale High. Teachers

are assigned custodial duties, like monitoring corridors or lavatories between classes, and three unit "housemasters" oversee discipline within their subdivisions. An intricate system of multicolored pass slips covers all teacher-sanctioned activity outside the classroom, and is used to report such offenses as tardiness, absence, or classroom disruption. Additionally, the department head circulates among the classes of his or her teachers, reminding them of administrative requirements ("I'd rather you didn't let them put their heads down on their desks") and expressing reservations about some academic practices (such as a book that might upset parents).

As a rule, students at Middletown High do little to disturb the daily flow of school life. I observed no student outbursts (in contrast to Central), and teachers reported very few disciplinary problems in class. On the whole, classes (except for those in the general track) were more orderly and restrained than those in either Central or Northdale. On the other hand, the natural, boisterous world of adolescents emerges in specific locations and situations. Raucous voices can be heard in the lavatories and cafeteria and during collective gatherings like assemblies. Additionally, as one teacher noted wryly, "They leave here a lot faster at the end of the day than they do in a fire drill."

In large part, the norms of school life are adhered to by the bulk of Middletown students. The order of school and classroom life only breaks down among largely alienated general track students or when a particular teacher is out of touch with the students. In contrast, there is a far greater gap between school and student norms at Central High, while school norms are far less rigid and more diversified at Northdale. Compared to its inner-city and suburban counterparts, Middletown High operates efficiently, with few ripples of discontent. None of the various actors seems in basic conflict with any of the others, although minor clashes do occur. The school administration is reputed to be conservative, cautiously mindful of the reactions of parents and the school board. Compared to those in the other two schools, teachers are relatively strict in behavioral terms, but several are fairly innovative in their curricular approaches. In its controlled environment, Middletown provides a strong contrast to the underequipped, agitated Central High and the more diversified, flexible Northdale school.

Northdale High School

Two impressions of Northdale High stand out in comparison to Central and Middletown. First, at least on the surface, the school is far more diverse than its counterparts in physical plant, curricular

activities, student behavior, and academic ability. Second, one is
struck by the relatively casual atmosphere of the school as a whole.

In part, the diversity at Northdale is reflected in the school
structure itself. Erected in the 1950s and early 1960s, the school
building is really a composite of several separate but interconnected
units. Administratively, the school is divided into eight units, each
with an assigned group of students, a guidance counselor, teachers,
and an administrative unit head. The school as a whole is blessed
with ample facilities, ranging from a well-endowed, much used library, to substantial audiovisual equipment, to a lavish art studio.

Additionally, students are able to choose courses from among
a broad selection of curricular alternatives. Instead of the usual
American history course, for example, a student can satisfy his or
her requirement by choosing from among a standard survey course,
a problem-oriented, interpretive course, or a course on the American presidency or the Supreme Court. Furthermore, Northdale High
offers a distinct school-without-walls program, housed in an independent unit. A kind of alternative subschool, this program has been plagu-
ed by problems of overenrollment and understaffing.

The other major characteristic of Northdale High is the relaxed,
sociable atmosphere throughout the school. Unlike the other two
schools, Northdale has an open campus that allows students to leave
the school grounds whenever they do not have a scheduled class or required activity. On pleasant days, it is not unusual to see groups of
students in the parking lot—talking, smoking, and sitting in cars—
while others sit or stroll on the school lawns. Additionally, teachers
are rarely strict about students being on time for class, although
there is a general expectation of punctuality. With 5 minutes between
classes, the corridor activity is generally more relaxed; students
move deliberately, stopping to talk or horseplay with friends. In conjunction with the relaxed atmosphere of the school, Northdale has a
liberal principal and a decentralized system of school discipline. The
latter allows closer attention to be paid to individual students. Overall, the major problem with the open campus has been student absen-
teeism (and related parental pressures).

Traditionally, the student body is diverse, with four or five distinguishable types of student groups, each with its own eating place
and behavioral style. In the midst of this diversity, however, it is
possible to discern characteristics of the Northdale student body that
distinguish it from those in Central and Middletown. Most noticeable,
perhaps, is the widespread evidence of student initiative in the life of
the school, particularly the proliferation of activities available to students. Bulletin boards throughout the school are covered with colorful
announcements of student club meetings, field trips, bake sales, or
guest speakers, and news items are distributed in a student bulletin

and in student dramatizations over the public address system. General student traits also are discernible in the classroom. In partiular, students can be observed conversing with each other about class topics more than their counterparts in the other schools. A relaxed atmosphere also prevails in classes, although students were sometimes intensely competitive.

Finally, all teachers reported that they felt no pressure from the administration regarding the way they ran their particular classes—within broad bureaucratic guidelines focusing on issues like student absences. The major constraints teachers felt were those of time (resulting from heavy teaching loads) and class size.

THE CLASSROOM: TYPES OF TEACHERS

Within the three schools, it is possible to make distinctions among individual classes according to observable traits of classroom interaction. The classroom groups defined here cross school and track lines. Because the criteria that distinguish one class from another are closely related to the way teachers teach, they suggest the outlines of a teacher impact that will be considered more carefully in Chapter 5. For present purposes, the classification of teacher types serves as a static picture of classroom variations. After examining structural patterns of inequality, we can examine the dynamics of classroom activity.

All 15 classes involved in the study are organized according to two control variables that prove in subsequent analysis to be democratically significant. On the basis of classroom observations, teacher interviews, and quantified measures of student behavior, classes are categorized according to the degree of teacher activism-passivism in managing and directing the class, and the degree to which the curriculum is relatively open or closed. The variable of teacher activism focuses on the degree of teacher leadership or domination in the classroom; in a sense, it reflects the degree to which the teacher takes charge of curricular exercises. In general, teachers classified as passive tend to be less assertive or less energetic in directing classroom activities, although they remain figurehead leaders. Teachers designated as active, on the other hand, tend to be more assertive in exercising leadership and control. Teachers of both types, however, differ in the quality of their activism, depending on a number of factors ranging from personality and experience to conscious pedagogical aims.

The second teacher trait focuses more specifically on curricular forces in classroom learning; in effect, it defines the quality of teacher input, whereas the activism variable defines the degree of input. Most fundamentally, it describes the degree to which student learning is constrained by the curricular structure. Teachers designated as open tend to stress two curricular qualities: content that is more open to personal interpretation and differing points of view (though usually not without a factual base) and approaches that allow greater diversity in learning activities. Teachers designated as closed tend to emphasize the opposite qualities. Content is narrowed to focus almost exclusively on factual or right-answer material, and there is far less room for individuals or groups to diverge from uniform assignments. A somewhat amorphous group of teachers, labeled flexible, employs approaches that are between the open and closed types.

Classification of teachers is aided by two quantitative measures of classroom interaction: the teacher-domination ratio and the convergent-question percentage. The former refers to the ratio of teacher-initiated to student-initiated comments that take place during of official, whole-class discussions. The latter measure depicts the percentage of all academic teacher questions that are right-answer or convergent as opposed to interpretive or divergent. The breakdown of teacher types according to these measures is illustrated in Table 3.2.

As can be seen in the table, far more observed teachers were active than passive, and there is a definite concentration of teachers tending toward the open side of the curricular constraint dichotomy. In considering the sample of teacher types, two qualifications need to be kept in mind. This scheme represents a relative rather than an absolute picture of teacher types, and teaching approaches and personalities vary within each group. Still, although the sample does not include totally authoritarian teachers who fail to develop a personal

TABLE 3.2

Teacher Categories

	Number of Teachers	Average Teacher-Domination Ratio	Average Convergent-Question Percentage
Active-open	4	4.9:1	44.3
Passive-open	3	2.5:1	40.5
Active-flexible	5	3.8:1	64.4
Passive-closed	2	7.0:1	82.2
Active-closed	1	10.9:1	76.4
Mean		4.6:1	57.3

Source: Compiled by the author.

TABLE 3.3

Teacher and Student Variables

	Teachers			Students		
	Teacher Activism	Curricular Constraint	Behavioral Control	Track	Curricular Initiative	Participation Distribution
Central High School						
Casey	Passive	Open	Relaxed	Business	Low	Moderate
James	Active	Flexible	Flexible	Business	Low	Wide
Hawkins	Active	Open	Firm	College	Restrained	Wide
Gianelli	Active	Closed	Strict	College	Low	Moderate
Pellagrini	Passive	Closed	Flexible	Business	Low	Wide
Middletown High School						
Backman	Active	Open	Firm	College	Restrained	Moderate
Ryan	Active	Flexible	Strict	College	High-restrained	Narrow
Baker	Active	Open	Firm	Honors	High	Narrow
Mitchell	Passive	Closed	Flexible	Business	Low	Moderate-narrow
Kopek	Active	Open	Strict	College	High	Moderate-narrow
Northdale High School						
Perez	Passive	Open	Relaxed	College	Restrained	Moderate
Crampton	Active	Flexible	Flexible	Honors	High	Wide
Schilling	Active	Flexible	Flexible	College	High-restrained	Moderate
O'Reilly	Passive	Open	Relaxed	College	High	Moderate-narrow
Ferris	Active	Flexible	Flexible	Business	Restrained	Moderate

Source: Compiled by the author.

rapport with students, there is a near-total range of diversity from the most passive-open teacher to the most active-closed.

To illustrate the various types of teaching activity, we can briefly consider the outstanding features of individual teachers in each group. An overview of the teaching sample is contained in Table 3.3. (Background data on each class are included in Table A.2.)

Active-Open Teachers

1. Hawkins (Central, college, seniors)
2. Baker (Middletown, honors, juniors)
3. Backman (Middletown, college, seniors)
4. Kopek (Middletown, college, seniors)

As a group, the active-open teachers stand out from all other teacher types by virtue of their highly active direction of class activities blended with a relatively open-ended curricular focus. With the exception of some teachers in the active-flexible group, these teachers are the only ones in the survey who combined a high level of class direction with curricular exercises that allowed a relatively broad range of individual student input. All other teachers were distinguishable by a more passive directing role, or a more constraining curricular focus, or both in combination.

Hawkins's social psychology class was marked by his energetic direction of class activities. An experienced young teacher, Hawkins directed his fairly passive group of students in a number of activities that drew on their own experiences and insights and built these into group generalizations that were then related to the appropriate literature. Baker's American history class also included a number of independent student projects and was particularly affected by his dynamic style and entertaining use of humor; students were largely involved, yet essentially in a reactive manner. Backman taught her sociology class in a businesslike manner that combined active leadership with a variety of individual and group projects; generally, students were passively attentive, although activity and informal contact with the teacher increased during the small group activities. Finally, Kopek's psychology class was firmly controlled, yet also included a number of individual or small group exploratory projects designed to fit into the external literature. Students were fairly compliant in their behavior, yet were highly involved in curricular activities.

Passive-Open Teachers

1. O'Reilly (Northdale, college, seniors)
2. Perez (Northdale, college, seniors)
3. Casey (Central, general, juniors)

As a group, the passive-open teachers are distinguishable from those in the active-open category by their low-key approach to the direction of curricular activities. All resemble the previous group, however, in the degree of diversity and student input allowed in the curriculum. Essentially, that input was allowed rather than required as in the active-open style.

One of the three, O'Reilly stands out as the most passive and open of all teachers studied, a classic laissez-faire type. Her political science students were consciously allowed to pursue activities of their choice. Much class time was marked by sporadic and largely directionless student activity, despite the fact that her students were visible more academically oriented than the norm. Both Perez and Casey exercised greater control over student behavior and supplied greater curricular direction, yet both included a wide range of curricular activities. Perez's American problems class was distinguished by the instructor's low-key and conversational manner and a largely passive, but attentive student group. Casey's American history class was marked by the instructor's intermittent efforts to engage a highly animated group of students who at best were sporadically involved in curricular activities.

Active-Flexible Teachers

1. Crampton (Northdale, honors, juniors)
2. Schilling (Northdale, college, sophomores)
3. Ryan (Middletown, college, juniors)
4. Ferris (Northdale, general, juniors)
5. James (Central, general, juniors)

The active-flexible group is the most disparate and indistinct of the five teacher categories. All the teachers tend to fall into a middle range in terms of curricular constraints, and while teacher activism varies widely from the most active (Crampton) to the least (James). Despite these differences, the five are best described as active classroom directors.

Crampton's American history class stood out from all others in the survey as a classic example of a highly academic, competitive class. Exhibiting a very high level of student ability and student ini-

tiative, the class was also distinguished by energetic, demanding
leadership on the teacher's part and highly structured curricular activities and expectations. Schilling's "Great Men and Women" class
included a number of chattering but involved sophomores and was actively directed by the teacher. The curriculum incorporated a variety
of activities and a mix of factual and interpretive material. although
few opportunities for individual study.

Ryan's American history curriculum was more disciplined and
uniform than that of the open teachers, yet she ran the class in a
fairly relaxed manner; her students tended to be curricularly active
and attentive throughout class time. Ferris ran his American presidency class with a firm hand and a highly focused curriculum. At
the same time, he made considerable allowance for individually paced
work. Seemingly, students whose basic school inclinations resembled
those of their low-track counterparts in other schools were more academically involved in Ferris's section. Finally, James had a quiet,
low-key classroom manner in a very small, passive American history
section. A young practice teacher (the only black in the group of
teachers, and one of few in the inner-city school), he took a predominantly fact-oriented approach to the curriculum, but left room for
more active and interpretive group projects.

Passive-Closed Teachers

1. Pellagrini (Central, general, juniors)
2. Mitchell (Middletown, general, sophomores)

One notable feature in both of these classes was the air of
teacher resignation toward the class being observed. Both teachers
confided that the unit in question was in some way their worst and
most difficult to manage. Both groups were made up of general track
students, and both contained two or three troublemakers.

Of the two, Pellagrini was somewhat more active in directing
his American history unit, although he had to counter greater disruptiveness on the part of some students. Without the disruptive students,
he might have been more accurately described as an active-flexible
teacher. A veteran of ten years in the city schools, Pellagrini combined a passive, or reactive, form of classroom direction with a curricular focus that was largely factual. Teacher contact with individual
students was informal and friendly. Mitchell, on the other hand, took
a less active stance in his world history class and consciously employed a more closed curricular structure. Of all teachers studied,
Mitchell asked the highest proportion of convergent or right-answer

questions (94.8 percent). Students were intermittently and passively involved, and a few were consistently if moderately disruptive.

Active-Closed Teacher

1. Gianelli (Central, college, sophomores)

Finally, of all the teachers studied, Gianelli came closest to an authoritarian type, by virtue of a tightly constrained curricular structure dominated by a highly active classroom director. Nearly all class time followed a uniform daily schedule in which the instructor led his largely passive group of students through factual material related to world civilization. Additionally, Gianelli, who was a large, tough-talking man, controlled student behavior far more tightly than any other teacher. Nonetheless, it is not difficult to imagine more dogmatic, authoritarian teachers. Numerous allusions were made to this kind of teacher by students and teachers, and one such former teacher was observed substituting for a Middletown class. Gianelli achieved a rapport with his students through frequent personal anecdotes and a kind of self-effacing humor.

Classroom Patterns

Consideration of the five categories of teachers reflects observable differences in the way teachers teach and what they teach. These differences center on the quality and degree of control exercised by the teacher and the curriculum in the classroom. At the same time, the level and quality of student involvement also varied visibly from class to class. Furthermore, these involvement traits revealed patterns corresponding to the five categories of teachers.

In classes categorized as active-open, students tended to be highly involved in their work relative to the norm. Where students seemed less academically inclined (Hawkins), there was more evidence of the teacher's struggle to activate students. In all four classes, however, student activity was consistently purposeful. Student initiative tended to be higher in the three passive-open classes, yet student activity was noticeably less purposeful and often strayed from the class activity at hand. With the exception of Crampton's highly academic honors section, the five active-flexible classrooms exhibited more evidence of student unrest or a sense of confinement; except for this characteristic, student behavior in these varied too widely to generalize about the whole group. In the passive-closed classes, students exhibited the lowest level of involvement in class and an air of apathy toward school in general. Curricular offerings seemed to have little relationship to their interests, except for an occasional informal discussion or a gamelike quiz. On the other hand, in the one active-closed class, students were more attentive, but far more passive in their behavior.

Throughout all this range of variation, a number of traits remained remarkably consistent from class to class. Most notably, student work was organized on a classwide basis, and tended to be almost entirely uniform in all classes. A handful of teachers tried to vary this structure with small-group or individual work projects, but these instances made up only a small part of the curriculum in each class. Cooperative work, where group performances were evaluated as such, was extremely rare. Finally, teachers seemed genuinely concerned about serving the needs of their students, and all espoused the principles of fairness and impartiality in grading and discipline issues.

Nonetheless, the variation represented by class and teacher categories suggests a dynamic of classroom interaction, namely, that the exercise of teacher control and the level and quality of student involvement in learning are related. However, this static picture of the variation in classes does not tell us which way the dynamic works. We do not know to what degree teaching approaches are determined by the kinds of students teachers encounter or to what degree the approaches used by a teacher determine the level of student involvement. Intuition tells us both are involved, and this view is borne out by the examination of teacher impact undertaken later in this work.

Two critically important questions are involved in considering the dynamics of classroom interaction. If some teaching approaches have an independent impact on the level of student involvement and the consequent democratic quality of learning (see Chapter 5), these approaches suggest the potential for democratizing school learning by pursuing certain teaching dynamics. On the other hand, if teaching approaches reflect student traits that are a function of the instrumental qualities of schooling, and this teaching variation subsequently teaches different lessons to the institutional groups of students, serious questions about the inequality in school learning arise. Reform concerns, as a consequence, would need to focus on the instrumental functions that result in these unequal lessons.

As we shall see, both situations exist. Teachers do have an independent teaching impact on the students who happen to gather in their classrooms, yet this impact pales next to the patterns of variation in classroom interaction that correspond to institutional groups of students, most particularly, student track level. The students' feeling of involvement in classroom activities emerges from the study as the variable on which students differ most widely and systematically.

By taking a closer look at this variable—first in the "snapshot" sense of involvement corresponding to student groupings and then in a dynamic sense of involvement affected by teacher input—we come closer to an appreciation of the critical reform needs of public schooling. As we shall see below, the level of student involvement proves to be the key to discerning the relative "democraticness" of classroom learning, and it is the variable that is most systematically tied to a student's track in school.

STRUCTURAL PATTERNS OF INEQUALITY

We can gain a preliminary sense of the pattern of inequality in classroom learning by scanning an organizational breakdown of the aforementioned teacher categories (see Table 3.3). With their associated traits of learning control and student participation, the five categories are unevenly distributed among groups of students. The teacher types marked by the highest level of purposeful student involvement tend to be somewhat overrepresented among upper-level student groups. Both honors sections are included in the active-open and active-flexible categories, along with five out of the eight college sections. Only two of five general track units are included, and neither is in the active-open groups. Similarly, these two categories include four of the five Middletown classes and three of the five Northdale sections as opposed to only one from Central High. At the same time, a slightly higher proportion of seniors and juniors is included.

On the other hand, the three classes associated with the most closed curricula and the most uninvolved or passive student behavior included two general track units and one from the college track; two are located in Central High and one in Middletown. While these patterns are suggestive, a far more reliable and dramatic picture of systematic patterns in classroom interaction results from examination of student questionnaire responses. Throughout the range of variables measured by the questionnaire, the most pronounced and consistent differences in student views are those corresponding to track level. Other structural groupings of students, namely, those corresponding to school and grade level, exhibit significant differences in student views; these differences, however, are less frequent, are usually smaller, and less frequently follow a steplike progression from bottom to top.

Student Participation

Analysis of student participation is divided into two sections, the first focusing on student involvement in class and the second on such variables as interest, opportunity, purposefulness, and efficacy.

Involvement

Student perceptions varied most widely on measures that reflect characteristics of student involvement in classroom activities.
Four measures were used to analyze involvement, each reflecting an
intuitively distinct element. These include three subjective attitude
statements: "The best thing about this class is the bell at the end"
(classroom alienation), "I find it hard to stay awake in this class"
(boredom), "A big problem with class is that you have to sit still in
one place the whole time" (confinement); and one self-evaluation measure, "How much of class time would you say you are paying close attention to the class?" (attentiveness).

As illustrated in Table 3.4, the four involvement measures*
are correlated with each other, although confinement is not significantly

TABLE 3.4

Student Involvement: Correlation Matrix

	Boredom	Confinement	(in) Attentiveness
Alienation	0.45	0.30	0.43
Boredom	—	0.17	0.48
Confinement	—	—	0.10

Note: Relationships between variables are most frequently represented by simple correlation coefficients. The sign of the coefficient
is based, where applicable, on the democratic interpretations of the
statements. Thus, for example, a positive correlation between involvement and constraint indicates that democratic aspects of each
(high involvement and low constraint) are positively related. Distributions throughout the study are considered significant at the 0.05 level.

Source: Compiled by the author.

---

*Attitude measures have five possible responses, from "agree
strongly" to "disagree strongly." Responses are scored from 1 to 5
in such a way that the most democratic response (for example, high
involvement) is given a score of 1 and the least democratic response
is scored 5. Thus, when groups of students are compared by their
mean scores, the lower score represents more democratic perceptions; a score of 3 is the midpoint.

correlated with either boredom or inattentiveness. Together the four
serve as the basis for examining involvement patterns among groups
of students.

The breakdown of student scores on the four involvement measures reveals the scope and consistency of track differences (see Table
3.5). One of the largest gaps of any measure used in the study separates track levels according to the degree of student alienation from
classroom activities. Translated into percentages, the differences
are equally striking. Only 10 percent of all honors students agreed
with the "bell at the end" statement as compared to 47 percent of all
general students; conversely, 76 percent of the honors students disagreed as opposed to 42 percent of the college students (22 percent
agreed) and 23 percent of those in the general track. By contrast, between-school differences range only from a mean of 2.69 in Middletown to 3.20 in Central; and grade scores range from a mean of 2.79
among seniors to 3.22 among sophomores.

The other involvement measures demonstrate that alienation is
not the only aspect of involvement that varies according to track level.
Only 17 percent of all honors students agreed that "sitting still" was
a "big problem" with their class, while 68 percent disagreed. On the
other hand, 36 percent of the college students agreed (39 percent disagreed) and 52 percent of the general students agreed (30 percent disagreed). School and grade differences were insignificant, except for
the gap between the relatively unconfined Northdale students (mean =
2.63) and their counterparts in the other two schools.

Overall, only 16 percent of all students found it "hard to stay
awake" in their classes, while 62 percent disagreed with the statement. Within this limited variation, however, track differences were
significant. Eighty-one percent of the honors students disagreed as

TABLE 3.5

Track Differences in Student Involvement (Mean Scores)

Track	Alienation	Confinement	Boredom	Attentiveness
Honors	1.98	2.27	1.78	1.54
College	2.80	3.05	2.40	2.28
General	3.43	3.34	2.51	2.62
Overall mean	2.87	3.03	2.35	2.28
Overall S.D.*	1.17	1.24	1.10	1.14

*Standard deviation.
Source: Compiled by the author.

opposed to 59 percent of both college and general students. Differences between school and grade groups were statistically insignificant.

Finally, student self-assessment on the pay attention scale follows a similar pattern. Student responses were divided into five spans of attentiveness, each corresponding to 20 percent of class time. On the average, honors students estimated that they paid attention to class activities 69 percent of class time, college students 54 percent, and general students 48 percent; overall, students averaged 54 percent attentiveness. School and grade differences were again insignificant.

Other Participation Measures

A more complete picture of the variation in student participation can be gained from measures that elicit student interest, perceived opportunities to participate, purposefulness, and student efficacy. Seven measures were used. Student interest was tapped by two descriptive terms: "interesting" and "boring." (These were part of a list of terms that students were asked to check if applicable to their class.) Opportunities were gauged by two attitude statements: "I have plenty of chances in this class to learn about things I am really interested in" ("chances to learn") and "This teacher gives everyone a chance to speak" ("chance to speak"). Purposefulness was determined by two class checklist items: "a challenge" and "you learn a lot in it." Finally, student efficacy was elicited by the statement "I feel I have a real influence on the way this class is run."

As can be seen in Table 3.6, these measures are all positively intercorrelated, and most correlations are of significant size (larger than 0.25). Student efficacy is the one measure that does not appear to be significantly associated with other participation variables, except for the perception of "chances to learn interesting things."

Similarly, these participation measures exhibit positive correlations with the four involvement measures considered above. At the same time, efficacy and confinement do not exhibit sizable correlations with any of the other items, and therefore are not included in Table 3.7. The perception of ample chance to speak in class is not significantly correlated with other measures, with the one exception of "it's hard to stay awake" (boredom).

These correlation patterns suggest a number of interesting insights into the dynamics of the classroom, for example, that "giving everyone a chance to speak" is related to students' "staying awake." For present purposes, however, the significant correlations demonstrate an interconnectedness among various aspects of student participation. As such, we would expect the participation patterns of dif-

TABLE 3.6

Participation Measures: Correlation Matrix

	Boring	Chances to Learn	Chance to Speak	Challenge	Learn a Lot	Efficacy
Interesting	0.37*	0.31	0.16	0.32	0.31	0.03
Boring	—	0.44*	0.21*	0.30*	0.46*	0.05*
Chances to learn	—	—	0.23	0.25	0.37	0.27
Chance to speak	—	—	—	0.10	0.08	0.11
Challenge	—	—	—	—	0.40	0.00
Learn a lot	—	—	—	—	—	0.05

*The correlations involving boring indicate a positive relationship between the democratic meanings, for example, a tendency not to check boring and to check interesting.

Source: Compiled by the author.

TABLE 3.7

Student Involvement and Participation: Correlations*

	Alienation	Boredom	Attentiveness
Interesting	0.43	0.34	0.37
Boring	0.35	0.50	0.37
Chances to learn	0.32	0.25	0.36
Chance to speak	0.17	0.31	0.11
Challenge	0.34	0.32	0.33
Learn a lot	0.34	0.39	0.32

*Between democratic meanings of measures.
Source: Compiled by the author.

ferent student groups to mirror student involvement patterns. This
proves to be the case, although the differences are not as pronounced.
   Distinctions on the two checklist items eliciting student interest
highlight between-track tendencies, although only a small proportion
of all students checked the term "boring." Twenty-three percent of
the total student population found their classes "boring"; 18 percent
of honors and 20 percent of college students agreed, while 29 percent
of the general students checked this item. School and grade differences were even smaller. The tendency to check "interesting" was
greater among students generally, and consequently track differences
are more pronounced. Sixty-four percent of all students checked the
term "interesting," including 42 percent of the general track students,
72 percent of college, and 84 percent of honors students. In both
cases, between-school differences were significantly smaller, although students in Central High were more likely to cite "boring" and
less likely to check "interesting." Between-grade differences were
insignificant.
   In terms of opportunities to participate, between-track differences persist, although student opinion in general varies less widely.
As can be seen in Table 3.8, the general track students perceived
significantly fewer "chances to learn about things I am really interested in" and somewhat fewer opportunities to speak in class. Student
sentiment on both statements is more positive than the statements
that elicit feelings of involvement. Differences between schools and
grades were insignificant. In terms of percentages, 71 percent of the
honors students agreed with the perception of ample chances to learn
as compared to 60 percent of the college students and 44 percent of
the general students. Eighty-eight percent of the honors students

TABLE 3.8

Participation Opportunities (Mean Scores)

Track	Chances to Learn	Chance to Speak
Honors	2.24	1.83
College	2.37	1.88
General	2.74	2.09
Overall mean	2.46	1.93
Overall S.D.	1.07	0.85

Source: Compiled by the author.

agreed that their teacher gave everyone a chance to speak in class as compared to 86 percent of the college students and 80 percent of those in the general track.

According to observational evidence, the perception of an ample chance to speak in class is not significantly related to the actual distribution of verbal participation itself. In other words, classes where students felt they had greater opportunity to speak were not necessarily the classes where a wider proportion of students did speak. Central High classes (with an average of 18 students in each class) were marked by wider distribution of verbal participation—28 percent made no verbal comments on the average. Middletown and Northdale classes (with attendance averages of 21.5 and 19.5, respectively) showed 50 and 40 percent of the students uninvolved. Comparably, general track classes were distinguished by wider participation. One can infer that the feeling of having an ample opportunity to speak in class reflects qualities of teacher domination and encouragement of student initiative more than it reflects the percentage of students in a given class who join in verbal commentary.

The sense of purposefulness in classroom activities mirrors the distribution of other participation variables among track levels. Overall, one third of all students considered their class "a challenge," yet the gap between honors students (71 percent considered their class a challenge) and those in college (28 percent) and general (14 percent) tracks is dramatic. Between-school and grade differences were minor.

Comparably, 47 percent of all students felt they "learned a lot" in their class; 72 percent of the honors students concurred as opposed to 48 percent of those in the college track and 34 percent in the general track. Again, between-school differences were far less significant (Central High students tended to "learn" less) and between-grade differences were negligible.

Finally, the most impressive characteristic of student efficacy is the consistently low sense students have of their influence over classroom activities. Nonetheless, the measure does reveal modest variation among student groups. Curiously, however, the feeling of efficacy does not follow the pattern of other student participation measures. In this case, the student groups that feel they have the most influence on the way their classes are run are those in Central High, in the general track, and sophomores. In fact, although differences among groups are not statistically significant, all classes in Central High exhibit a higher degree of student efficacy than is found in either Middletown or Northdale.

In a sense, the efficacy statement appears to have little bearing on other democratic traits of involvement; the feeling of influence tends to be higher in classes that are less curricularly involving and interesting. One might infer that the extrinsic, functional controls of schooling, which are more pervasive in upper-level classes, result in less student efficacy than teacher controls in classes "freed" from the success syndrome. More will be said of student efficacy when the unequal lessons of schooling are considered in Chapter 4.

A different, albeit limited, perspective on student participation can be gained from tabulating the total number of verbal student comments in a representative class discussion. Although differences among groups were not very large, classes in Central and Northdale were far more verbal than those in Middletown. Additionally, general track classes were more verbal than either college or honors sections. Little difference was observed between grade levels.

As purely quantitative measures, the figures on verbal participation do not reveal anything about the quality of student comments. The three most verbal classes were clearly verbal in different ways. Casey's class included a large proportion of scattered "buckshot" verbalization, with comments and questions tossed rapidly back and forth between the teacher and his vocal students. On the other hand, Crampton's honors class involved a high degree of continuity in verbal interchange; student comments were directed to those made by the teacher or other students in a fairly continuous flow of ideas. The high verbality in Hawkins's class reflected the teacher's conscious effort to achieve a degree of continuity by asking individual students two or three consecutive questions. In general, the high degree of student verbality among Central High and general track classes reflects the tendency of those teachers to ask a large number of rapid-fire questions.

The picture that emerges from these data is one of substantial inequality in learning participation among different track groups.

Honors track students feel far more involved in their classes, are more attentive, find classes more interesting and more purposeful, and perceive greater opportunity for meaningful involvement. General track students tend to have the opposite experience. Individual classes in these groups consistently follow the group pattern. College track classes, on the other hand, include a wider range of classroom types, generally lying between the other two groups.

Classroom Control

As a rule, student perceptions of classroom control exhibited far less variation than most measures of participation. Honors students tended to feel less controlled by the teacher's instructional activity, yet they felt most controlled by the grading function. Overall, however, perceptions of control decreased among higher-level students, although distributions were not always statistically significant.

Dramatic gaps among student groups emerge from the two observational measures, teacher-domination ratio and convergent-question percentage. As noted earlier, the average teacher-domination ratio across the spectrum of classes was 4.6 teacher-initiated comments for each student-initiated comment. Between-track and between-school differences were substantial. In honors classes, the ratio was 1.6 to 1, the lowest of any group; in college classes it was 4.7 to 1, and general classes, 5.7 to 1. Central High had the highest ratio of any group, 8.2 to 1, while the ratio in Middletown was 3.3 to 1 and in Northdale, 2.4 to 1.

These group differences mirror observational impressions of the way teachers tended to teach in each of the schools and tracks. The quality of teacher domination becomes more clear when we consider the convergent-question percentage. Although more subject to the chance activities and subjects encountered in individual classes during the extended period of observation, this measure reveals an interesting pattern of variation. As noted earlier, an average of 57.3 percent of all academic questions was convergent or right-answer. In Northdale, the percentage was lower than the mean (51 percent), while in Middletown it was higher (64 percent). (Central's figure was 57 percent.) However, the exclusion of two classes (O'Reilly and Ferris), where the measures are based on an unreliable sample of teacher questioning, lowers the Northdale score to 43 percent, making Northdale the only school where interpretive questions outnumbered factual ones.

Track differences are not steplike on this measure; college classes had the lowest percentage of convergent questioning (48 percent), while the honors figure was 62 percent and the general, 71 percent. This deviation from the normal pattern can be explained in part by the low degree of convergent questioning in three college classes (Perez, Kopek, and Hawkins), each reflecting a particular subject focus and teacher approach. Additionally, the honors score is raised by the unusually high percentage (82 percent) in Baker's class during the period of quantified observation. The exclusion of these classes would bring the honors score down to 42 percent, while the college score would rise to 61 percent, resulting in steplike differences among the three tracks.

The most dramatic and consistent difference in convergent questioning emerges among grade levels. Teachers tended to ask more interpretive and open-ended questions of older students, not surprisingly, considering the changes in social awareness and intellectual development that may occur during these years (as well as the fact that senior classes were generally electives). Only 33 percent of the questions in senior classes were convergent as opposed to 66 percent in junior and 78 percent in sophomore classes.

Turning to student perceptions, a number of measures elicit characteristics of the control environment. Overall extrinsic control represented by the teacher's grading function was measured by the statement "You have to do things the way the teacher wants if you want to get a good grade" (grading control). Additionally, feelings of personal freedom in the class are represented by the statement "In this class I am free to be myself" (personal freedom). Students were also asked to describe classroom discipline according to a four-part scale: "too harsh," "strict but fair," "relaxed," and "too easy" (discipline). And "relaxed" was one of the descriptive terms they could check if appropriate to their class. Finally, perceptions of teacher authority were elicited by the statement "Listening to the teacher is important because he (she) knows what he's (she's) talking about" (teacher expertise).

Although the five control variables tend to be positively correlated with each other, most correlations are not of significant size. Only discipline and "relaxed" (0.33) and grading control and feeling free (0.23) were significantly associated.

As might be expected from the description of teacher types, the control variables exhibit a positive and usually significant correlation with several measures of student involvement. The most consistent and significant correlations are those between student involvement and interest, on the one hand, and democratic qualities of teacher control, on the other (see Table 3.9). In general, the more students tend to "feel free to be themselves," to perceive the teacher's grading control as inconsequential, and to see the teacher as "knowing what he's talking about," the more they tend to feel involved and interested in classroom activities.

TABLE 3.9

Student Involvement and Classroom Control: Correlations

	Alienation	Confinement	Interesting	Chances to Learn
Grading control	0.26	0.26	0.24	0.13
Personal freedom	0.32	0.26	0.33	0.26
Teacher expertise	0.31	-0.05	0.20	0.41

Source: Compiled by the author.

Most of the remaining variables are only slightly and sporadically associated. Paying attention, for example, is associated with teacher expertise (0.29) and discipline is negatively associated (-0.15) with chances to learn. (In other words, less discipline is associated with fewer chances to learn.) "Learning a lot" is significantly correlated with the feeling of a "relaxed" classroom (0.29) and with teacher expertise (0.35). Finally, feeling free to be one's self is associated with an ample opportunity to speak (0.26) and the feeling of efficacy (0.27); it is negatively associated with the tendency to describe class as "boring" (0.32).

Not surprisingly, most intergroup differences in classroom control follow the pattern of student involvement. The single most striking exception is reflected in extrinsic grading control. As observed in Chapter 2, a majority of students in all three schools, all tracks, and all grades agreed that they "have to do things the way the teacher wants to get a good grade." Yet honors students tended to agree more than college students, as can be seen in Table 3.10. In all, 58 percent of the student sample agreed with the statement and only 24 percent disagreed. Eighteen percent of the honors students and 20 percent of the general students disagreed, while a larger proportion (27 percent) of college students disagreed. Between-school and between-grade differences were also modestly significant. Overall, Northdale and senior classes felt less controlled, while Central and sophomore classes felt more controlled. (Crampton's actively directed, high-powered honors class had the highest control score and O'Reilly's laissez-faire class had the lowest score.)

Both classroom discipline and personal freedom mirror the general pattern of variation, as the table illustrates. Honors students

were least likely to perceive classroom discipline as harsh and more
likely to feel free in class (59 percent agreed). General students were
most likely to classify discipline as harsh or strict and were least
likely to feel free (41 percent agreed). Between-school and between-
grade differences were also revealing, if modest. Northdale students
felt discipline was most relaxed and felt most free, while Middletown
students were least likely to share these views. Among grade groups,
seniors felt most free and relaxed and sophomores least free.

In viewing the teacher as an authority or expert worth listening
to, students tended to be at the same time respectful and deferential,
with little variation among groups. Still, honors and Middletown students were more inclined to view their teachers as worth listening to;
of all groups, seniors and Northdale students were least inclined to
hold this view.

TABLE 3. 10

Classroom Control (Mean Scores)

Track	Grading Control	Personal Freedom	Discipline	Teacher Expertise
Honors	3. 64	2. 42	2. 46	1. 93
College	3. 43	2. 57	2. 59	2. 26
General	3. 66	2. 85	2. 71	2. 22
Overall mean	3. 52	2. 63	2. 62	2. 20
Overall S. D.	1. 16	1. 11	0. 86	0. 95

Source: Compiled by the author.

Fairness

In addition to measures that elicit characteristics of classroom
control, two questionnaire items sought student perceptions of the
fairness with which control is exercised. One measure focuses on
impartiality in grading, asking students, "Do you feel that your teacher grades you on the same basis as everyone else in the room?" with
five possible responses: "always," "usually," "sometimes," "rarely,"
or "never." The other measure elicits an overall sense of justice in
the classroom, of being rewarded for one's efforts; the statement
reads "You really can't make excuses in this class because you get
out of it what you put in. "

The two fairness measures are interrelated (0.27 correlation) and both are positively correlated to nearly all the participation and control measures. Still, with few exceptions, the size of these associations is not significant. The only significant correlation is that between classroom justice and teacher expertise (0.32). Classroom justice and impartiality perceptions are also associated with the perception of chances to learn interesting things (0.24 and 0.23, respectively) and of the chance to speak in class (0.23 and 0.15). Most of the remaining correlations range between 0.10 and 0.20.

As Table 3.11 indicates, students tended to view the exercise of control as fair, yet significant and steplike differences emerge among track levels. Eighty-three percent of all honors students felt their teacher graded them impartially "always" or "usually," while no students in this group cited the responses "rarely" or "never." On the other hand, 77 percent of the college and only 52 percent of the general students were in the former category, while 11 percent of college and 17 percent of general students were in the latter. Between-school and between-grade differences were modestly significant on both measures. In both cases, Middletown students and seniors saw their classes as most fair and Central students and sophomores least fair.

To summarize, classroom control tends to follow a steplike progression from less democratic characteristics in low-track classes to more democratic traits in high-track classes. Honors students are less overtly controlled and less teacher dominated, feel more free to be themselves, perceive classroom discipline as more relaxed and the teacher as more worth listening to, and feel classroom control is exercised fairly. General track students tend toward the opposite views, while the perceptions of college track students lie in between.

TABLE 3.11

Classroom Fairness (Mean Scores)

Track	Grading Impartiality	Overall Justice
Honors	1.94	1.76
College	2.02	2.25
General	2.58	2.49
Overall mean	2.18	2.25
Overall S.D.	1.09	1.01

Source: Compiled by the author.

The one notable exception was the perception by honors students of tight and unilateral grading controls equal in force to those perceived by general track students.

Classroom Community

Finally, four measures were used to elicit qualities of the classroom community. Two statements focus on personal characteristics of the teacher: "I don't feel the teacher cares very much about what I think" (teacher cares) and "Even if I don't do well in class, I feel the teacher respects me as a person" (teacher respects) (correlation = 0.39). Additionally, students were able to indicate if they feel that "competitive" was an appropriate description of their class. Finally, perceptions of peer-group pressures were tapped by the statement "I sometimes don't speak out in class because of what other students might think of me" ("don't speak out").

Of these four measures, the perception of the teacher caring about what students think is highly correlated with a number of participation-related measures, including alienation (0.34), boredom (0.35), attentiveness (0.29), interesting (0.26), boring (0.27), chances to learn (0.30), chance to speak (0.40), and personal freedom (0.40). The perception of the teacher respecting students as persons regardless of performance is most significantly correlated with personal freedom (0.27) and the chance to speak in class (0.29). The perception of class as competitive is significantly correlated with the perception of class as a challenge (0.29); it exhibits a somewhat less than significant correlation with boredom (0.22). Finally, the hesitancy to speak out in class is not significantly correlated with any of the other variables.

Overall, student responses to these measures tend to be positively correlated with most other questionnaire items, even if the size of the correlation is small. As a result, it is not surprising to find between-group differences following the normal pattern. As Table 3.12 indicates, differences among tracks were generally small, yet they follow a steplike progression. In each case, honors students were the most favorably inclined in their perceptions and general students the least. Seventy-eight percent of all honors students viewed their teachers as caring about what they think as opposed to 72 percent of the college and 61 percent of the general students. Between-school differences were smaller, with Northdale students having the most favorable view and Central students the least. Between-grade differences were insignificant.

Perceptions of teacher respect varied even less. Seventy percent of all honors students agreed with the favorable view of their

TABLE 3.12

Classroom Community (Mean Scores)

Track	Teacher Cares	Teacher Respects	Don't Speak Out
Honors	2.05	2.28	2.54
College	2.17	2.26	2.60
General	2.41	2.48	2.65
Overall mean	2.23	2.33	2.61
Overall S.D.	0.93	0.96	1.24

Source: Compiled by the author.

teachers, while 66 percent of college and 57 percent of all general
students concurred. Between-school and between-grade differences
were statistically insignificant. The universal tendency for most students to perceive teachers as respecting them regardless of performance underscores the basic teaching prerequisite of establishing a
personal rapport with students.

Responses to the statement "I sometimes don't speak out in
class" revealed a unique pattern. None of the between-group differences was statistically significant, although older students were less
likely to agree. Instead, student views were amazingly consistent
from class to class. Yet, the overall range of individual student responses was wider than many of the other measures (standard deviation = 1.24). In short, a fairly consistent proportion of students in
every class felt sufficiently uneasy about their peers' views that they
were hesitant to speak out, regardless of the particular teacher and
class involved. Roughly between 20 and 30 percent in all classes felt
this restraint, while a larger proportion either disagreed or was
neutral toward the statement.

Finally, the perception of class as competitive reveals substantial between-track differences. Thirty-seven percent of all honors
students concurred with this view as opposed to 23 percent of all college and only 7 percent of all general track students. Slightly more
Northdale students (24 percent) than Middletown (20 percent) or Central (16 percent) students held this view, while between-grade differences were insignificant. The most competitive classes were Crampton's honors section (45 percent) and Schilling's college unit (42 percent), both in Northdale High.

For the most part, variations in the community measures were
slight. Honors students felt a stronger bond between themselves and

their teachers and greater competition with their peers. General students had perceptions that tended in the opposite direction and college students fit in between.

CONCLUSION: INSTITUTIONAL INEQUALITY

We have seen in this chapter a consistent pattern of variation in the schooling experience of different students. From the perspective of democratic socialization, the quality of schooling varies most fundamentally in the degree to which it involves students in purposeful learning activities. To some degree, this variation is simply a function of standardized classroom learning as we know it. Several students in nearly every observed session spent their class time daydreaming, absently fidgeting with pencils, or passively slouched in their seats. Overall, an average of 38 percent of the students in a given class made no verbal comment during discussions and more than half (54 percent) made at the most only one comment.

On the other hand, teachers were able to affect the distribution of student participation within the classroom, some by diversifying the subject material and others by diversifying the method of study. Most teachers constrained dominant students during discussions, and most saw the effort to induce student participation as a significant part of their teaching function. Nonetheless, some teachers were far more successful in these ventures than others. Almost all teachers cited systemic constraints that frustrated their efforts.

The within-class variation in student involvement raises interesting policy considerations. Most fundamentally, it challenges the degree to which we rely on standardized classroom instruction. However, differences among individual classes, particularly among such class groupings as school, track, and grade level, have a more direct bearing on the issue of inequality in education.

In very few instances the most significant variation in learning involvement was age or grade related. In fact, the only measures in which this was the case, peer intimidation and convergent questioning, are intuitively related to a student's age and experience. Moreover, because grade-level differences are eventually equalized over time (if students stay in school), they are not significant for policy considerations.

More prominent differences emerge among school groupings. Each of the three schools exudes a distinctive institutional atmosphere, and each reflects an identifiable type of community input. Differences in such environmental factors as building efficiency, availability of teaching resources, school policies and administrative practices, the degree and quality of school control, the degree of curricular choice, and general patterns of student behavior: all suggest that many things about a student's encounter with public schooling depend on what school he or she happens to attend.

Furthermore, it is possible to trace these differences into the classroom. Perhaps the most significant difference among schools lies in the variation in teaching control and the manner in which teachers direct their classes. Central High classes were far more teacher dominated than those in either of the other two schools, while both Central and Middletown classes treated subject material in a more narrow, factual manner. The sample of teachers suggests that we would find far more active-open and active-flexible teachers in Northdale and Middletown and a more closed curricular focus in Central High.

The between-school learning structure, moreover, varies in the eyes of the students. Significant differences emerge on questionnaire items measuring student involvement and interest, teacher grading practices and perceptions of fairness, and student efficacy. Northdale students find classroom discipline significantly more relaxed than students in the other two schools, and they feel far less constrained from active involvement in class activities. Along with Middletown students, they are far less alienated from their classroom experience than students in Central High, and they feel their teachers are more impartial. Middletown students perceive the greatest chance to learn about topics of interest in their classes; they are most inclined to feel they get out of class what they put in; and they feel they learn a lot in their classes, more so than students in the other schools. Central High students are more alienated, feel teachers and classrooms are more confining and less fair, but still feel they have some influence on the way the class is run.

Despite these significant distinctions among schools, however, the most dramatic and consistent differences in school learning, across the entire range of variables, exists among track levels. Of all structural groups in schooling, honors track students have the most democratic learning experiences and general track students have the most profoundly undemocratic experience. Relative to their counterparts, honors students tend to be highly involved in class, significantly less confined, attentive and alert, and very interested in subject material. Also, they perceive many more chances to learn interesting things and somewhat greater opportunity to speak in class. They feel far more challenged and are far more likely to feel they learn a lot.

Honors students also encounter a more democratic learning environment in the class. Teachers are more likely to be active-open

or active-flexible among the upper-level groups. Teacher domination
is very low in honors classes, and (at least in the more academically
rigorous class) the percentage of convergent questioning is also very
low. Still, honors students do not differ markedly from other groups
in feeling that they have little influence over their class and in per-
ceiving tight grading control in their teacher's activities. On the other
hand, they feel more free to be themselves, discipline seems less
constraining, and their teachers seem more worth listening to. Grading is perceived as very impartial, and the overall reward system as
a just reflection of personal effort. Honors students are somewhat
more likely to see their teacher as caring about what they think and
respecting them as persons regardless of their performance. Peer
pressure is rarely an impediment to classroom participation, even
though honors students are likely to see their class as competitive.

   With the sole exception of the one student efficacy measure,
every single classroom variable exhibits the opposite or less democratic trait among general track students. Alienation and confinement
in class are very high and attentiveness and interest are low. General
track students also find it harder to stay awake in class, and they perceive fewer chances to learn interesting things, as well as less opportunity to speak in class. Furthermore, they are not likely to view
their class as a challenge and do not feel they learn a lot in class.

   Of all the classroom environments, the type encountered by general track students is the most external and tightly constraining.
Teacher domination is very high, as is the percentage of convergent
questions. Still, in the frequently disruptive atmosphere, general students feel they have somewhat more influence in class than either of
the other two groups (although efficacy is still low). The teacher's
grading control is perceived as pervasive and discipline as more constraining, while personal freedom is lower. Teachers are also perceived as less worth listening to.

   While overall student sentiment on fairness and community
measures tends in a democratic direction, general track students
perceive grading as less impartial and the overall reward system as
less just, that is, less grounded on personal effort. Teachers are
seen as less caring about what students think and less likely to respect
students as persons. Peer intimidation is slightly higher than in the
other two groups, while the perception of class as competitive is
much lower.

   In sum, we can say that honors and general classes reflect distinct types of learning experience, regardless of the particular school
setting. General track classes in particular resemble each other far
more than they resemble other classes in the same school. On the
other hand, college track students tend to have learning experiences

that lie in between honors and general track students. Yet the eight
college track classes studied were a more disparate group, ranging
from O'Reilly's laissez-faire section to Gianelli's authoritarian class.
The variation in college classes seems to reflect the style and objectives of an individual teacher; more systematically, college classes
seem to reflect the dominant styles of a particular school. Thus, for
example, the three college classes in Middletown (Backman, Kopek,
and Ryan) were distinguished by active teacher direction and a relatively open curricular focus in conjunction with generally low student
initiative. The three college classes in Northdale High (Schilling,
Perez, and O'Reilly) were marked by a more relaxed atmosphere,
greater student initiative, and broader curricular diversity. The two
college classes in Central High (Gianelli and Hawkins) included a large
proportion of passive, uninvolved students, although the two teachers
took very different appraoches in directing class activities (with different results).

　　These between-school differences may reflect the differences
in student population traits that are usually associated with track level.
Indeed, judging from appearances, college students in Northdale High
were far more upper-level college students than those in Central High.

　　In sum, one emerges from the analysis of school inequality with
strong documentation that the within-school differences in school
learning—whether these reflect pure or school-socialized student
traits—are the most profound and systematic in public schooling.
Furthermore, an important distinction can be made between inequality
within schools and inequality between schools. The latter is tied, in
part to the "accident" of residence—an accident that is not, however,
random, but is a function of family background, wealth, and occupational status, as well as the relative socioeconomic homogeneity of
many American communities. To this degree, egalitarian reforms
aimed at between-school differences rightly concentrate on policies
like equalized school funding or social and racial integration.

　　At the same time, however, differences among schools are a
reflection of differences within schools, in particular, the predomi-
nance in each school of a type of student population associated with
track level. Within-school differences are inherently tied to institutional functions of schools, and thus the aforementioned egalitarian
reforms will leave such systematic inequalities untouched.

　　By highlighting the differences in the kinds of learning environments encountered by students, we have qualified the monolithic ap-
pearance of school learning suggested in the previous chapter. Still,
insofar as different schools pursue common institutional functions,
schooling remains a universal phenomenon. As argued in the preceding chapter, the most universally antidemocratic traits of school
learning reflect instrumental functions that schools perform for society,

most particularly the functions of social selection and equal opportunity. As we have seen in this chapter, the most dramatic variation in the way schools and school personnel treat students is tied to student track level—again, reflecting the pursuit of instrumental functions.

In an ideal sense, one might suggest that tracking provides a means of structuring learning experiences to fit different identifiable types of student needs. Documentation of the ways in which tracking is implemented suggests, however, that tracking closes far more opportunity doors than it opens,[1] and we have seen here that the tracking experiences of different groups hardly work for the betterment of those at lower levels. Ultimately, tracking serves the instrumental function of social selection, for through tracking, schools select types of students for appropriate educational experiences.

In a sense, tracking is a bureaucratic answer to the need to distinguish among students. Bureaucracies operate efficiently by placing people into categories. In order for the treatment of persons to be legitimate, these categories have to fulfill the particular functions of the given organization. In schools, tracking theoretically fulfills instrumental functions and is therefore fair. In theory, students have had a chance to exhibit their abilities through their school performance, and thus they can be separated into different tracks.

Given the bureaucratic structure of schools, it is not really surprising to find that a great many practices satisfy (at least in theory) the requirements of fairness. Most teachers upheld democratic principles of fairness, universality, respect for persons, and equal opportunity within the classroom; at least such was their intention, and student perceptions tend to corroborate this effort. Students are also continually measured in order to place them in the most appropriate learning category or track.

However, even if we allow that the principles of fairness are universally upheld in the schooling experience (highly dubious), that all are treated equally, the results of this treatment contradict democratic principles of equality. By examining the varying quality of learning experiences encountered by different groups, we can detect two ways in which antidemocratic inequality results.

In the first place, even if selection is done fairly, tracking results in experiences that in effect close off paths for personal advancement among students in the lower levels. Of all students, those in the general track encounter environments that are the most closed and most alienating. In the process, whether legitimately assigned or not, lower track students learn to be uninvolved in the public environment they encounter. In the individualistic sense of the term, tracking results in the violation of equal opportunity, even if administered with the utmost fairness.

Second, the results of tracking are profoundly dysfunctional in a democracy because the varying tracking experiences teach lessons that have direct implications for adult social and political behavior in society. As we shall see in Chapter 4, the antidemocratic traits of schooling have a different impact on different students. Thus, we can translate the antidemocratic constants into three types of political lessons learned by three types of students. Most systematically, these types of students correspond to the three track levels.

Both the individual and social implications of school inequality are made far more serious by the fact that tracking affects different socioeconomic groups differently. In this study, a student's track level was significantly correlated (0.38) with his or her self-reported socioeconomic status, an association that is generally true in the schools. As a result, the tracking experience denies the equal opportunity of lower socioeconomic groups, and it fosters and reinforces unequal patterns of social and political participation. Chapter 4 suggests that the three lessons of schooling essentially reinforce the disadvantages and nonparticipatory orientations of several identifiable lower-level groups. At the same time, however, even those at the top are not pure winners in democratic terms.

NOTE

1. See, for example, Aaron V. Cicourel and John I. Kitsuse, The Educational Decision-Makers (Indianapolis: Bobbs-Merrill, 1963), Ch. 5.

4

THE UNEQUAL
POLITICAL LESSONS OF
SCHOOLING

In the previous two chapters, we examined empirical evidence
of two aspects of the schooling experience. Chapter 2 focused on
those characteristics that diverse high schools share in common. In
terms of the norms of democratic citizenship, these were found to be
essentially antidemocratic. Chapter 3 analyzed the ways in which the
schooling experience varies most systematically. From this analysis
emerges a picture of more and less democratic learning experiences
encountered by different groups of students.

Both aspects of schooling, the constants and the systematic variations, have serious implications for democratic society. In effect,
we can say that schooling is experientially hostile to the citizenship
norms of personal autonomy and sociopolitical participation. Yet, in
its impact, schooling is unevenly hostile; it is more democratic for
some students than for others. As a result, schooling violates the
third norm of citizenship: universality.

By concentrating on this uneven impact, we can distinguish ways
in which schooling is inherently unequal. We can begin by extrapolat-
ing four antidemocratic "lessons" embedded in the schooling process
itself. These are largely deduced from the empirical analysis undertaken in Chapter 2.

We can go beyond this theoretical exercise, however, to examine
the lessons that different groups of students actually learn. These
lessons can be discerned most clearly in the behavior and perceptions
of students in the three track levels. Yet we also can speak more generally of lessons learned by various groups of students in "upper,"
"middle," and "lower" categories—each of which contains a disproportionate number of from upper, middle, or lower socioeconomic

status (SES). In essence, each group learns a political lesson that
undermines certain qualities of democratic citizenship. At the same
time, however, the three lessons have unequal implications for effective democratic citizenship. Each of the three reinforces behavioral
and attitudinal traits frequently associated with the class and subcultural structure of society.

Furthermore, as we will see in Chapter 5, we can point to ten-
ative evidence that schooling not only reinforces student inclinations
but teaches unequal citizenship, even at the secondary level. Because
the three lessons have unequal implications for the likelihood of occupational success and political influence, insofar as these depend on
individual behavior, the schooling process performs a vital function
in maintaining unequal opportunity in society. Before describing the
three lessons learned by different student groups, we can draw a
static picture of the four lessons inherent in the universal schooling
process.

THE FOUR LESSONS OF SCHOOLING

Drawing on the description of antidemocratic traits inherent in
the schooling process, it is possible to deduce four behavioral and attitudinal lessons embedded in the structural constants of schooling.
These, in turn, reflect the instrumental functions performed by the
public schools. In brief, the four lessons are acquiescence, fostered
by the largely passive and externally controlled learning process; a
psychological stance of dependence, fostered by the binding, extrinsic
incentives that reinforce the control structure; social isolation, or
privatism, fostered by a learning process that separates learners and
rewards self-pursuits; and alienation from one's public environment,
fostered by a uniform, external learning process. In one way or another, all four lessons reinforce adherence to the social and institutional
status quo.

Acquiescence

In the institutional environment of the school and most directly
in the classroom, the student's major task is to assimilate and conform to externally imposed constraints. All students are required
continually to yield personal needs and interests to external constraints,
to suffer through the schooling experience. In the classroom, the most
pervasive activity is seeking the right answer to give the teacher in a
predetermined subject area. This purportedly intellectual activity is
socially an act of compliance that is repeated over and over again. As

Seymour Sarason has observed of the "regularities" of the classroom, " . . . one of the most significant effects of school on children is to get them to accept existing regularities as the best and only possible state of affairs, although frequently this is neither verbally stated nor consciously decided."[1] As Robert Hess and Judith Torney have observed, even civics classes emphasize the assimilation of information rather than student participation in democratic ideas and activity.[2]

Beyond the fundamentally passive nature of classroom give-and-take, acquiescence is reinforced by bureaucratic and autocratic controls in the school at large. Classroom interaction is affected unavoidably by the compartmentalization of learning into standardized packages delivered in disconnected quantities and interrupted by bells. The efforts of teachers to involve students in learning are undermined by controls that are purely arbitrary when viewed from the perspective of individual learning activity.

Dependence

The second lesson of the control structure emerges where schooling has its most total effect. Acquiescence to external controls takes on a psychological quality of dependence when the extrinsic incentives of schooling are seen as critical by the student. Robert Dreeben has argued that schools foster a quality of independence—of "doing things on one's own, being self-reliant, accepting personal responsibility for one's behavior, acting self-sufficiently"[3]—that can be distinguished from the personal dependence on maternal affection and controls in the home.

One can argue, however, that the process by which students work independently requires an adjustment that substitutes one form of dependence for another. Instead of depending on the warm, supportive traits of the home, the individual depends for his or her social standing on the external outcomes of the schooling process. The student needs the success that can be gained through school rewards, and the path to those rewards is one that demands conformity to external standards.

The lesson of dependence is most acutely felt in connection with the threat of failure that pervades the learning process. Students cannot help but be aware of the presence of failure in learning and its costs. The grade structure rests on the presumption of a failing bottom line; more than one teacher involved in the study lamented the fact that failure was built into the learning process, with clear social and intellectual costs. Finally, students need only look around them in class (and outside the school) to observe the self-defeating coping

strategies adopted by those who have previously failed. Where failure
is present and costly, it reinforces student dependence.

From the perspective of the individual personality, dependence
is most critical when it requires conformity to controls from above.
As David Riesman has observed: "The point is that the individual is
psychologically dependent on others for clues to the meaning of life.
He thus fails to resist authority or fears to exercise freedom of choice
even when he might safely do so. "[4] As students come to see the external world of the school as the definition of public reality, they lose
the social independence that emanates from their individual personalities.

Privatism

The quality of independence that is fostered by the learning process is that of independence from one's peers. As we have seen, the
structure of work requires each student to work on his or her own in
pursuit of an isolated self-interest. The social side of school is pursued largely outside the official functions of schooling. In the process,
students learn that their interaction with others has little to do with
those aspects of learning that society values. By implication, they
learn that public life is largely a matter of pursuing one's own self-
interest according to existing standards, if necessary, pushing harder
to stand out from one's peers. The social group is not something one
interacts or cooperates with in order to serve collective needs and
maximize the social good. As noted earlier, this aspect of learning
reinforces existing conditions. It mirrors characteristics of a race
rather than of a human community where the individual interests and
contributions of each person are significant.

In such a context, efforts to satisfy needs for community—for
warmth, friendship, and social cooperation—are forced outside the
learning process. These ends are pursued in the back rows of classes
where students are uninvolved and most pervasively in the corridors
between class periods. Judging from the views of students in the study,
the schooling process fails to take advantage of opportunities for
meaningful social interaction.

Alienation

Finally, the schooling process is one that teaches the lesson of
social alienation. In fact, it is possible to argue that the universal
lesson of the schooling structure is alienation of one kind or another.
When we examine the three lessons learned by different groups of stu-

dents, we will see how one group learns the lesson of alienation from peers, one group learns the lesson of alienation from self, and one learns the lesson of alienation from participation in public institutional life.

In a sense, all three lessons derive from the fact that the schooling process is so pervasively external to the felt needs, interests, and abilities of young people. Schooling is most fundamentally undemocratic for two related reasons: the learning process fails in any systematic manner to emanate from the needs and interests of the young, and the institutional functions of schooling are not primarily concerned with meeting student needs and developing student interests, despite rhetoric to the contrary. In short, because schooling is primarily shaped by instrumental rather than educational functions, it is encountered by the learner as an alien environment.

Insofar as the institutional life of school learning teaches a universal lesson of alienation, our critical attention is drawn to the structural constants of public schooling. To the extent that this universal experience is functional, that is, it prepares young people for existing adult roles, our attention moves beyond the school to criticize institutional life in society at large. To gain a better sense of the three types of alienation fostered by schools, we now examine the three political lessons that different students learn in school.

UNEQUAL POLITICAL LESSONS

In the previous chapter, we saw how the most systematic variation in the schooling experience corresponds to the particular track a student happens to be assigned to. This structural inequality has two important implications for our consideration of the unequal political lessons of schooling. First, a student's track level also corresponds with a number of other background traits. Lower-track students include a disproportionate number of students who come from lower- and working-class backgrounds, and, in the inner-city school, a disproportionate number of nonwhite and non-English-speaking students. In other words, while categorizing students into tracks, schools also categorize students by class and race, although the association between track and background is far from perfect.

Furthermore, the preceding chapter suggested ways in which the major qualitative differences among schools reflect the dominant student type in a particular school's population. The schooling experience in Northdale High was tailored to the kinds of academic pursuits best fulfilled by honors track sections. Comparably, the dominant ethos in Middletown High reflected a middle-level population—students with largely passive academic interests and a concern for upward mobility. Finally, learning in Central High was largely tailored to fit the nonacademic and largely uninvolved general track population.

Consequently, in this section, the three political lessons learned by three groups of students are not strictly a reflection of track level. Tracking and the functions it serves are at the root of these unequal lessons in two ways: descriptively, track differences are the most consistent of any variations uncovered in the study and causally, the functions served by tracking also explain other significant group differences (for example, grade average or postgraduate plans).

In distinguishing among the three lesson types, the three groups of students will be referred to as "upper," "middle," and "lower," according to the way in which different students are sorted by schools. These are roughly defined categories rather than pure types; each contains a disproportionate number of certain student groups. (For the distribution of student groups, see the appendix.) Categories, such as track level, self-reported grade average, and postgraduate plans, are a direct reflection of the schools' social selection function. Sociological categories, such as socioeconomic status and race, are referred to as upper, middle, or lower only in the sense that the selection function results in disproportionate numbers of some groups in school levels corresponding to these terms.

Students in the upper level group include those in honors or accelerated learning units, those with the best grade averages, and those who plan to go on to attend select colleges. These students are more likely to be found in Northdale High than in the other two schools. This group also tends to consist of upper-middle-class, white students.

The middle-level group is functionally made up of those in the college-preparatory track who nonetheless are not likely to attend select colleges. These students also receive lower grades than the top group. Because college track classes are most likely to reflect general characteristics of a particular school, these students are most likely to be found in Middletown High. This group also tends to consist largely of middle- and working-class students from upward-mobile backgrounds; it also tends to be the most racially mixed group of the three.

Finally, the lower-level group is most clearly defined by track level. Of all structural groups, students in the general track encounter the most distinct learning environment, regardless of which school they attend. Central High includes the largest proportion of students in this group and thus best typifies the lesson learned by those at the bottom. This group also receives the lowest grades and is much less likely to pursue an education after secondary school. These students tend to come from lower- or working-class families and include a disproportionate number of nonwhites.

The three unequal lessons learned by these groups are substantiated by questionnaire responses. They are also based on descriptions of the learning experiences and perceptions that vary according to track level. The variable that most dramatically distinguished the learning experiences of one track from those of another, student involvement, provides the key to understanding the three types of lessons considered in this chapter. Essentially, we can distinguish three types of student involvement, varying in quality and degree. Through these, we can distinguish the three lessons of schooling.

At the outset, it is possible to define three profiles of student involvement in learning:

1. Students in the bottom group are essentially uninvolved in school learning. They are the students who feel least engaged, who feel they have the least stake in schooling. It is not difficult to understand why this is the case. These students experience the most rigidly external form of teacher domination and curricular constraint. They encounter a schooling mainstream that is essentially alien. If they had illusions about their place in society, schooling confirms that they are society's losers.

Although the most policed of all groups, students in the lower level encounter a control that is emptied of meaning, in other words, control for its own sake. These students feel less controlled by school than do other groups; in fact, they feel they have more influence over their classroom environment. They are the least acquiescent, for they have learned that dependence on schooling doesn't pay off. As a result, we can say that they learn the lesson of alienated freedom. Their freedom is gained at the personal cost of educational (and thereby social and occupational) success. As have-nots, they tend to concentrate their school criticism on tangible targets, such as the need for a smoking lounge, instead of the overwhelmingly external schooling environment.

2. Students in the middle group are noticeably involved in school learning. They are attentive in class and report that they feel very involved in learning activities. Yet there is a quality of deference and intellectual passivity in their involvement. They conform most totally to the externally imposed standards of schooling. They are most compliant in behavior and least critical in attitude.

Again, it is not hard to understand why this group acts as it does. The control they experience is full of meaning. With a chance for relative success and the drive to achieve it, they tend to internalize the norms of schooling as a definitive picture of reality. They learn the lesson of dependent acquiescence. In the process, they experience the most severe alienation from self. The school critiques of this group reveal a plaintive yearning for something lost; of all groups, they most frequently volunteered the simple word "freedom" as the element "missing most" in school.

3. The third group of students, those at the top, are also relatively involved in school learning, yet their involvement differs in quality from those in the middle. They are involved for both intrinsic and extrinsic reasons. They are also driven by a need to succeed or, more accurately, to excel. Yet they are more likely to be involved in a learning process which encourages intellectual independence. They are also more likely to encounter flexible teachers.

Like the middle group, students at the top conform to the requisites of schooling; they acquiesce. Yet, unlike the former, these students maintain a critical attitude toward their schooling experience. They are more likely to chafe under tight constraints, and are more outspoken in challenging the controls they encounter. Acquiescence is seen as an essentially situational necessity, not a fact of life. In the process of acquiescing, these students hold a portion of themselves apart from the embrace of schooling; they maintain a degree of personal independence. They learn the lesson of independent acquiescence.

At the same time, students in this group best learn the lesson of privatism and independence from their peers. Their learning experience is most competitive, most tailored to the pursuit of self-interest. Of all students, those at the top tend to be most critical of the lack of warmth and community in schooling.

Having sketched these student profiles, we now consider each of the lessons in greater depth, with additional empirical documentation.

Alienated Freedom

We have already seen how those in the general track are by far the most alienated from their classroom experience of any track group. More than twice as many general students agreed as disagreed that the "bell at the end" was the "best thing" about their class (among honors students nearly eight times as many students disagreed as agreed). Similarly, a majority of all general students felt that sitting still in one place was a big problem with their class.

These sentiments appear to be well grounded in the schooling reality these students encounter. The teacher–domination ratio among general track and Central High students was between three and four times as high as that of other groups. Similarly, the percentage of teacher questions that were purely factual was highest for these students (71 percent among general classes). Not surprisingly, these students were least likely to feel they learn a lot in class and least

portant to listen to the teacher. They felt they had the fewest chances to learn things that interested them. In essence, the classroom is largely an alien world for these students.

These sentiments clearly carry over into the school at large. In the first place, students in identifiably lower groups were far more likely to feel alienated from school in general, as revealed by responses to the statement "When I'm in school, all I can think of is other places I'd rather be." The most dramatic differences emerge between track and grade-average groups. Forty-eight percent of all general students agreed with the statement as opposed to 30 percent of the college and 9 percent of the honors students. Fifty-four percent of those with C's or below agreed, while that percentage dropped to 21 percent among B average and 4 percent among A average students. Forty percent of all students from lower- and working-class families agreed as opposed to 27 percent of all middle-class and 25 percent of all upper-middle-class students. Finally, more students in Central High (44 percent) agreed than in Middletown (28 percent) or Northdale (30 percent), and more blacks (42 percent) than whites (29 percent) agreed—although both of these response distributions are not statistically significant. Correlation coefficients between the alienation measure and grade average (0.40) and track (0.26) were significant, while those between alienation and socioeconomic status (0.18) and school (0.06) were insignificant though positive.

Other schoolwide measures add to our understanding of alienation, although they reveal less striking and less consistent differences among student groups. In response to the statement "Most of my teachers are people I can talk to about things that are important to me," general track and C average students were least likely to agree. A small but steplike difference can be seen in track group responses. Fifty percent of general track students disagreed with the statement compared to 47 percent of all college and 31 percent of all honors track students. Sixty-four percent of all C average students disagreed compared to 42 percent and 17 percent of those with B and A averages, respectively. (Grade average had a correlation of 0.28 with this measure.)

On the other hand, Central High and nonwhite students agreed with the statement more than their counterparts, suggesting a particularly strong bond between Central High teachers and their more academically oriented and successful students (many of whom, in Central, are likely to be nonwhite). Students heading toward four-year colleges were least likely to view their teachers as unapproachable (39 percent disagreed), while those planning on attending two-year colleges (46 percent) and those planning to seek employment (61 percent) were more likely to hold this view.

Differences in student responses to the statement "Most days I look forward to going to school" were slight, but revealed an interesting qualification of student alienation. The most significant differences occurred among school, grade average, and racial groups. Only 17 percent of A average students disagreed with the statement as opposed to 34 percent of B average and 42 percent of C average students. On the other hand, Central High and nonwhite students looked forward to school more than their counterparts. Forty-one percent in Central agreed as opposed to 36 percent in Middletown and 23 percent in Northdale; 58 percent of the black students agreed as compared to 36 percent of all white students.

This tendency may reflect the teacher-student bond described above. It may also reflect the relative social attractiveness of school for these students when inner-city alternatives are considered. These findings reinforce the view that a quality school experience is more critical for inner-city students than it is for those who have ample options for self-development outside the school. Yet, sadly, these views largely reflect a picture of the potential for personal involvement rather than the reality. The overall pattern of alienation in classes and in school generally demonstrates that these students are most systematically confined to the lower levels, and thus are the most consistent losers in schooling.

In sum, one can say that all groups categorized as lower level are alienated by the formal learning functions of schooling. Inner-city, low socioeconomic status, general track, nonwhite, and low grade-average students exhibit consistently greater alienation from school while in school. As a result, it is not surprising to find patterns of alienated student behavior most prominent in the school where lower-level students were most concentrated. Evidence of this behavior was readily observable in Central High. For example, a group of male students waiting outside school shared some liquor hidden in a paper bag. Two girls cursed under their breath as a teacher hurried them to class. One fairly conscientious student remarked, "You should see how many kids in school are high." Another commented, "This school is crummy. No one puts out."

Within the classroom, students in the lower group were most likely to encounter an overtly autocratic environment. Behavioral discipline tended to be stressed by teachers and was perceived as more strict or harsh by students. Additionally, students in the lower track felt less relaxed and less free to be themselves. They were most likely to view the teacher as unilaterally controlling through the grading function. And, as mentioned earlier, these students tended to encounter a teacher-dominated, closed curriculum.

Despite this classroom control, however, students in the lower level were most likely to feel they could influence the "way this class is run" (although even among low-level students, more disagreed than agreed with the efficacy statement). Lower-working-class students and those with a C average were slightly more likely to agree, although differences are statistically insignificant. However, differences among track levels and schools were more significant as noted in the last chapter. In part, this perception may reflect a reality of low-level classes, namely, that teachers are less bound by college-preparatory curricula and can be more informal and personal in directing the class. Some teachers in low-track classes, as noted earlier, displayed a more resigned, casual approach to the class.

Two kinds of efficacy are possible in such an environment. One derives from the fact that teachers are more accessible to students who are willing to make an effort in class. These students stand out. The other kind of efficacy carries with it a more negative lesson. Students in lower-level groups were more likely to disagree with the statement "The grades I get have a lot to do with how I feel about school." Having less to lose, these students can be more outgoing and disruptive. There was considerable evidence in general track classes of individuals or small groups influencing the class by acting disruptively or speaking loudly.

One can argue, then, that the classroom control structure teaches lower-level students two simultaneous lessons. On the one hand, by emphasizing order and tight constraints, it reinforces authoritarian patterns of dealing with institutional control. On the other, since the learning process is not intrinsically interesting, and there is less hope for success and more awareness of failure, low-level students learn a negative lesson of personal efficacy. The most likely way to influence the school environment is by the kind of disruptive, uninvolved behavior that reduces chances for academic school success.

This characteristic of lower-level classes suggests the kind of alienated freedom learned by these students. Confronted by relatively meaningless control, these students seek channels of individual expression within a policing atmosphere. They learn to cope with the school controls, but act out whenever and wherever they can. Theirs is a conformity of appearances only. Thus, students in low-level classes are likely to chatter with each other as much as the teacher allows them. In the less chaotic classes, students could be observed talking among themselves with an eye out for the teacher, only to bury their faces in books when the teacher looked up from his or her work. They made a show of keeping busy, the most basic requirement of classroom control. As Willard Waller has observed:

> Whatever the rules that the teacher lays down, the tendency of the pupils is to empty them of meaning. By the mechanization of conformity, by "laughing off" the teacher

or hating him out of existence as a person, by taking
refuge in self-initiated activities that are always just
beyond the teacher's reach, students attempt to neu-
tralize teacher control. [5]

Within this environment, students not only retain a degree of
personal freedom but they simultaneously come to view the exercise
of control in authoritarian rather than democratic or rule-governed
terms. All students were asked to classify a series of 15 hypothetical
teacher practices as "fair" or "unfair." Many of these involved issues
of arbitrariness or favoritism on the part of the teacher. On these
measures, low-level students were least critical. For example, only
41 percent of all general track students felt it was unfair for teachers
to grade students on the opinions they expressed as opposed to 53 percent of college and 68 percent of honors students. Similar differences
emerge among grade-average groups: 46 percent of the C students
judged these practices unfair compared to 55 percent of the B's and
70 percent of the A's; and among socioeconomic status levels: 45 percent of lower-working-class students, compared to 53 percent of middle class and 65 percent of upper-middle class. Central High students
were least critical; only 29 percent felt this practice was unfair.
        A similar pattern emerged when students were asked to judge
the teacher's practice of paying more attention to students who agreed
with him or her. All lower-level students were more likely to accept
this practice as fair (including nonwhite students). Differences among
groups were not as pronounced; an overall average of 85 percent were
critical. The most pronounced differences occurred between white
and black students; 90 percent of the former felt this practice was unfair as opposed to 68 percent of the black students. One possible explanation for this difference is that black students are more accustomed
to their predominantly white teachers paying less attention to them.
Consequently, they may find that a strategy of agreeing with the teacher
in order to gain attention is productive and therefore legitimate.
        Finally, the lower-level students were least concerned about the
teacher's forbidding students to criticize him or her. Again, black
students were least critical of any group; 42 percent felt this practice
was unfair as opposed to 74 percent of all white students. Race and
socioeconomic status were both significantly correlated with student
responses on this measure (0.32 and 0.23, respectively). Forty-nine
percent of Central High students found the practice unfair as opposed
to 69 percent in Middletown and 80 percent in Northdale. In general,
low-level students encountered more autocratic controls and as a consequence may have been more accustomed to practices like this one.
        The pattern of compliance with arbitrary teacher practices is
reversed, however, when students were asked to judge teacher actions

that reflect the basic norms of academic involvement. Low-level students were significantly more critical than their counterparts of four such practices: the teacher downgrading a late assignment or test, the teacher telling a student who is talking to a friend to be quiet, the teacher sending a late student to a school official, and the teacher changing a student's seat so he can keep an eye on him. In each of these cases, students in the general track, those with a C average, students in Central High, and those from lower-working-class backgrounds were more critical of these practices. Racial differences were insignificant. The most substantial criticism was directed at the teacher's downgrading a late assignment.

In general, then, lower-level students, particularly those in the general track and with a C average or below, tended to criticize as unfair those teacher practices that they are most likely to experience as obstructive controls. They were not nearly as concerned about violations of rule-governed authority, in part because they may see teacher partiality as a real path to school success. Clearly, these views reflect the self-interest of these students in the learning environment they encounter. Lower-level students are far more likely to experience disciplinary measures for tardiness or disruptive behavior. On the other hand, upper-level students rarely experience such discipline.

To some degree, upper-level students may achieve their higher status because they are less likely to be tardy or disruptive. Conversely, however, they may be less likely to encounter reprimands because they are "better" students. In either case, the pattern of lower-level criticism reflects real conditions, for the teachers of low-level classes placed far greater emphasis on behavioral controls.

The criticisms expressed by lower-level students can also be seen as a reflection of their alienation from schooling. Since they feel largely uninvolved in learning, they do not tend to criticize violations of the norms of intellectual inquiry. Being more inclined to seek unsanctioned outlets of behavior, they are more critical of those practices that punish this behavior.

The pressure of academic constraints on unsanctioned behavior is felt most directly within the classroom. In fact, the overall schooling experience for low-level students is sharply divided between classroom and schoolwide environments. As one teacher in Central High observed, there are two different worlds in an inner-city high school: "The classroom, despite all we say about it, is relatively sane. The rest—halls, cafeteria, administration, outdoors—is crazy." Although classes in Central High varied in their orderliness and were generally more agitated than in the other two schools, student behavior was more passive and purposeful in the classroom than elsewhere in school. Students who were very reluctant to speak in class could be seen shouting in the corridors. Nowhere was the contrast more universally pronounced than in the transformation of student behavior (particularly in Central High and general track classes) from the controlled and subdued manner of the classroom to the animated laughing, yelling, and chattering that took place immediately as students left class.

Not surprisingly, then, students in the lower-level groups were less inclined to agree with the statement "To get along in school, you have to do what people say." Central High, general track, low SES, nonwhite, and students who plan to work after graduation all disagreed significantly more than their counterparts; the sole exception was the grade-average grouping, where differences are not so pronounced. Yet these students were more overtly policed; they were most likely to encounter locked doors, patrolling monitors, and the commands of school officials than students in other groups.

A number of inferences can be drawn from the distinct experiences and perceptions of lower-level students. In the first place, it is possible to see how a policing atmosphere and student alienation go hand in hand. On one side, schools and teachers are more overtly autocratic because low-level students are alienated from the controlling functions of schooling. On the other, because low-level students encounter a learning environment that is most closed—where control appears to exist for the sake of control—they find little meaning in the learning environment; they withdraw and become alienated.

At the same time, however, the constraints built into the functions of schooling—those associated with school and occupational success—are more totally controlling. To the extent that students at the bottom are alienated from schooling, they tend to experience only an autocratic, policing control. Yet because they are alienated, they are more disruptive and expressive of unsanctioned behavior. Because of the diminished control they experience and their pursuit of personal expression, these students are more free. Hence, the lesson of alienated freedom.

In social terms, however, lower-level students have learned a costly antidemocratic lesson. They are free because they have given up trying to conform to the schooling race; they have forgone a real chance to get ahead. Furthermore, in experiential terms, their schooling encounter has disabled them from participation in public life. They have learned to withdraw their personal needs from the grips of public institutions; in the process, they learn not to bother or care about playing a constructive, participatory role in shaping the life in common. For the most part, they reduce their demands to a wish for decent facilities; thus, for example, the major complaint of Central High students was that their school needed modernizing (it did) and better tangible facilities.

We need to bear in mind that the lower-level students in this study were at least conforming to the minimum prerequisite of schooling: school enrollment and attendance. Others had already been more severely displaced and had become society's dropouts. The implications for both groups, however, are clear. There is substantial evidence in social science that lower-class groups are far less prone to participate in political life, [6] and are more prone to experience severe displacement from their social environment, including higher rates of mental illness, alcoholism, and crime. [7] Some commentators argue that these traits are the result of psychological or subcultural orientations of different groups in society. Edward Banfield, for example, defines low social class according to such criteria as a low sense of "fate control," a "time horizon" limited to the immediate circumstances, and an inability to abstract or detach oneself from "immediate gratifications." [8]

There is little doubt that these behavioral patterns exist to some degree. [9] However, it is not hard to see that, to some extent, these traits are caused by the unfolding individual's first major encounter with public life: the schooling experience. Except for the demonstrable, independent, teacher impact on student involvement considered in Chapter 5, the methodology of this study cannot provide a statistical test for determining the school's causal role in teaching the lesson of alienated freedom. Nonetheless, based on the empirical evidence, we can construct an intuitively plausible explanation.

How do schools teach the lesson of alienated freedom and its associated characteristics? In the first place, schools encounter students who exhibit various ways of dealing with authority and various levels of verbal facility. [10] Because of the social selection function, schools and teachers immediately begin the necessary task of sorting and separating students according to mainstream learning criteria. One instructor of teachers has estimated that informal tracking begins within four months of the start of first grade. [11] Quickly, students who do not fit into the school's select groups experience failure in the school's terms. Having once experienced failure, and having the lesson reinforced by subsequent experiences, these students try to maintain a semblance of personal dignity and individuality by withdrawing a portion of themselves from involvement in the schooling process. Having done so, they become more difficult to involve in learning, and teachers resort to an easier route, namely, the use of factual "games" where students can be situationally motivated to do well.

These games, however, are essentially external to the students' personal needs and interests; they have little meaning beyond winning or losing. Games and knowing facts, after all, are of limited holding power unless they are directed to an attractive and realizable end. As

a consequence, students become more restless and more alienated.
Encountering greater student disruptiveness, schools resort to more
autocratic controls; as long as students are "busy," the schools and
teachers are "succeeding." These patterns become built into the
structure of schooling through high school tracking. Since tracking
becomes overt at a time when adolescents are internalizing society's
expectations for their future adult roles, the implications are obvious.
Students at the bottom—to say nothing of those students who opt out of
the bottom by dropping out of school—"choose" a path that at least allows a realizable element of personal freedom, but they pay an im-
mense social price. Furthermore, because these students do not become participating members of society, but frequently need to be controlled as adults, society also pays a large price.

Dependent Acquiescence

The two remaining schooling lessons are far more distinct when
compared to the lesson of alienated freedom than they are when compared to each other. Both the middle- and upper-level students tend
to be involved, objectively and subjectively, in learning and the schooling process. Yet a significant qualitative difference in that involvement emerges in their classroom and school behavior and in some
questionnaire responses. The middle group exhibits signs of dependence on the external controls and rewards of schooling, while the upper group exhibits a more independent stance toward school involvement.

In addition, however, it is less clear empirically who the students are in each of the upper two groups. Crampton's honors class
in Northdale, on the other hand, seems to be the paradigm of the upper-level group. In many ways, college track students in Middletown
High best fit the middle-level criteria, but they could easily be joined
by students in Gianelli's college track class in Central High and
Perez's students in Northdale. This group included disproportionate
numbers of students with a B average, those who planned to attend
two-year colleges, and those from middle-class backgrounds. Because college track classes tended to fit school types, the purest middle-level group was the Middletown students in the college track.

Middle-level students are visibly involved in school. They are
quietly attentive in class, and they do not disrupt classroom activities.
They also do not feel so alienated that the bell at the end is the "best
thing" about the class. Still, they tend to feel somewhat confined by
the class; opinion among all college track students was evenly divided
in response to the statement that "sitting still in one place is a big
problem in class." Students in Middletown High were most likely to

agree that confinement was a problem, while students in Northdale were least in agreement. On the other hand, Middletown students were less likely to find it hard to stay awake in class, and they also claimed to be most attentive in class.

Middle-level students also encountered classroom environments that were more controlling than upper-level and less controlling than lower-level classes. Teacher-domination ratios in Middletown High were fairly close to those in Northdale, while those in college track classes were distinctly higher than those of honors sections. Middletown students also encountered the highest percentage of convergent questions of all school groups (in part because of the extremely high scores in Baker's honors unit and Mitchell's general class). Finally, Middletown students were closer to Central students in agreeing that they had to do things the way the teacher wanted in order to get a good grade.

In sum, middle-level students encountered a more closed and controlling classroom environment than students at the top, yet they differed from lower-level students in the degree to which they were engaged by the extrinsic controls of schooling. Middletown students were most likely to view the grading function as controlling and grades as important. Along with students in Northdale, they were most likely to agree (58 percent) that "The grades I get have a lot to do with how I feel about school." They were far more likely than either Northdale or Central High students to agree that "If it weren't for grades, school could be really interesting." (A significant percentage of the students in Central High seemed to feel that school "could not be interesting" regardless of grades.) Fifty-six percent of all Middletown students held this view, as opposed to 33 percent in Northdale and 27 percent in Central. Although noticeably less alienated from school than students in Central High or the general track, Middletown students were only slightly more likely to agree (35 percent) than disagree (28 percent) with the statement, "When I'm in school, all I can think of is other places I'd rather be."

Middletown students were also most conscious of the comparative effect of grades. Fifty-three percent of all Middletown students agreed that "Grades make me feel like I'm always being told I'm better or worse than somebody else" as opposed to 49 percent in Northdale and 31 percent in Central. Only 20 percent disagreed, compared to 31 percent in Northdale and 49 percent in Central. Additionally, although Middletown students were less likely than Central students to view grades as important for jobs (50 percent agreed in Middletown, 64 percent in Central, and 49 percent in Northdale), this difference overshadows a within-school distinction; students with a B average were more likely to look to the job outcome of school grades than those with either higher or lower grades.

Still, Middletown students stood out from others in the degree to which they feel pressure to do well in school from outside sources. More cited as the reason for doing well in school that "it makes my parents happy"; school success was also more likely to make them feel they've accomplished something. It is not difficult to trace the roots of dependence among middle-level students to their felt need for school success, particularly the pressures they are likely to feel from parents who see school as a path to upward mobility. Middle-level students therefore feel a strong pressure to do well, yet they, themselves, don't view the drive to school success in purely utilitarian terms. They are most likely to define their feeling of accomplishment according to their standing in school.

In this sense, these students are most likely to absorb and internalize the norms of school life. In reality, they are doubly controlled in school. They encounter teachers and classes that involve them yet dominate them, and they feel the constraints of grade pressures, which reinforce their compliance. It is not surprising to find that students in a school like Middletown were most likely to agree that "To get along in school, you have to do what people say." Sixty-one percent of all Middletown students agreed with this view compared to 56 percent in Northdale and 25 percent in Central. In fact, middle-level students consistently agreed with this statement more than their counterparts above and below (except for grade-average groups). Students in the college track, from middle-class families, and those planning to attend two-year colleges were all more likely to agree.

Despite this pervasive control, middle-level students are most likely to see the schooling environment as a fair one. They are most likely to view grading practices as fair. Sixty-three percent of all Middletown students agreed that "No matter what people say about grades, you usually get what you deserve" as opposed to 53 percent in Central and 45 percent in Northdale. In terms of their attitudes toward various hypothetical teacher practices, middle-level groups consistently fell between the upper- and lower-level groups. On issues of rule-governed authority, they were less critical of violations than upper-level students and more critical than those at the bottom; on basic classroom norms, they viewed teacher constraints as more fair than bottom-level students and less fair than those at the top.

The behavior of middle-level students also bears out their basic acceptance of the necessity of school controls and the manner in which these are exercised. One can distinguish a quality of deference in their attitude toward school authorities, particularly teachers. Middletown students were most likely to agree that "Listening to the teacher is important because he (she) knows what he's (she's) talking about." They also felt they learned a lot more than lower-level students, de-

spite the constraints in their environment. They were most likely to
agree that "You really can't make excuses in this class, because you
get out of it what you put in" and were most likely to feel that their
teachers graded them impartially.

Teachers in Middletown High frequently commented on these
characteristics of their students. One described her students as "well-
disciplined kids," while another made a more negative assessment,
noting that the students often exhibited a "rigid, unchanging code of
thinking, which they get from their parents." Comparable comments
could be heard from Perez in Northdale as he described his middle-
level class as "too quiet" and "too passive," and from teachers in
Central High who felt that many of their students had been "too well
trained" by years of passive, rote learning.

Despite their behavioral compliance and a tendency to accept
and internalize school norms, we cannot conclude that middle-level
students are satisfied with their schooling environment. Middletown
students were least likely to agree that "Most days, I look forward to
going to school." Additionally, compliance with orderly bureaucratic
efficiency disappears when it is no longer required. The final bell at
the end of the school in Middletown was greeted by a sudden burst of
student activity and animated behavior, and students normally evacu-
ated the building in less than 5 minutes. Finally, students in Middletown were far more likely to feel that "freedom" was the quality missing most in their school. Thirty-eight percent of all Middletown students volunteered this response when asked, "What do you feel is missing most in your school?" while only 9 percent in Northdale and 8
percent in Central concurred with this view. Middletown students
were also more likely to feel that "school spirit" was lacking.

In sum, students in the middle-level feel most controlled by
their schooling experience, and they are not entirely happy with that
control. Yet they are least likely to challenge or evade the controlling
environment. They behave most compliantly and tend to be passively
attentive in class. They draw a sense of accomplishment from how
"well" they do according to external grading criteria. They are most
aware of the pervasiveness of grading, yet they tend to feel that "you
can't complain" or "make excuses" about grades because they are
awarded fairly.

We can see in this experience the groundwork for a largely passive and acquiescent adult population. Students in this group seem
more likely to become adults who view as legitimate the way institutions define their needs, despite a feeling of chafing under external
controls. They are most likely to be those whose consumption patterns
are largely shaped by external incentives produced by advertising.
They are likely to work hard and achieve modest success and to value

loyalty to a political party or a leader. They do not place substantial demands on their public institutions; feelings of personal community are derived from sources other than institutional life in common. Yet those in the middle level need to feel that their efforts are rewarded, at least modestly. They are unlikely to reject the status quo until they perceive that their loyalty is no longer appreciated. Understandably, they are particularly sensitive when those who do not "make an effort" (such as uninvolved students) are rewarded.

Again, it is possible to piece together a dynamic picture of the ways in which the schooling experience teaches these characteristics. Middle-level students first encounter the school environment as a "very important place." They are not likely to have traits like personal initiative encouraged in their preschool background, yet they may receive some "training" in school-related functions like reading and arithmetic. If they are fortunate, they may have a parent who spends time stressing these activities.

Once these students encounter the school, they readily fall into a middle category in the selection process. They are capable, but not seen as a challenge to the teacher; they are also not perceived as a problem in behavioral or academic terms. Their efforts are duly rewarded, but they are not given special attention; in fact, they might tend to feel ignored when teachers pay more attention to problem children or to students who show considerable learning initiative. In short, these children best fulfill the structural requirements of schooling and require the least personal input from teachers. They may, however, feel the teachers' gratitude, and find their teachers warm and rewarding.

By the time these students arrive in high school, they are most likely to be grouped together. The most actively academic (bright) students are put into accelerated sections, while the problem students are tracked into nonacademic groups. As a consequence, middle-level students receive concentrated attention from their high school teachers. Yet the teachers are not likely to have high academic expectations of these students. In fact, the teachers are somewhat likely to be middle level in their own origins. As a result, these students encounter learning environments that are moderately involving and teachers who work with watered-down academic requirements to reach the students' interests. Teachers are more likely to be active in directing classes, and the curriculum is open enough to engage interests and occasionally to be fun.

However, in the high school experience, these students are most likely to encounter the direct channeling functions of schools. Although important decisions about their futures have already been made, these students, themselves, become aware of the instrumental function of schools, of the need to make a good record in school in order to enjoy relative success after school. Acquiescence is already something of a habit that is reinforced by the well-oiled high school bureaucracy. The awareness that they are dependent on the controls to which they acquiesce makes these students most totally controlled.

Independent Acquiescence

Like their counterparts in the middle, students at the upper level are a less distinct group than those at the bottom. Two structural groups tend to embody most traits of upper-level students: those in honors or accelerated classes have the most democratic classroom experiences, while students in Northdale High are most likely to encounter a comparably democratic school environment. Additionally, upper-level groups tend to consist almost entirely of upper-middle-class students, although not all of the latter are in the upper levels of the school. The purest type of upper-level experience is represented by the honors section in Northdale High, Crampton's American history class.

Students at the top of the schooling ladder are most involved in intrinsic qualities of their learning experience. They are most interested in classroom topics and activities; they feel least confined in class; they are most attentive and least bored. They are most likely to find class a challenge and most likely to feel they learn a lot in class. They also encounter a classroom most shaped by intellectual concerns, most demanding of intellectual independence and initiative. Teachers are least dominating, and teacher questions, particularly in Crampton's class, are divergent; they demand interpretation and analysis rather than simple factual reporting. Discussions in a class like Crampton's exhibit the greatest substantive continuity; students were more likely to respond to each other's comments and questions. Finally, these students were more likely to carry on classroom discussions outside of class.

Upper-level students thus come closest to experiencing a learning environment that develops individual autonomy and encourages active participation. Yet these students are also highly subject to extrinsic controls in schooling, most particularly the drive to excel according to the school's most rigorous demands. They were as likely as students on the bottom to agree that "You have to do things the way the teacher wants if you want to get a good grade" (students in Crampton's class stood out from all others in their overwhelming agreement with this statement). They were most likely to view their class as "pressured," and they were more likely to suggest that "getting into a good college" was an important reason for doing well in school.

Students at the top also view teacher actions that enforce the classroom norms as completely fair, and view violations of impartiality and teacher objectivity as extremely unfair. Seventy percent of all A students, 67 percent of all honors students, and 65 percent of all upper-middle-class students felt it was unfair for the teacher to grade students on the opinions they express (overall the average for this view was 52 percent). Ninety-one percent of the honors students, 88 percent of those with A's, and 98 percent of the upper-middle-class students criticized the teacher's paying attention to students who agree with him or her, and were least critical of such punitive measures as downgrading late assignments or telling noisy students to be quiet. Obviously, these sentiments reflect the self-interest of students who find the norms of punctuality and orderliness a relatively easy burden, and who have profited by impartial standards of evaluation. Also, as more articulate students, they would expect those in authority to base their actions on rules and explanations.

Because upper-level students are most involved in intrinsic learning processes and are controlled by the extrinsic incentive structure, overt, autocratic controls are largely unnecessary. Teachers relax classroom discipline as disruption and tardiness become inconsequential. Comparably, schools that are tailored to these kinds of students are able to adopt flexible scheduling and open campus programs. As noted earlier, the atmosphere at Northdale High was highly relaxed and informal compared to those of the other two schools, and students exhibited the greatest initiative in school and classroom activities.

In part, autocratic control must be downplayed because these students are learning to be more intellectually independent; they demand reasons for controls they encounter. In this sense, school control reflects democratic traits. However, the one kind of control that is pervasive and legitimate is that embodied by the instrumental function of schooling. Upper-level students are like those in the middle in viewing the grading function and related controls as pervasive forces in their schooling experience. Students in Northdale, for example, were just as likely as those in Middletown to agree that "The grades I get have a lot to do with how I feel about school" (59 percent agreed). Similarly (although less so), they tended to agree that "Grades make me feel like I'm always being told I'm better or worse than somebody else" (49 percent agreed; 31 percent disagreed). They were slightly less likely to disagree (23 percent to 36 percent in Middletown) with the view that "Grades are important because they have a lot to do with what kind of job you end up getting."

On the other hand, Northdale and upper-level students tended to be more critical of the school reward system. Whereas 63 percent of all Middletown students agreed that "No matter what people say about grades, you usually get what you deserve," only 45 percent in Northdale held this view. They also felt that their teachers were somewhat less impartial and that they were less likely to "get out of class what they put in" than students in Middletown.

In general, students at the top tend to be more articulate and outspoken in their criticisms of the institutional environment. In part, this may be because the learning process they experience is more tailored to instill this quality; in part, it may reflect their upbringing. While they may accept the legitimacy of the instrumental functions of schooling, they criticize its social by-product, competitive isolation. Honors track and Northdale High students were far more likely to view their classes as "competitive" than students in lower groups. Because more students are likely to become involved in classroom interaction, they have to struggle more to make a mark, to attract the teacher's attention. When asked what was missing most in their school, students in Northdale High were most likely to cite traits such as "closeness," "warmth," "caring," "personal attention" (even though there were far more counselors in Northdale than in the other two schools), and "happiness." They also felt "more good teachers" were needed in their school, while Middletown and Central students were unlikely to cite this need. Finally, Northdale students were likely to agree that "School is most interesting as a place to see friends."

Students at the top have encountered a learning process that is (relatively) geared to intrinsic interest and independent activism; yet their overall encounter with institutional life controls them by extrinsic incentives. In many respects, schooling becomes a struggle, a competitive struggle to reap the rewards of the schooling race and a personal struggle to find and carve out meaningful encounters. Schooling control is largely perceived as situational, a control that these students have to yield to temporarily while they hold apart the things they "really believe in." Yet, as a process reinforced in later life, schooling threatens to submerge the person's independence the way it does with students in the middle. Some may lose the element of personal control and become effective manipulators in society; others may hold on to personal values and experience continued conflict in their occupations; others may drop out.

Although students in the upper levels have the most democratic learning experience of any group, it is not without its social and personal costs. The keen interest in this study displayed by students in the honors sections and their comments on some questionnaire items suggest an element of unhappiness with the schooling process. These students might concur with Kenneth Keniston's statement, "You have to grow up in Scarsdale to know how bad things really are."12

In the process of becoming involved in school learning, students at the top learn the lesson of privatism. Their learning process is most acutely atomistic, requiring the relentless and isolated pursuit of self-interest. At the same time, because they are set apart as the select of the school race, upper-level students learn that their collective interest, insofar as it exists, has little in common with those below them. Regardless of how much social class and racial groups are mixed in schools, they are likely to become separated within the school by the existing selection function.

In sum, then, upper-level students learn to be political activists, pursuing their self-interest through participation in public institutions. They are smart, intellectually independent, and less likely to be swayed by appeals to emotion or irrationality. They have learned the lessons of craft, enterprise, initiative, and autonomy. They are skilled at detecting and following established paths to success, even if these only stress the ability to psych out the teacher, the ability to work diligently at specified times, to draw attention to oneself in group situations, or to produce punctually.

We can see how these activists are most successful in a political system geared to competitive interaction among interests. They are the most likely to participate politically to gain their own ends, and in the long run to shape the social and political environment in such a way that it reinforces and perpetuates these very traits. Yet their loss is a sense of communal interdependence; they are most likely to bemoan the absence of community.

Dynamically, the lesson of independent acquiescence is easy to comprehend. Students who come from academically oriented backgrounds are ahead of the game when they encounter the schooling process. They are more likely to be articulate and to expect explanations for practices that affect them. [13] Teachers who encounter these students may find the challenge uncomfortable or time consuming, or they may respond positively. In either case, it is likely that these students will be directed to learning experiences that require greater student initiative. To some degree, however, the more gifted students will be forced to restrain their curiosity as they undergo pedantic learning procedures; the mainstreaming qualities of schooling have at best a limited amount of "give."

By high school, these students will continue to stand out as the most articulate and self-initiating in a school's population. They will be tracked into experiences that tend to reinforce these tendencies at the same time that they isolate these students. And they will come face to face with the dominant need to do well, to get into a good college, to get into a good professional school, and so on. They will acquiesce, but will retain at least an intellectually critical stance, if not a semblance of personal independence.

CONCLUSION

The major portion of this chapter has drawn on empirical find-ings to construct a picture of the three unequal lessons taught by the schooling experience to different groups of students. In a sense, we have documented ways in which the types of lessons that Everett Reimer describes are taught by the process of schooling he has ob-served:

> . . . different students learn in varying degrees to con-form, to ignore the rules and to take advantage of them. Those who ignore them in the extreme become dropouts, and learn mainly that they do not belong in school or in the society it represents. Those who conform to the rules become the dependable producers and consumers of the technological society. Those who learn to beat the school game become the exploiters of this society. Those on whom the discipline of the school falls lightly, who easily perform its assignments and have little need to violate its rules, are least touched by school. They are, or become, the social aristocrats and the rebels. [14]

In documenting this picture of inequality in schooling, however, the empirical study points to forces broader and more systemic than the rules that students encounter in schooling. A more accurate ex-planation for the unequal lessons would evolve from the controls at work in the schooling experience, particularly the control over stu-dent learning embedded in the social selection function. As schools and teachers seek out efficient ways of selecting and sorting students according to school-related criteria, students come to encounter in-creasingly distinctive types of learning environments.

At the high school level, where the instrumental functions of schooling become most pronounced, these distinctive learning environ-ments become built into an overt tracking structure. Of all identifi-able categories of students, track level was most closely associated with the patterns of variation in school learning; differences also emerged among grade-average groups and among the particular types of college preparation found in each school. All of these are clearly tied to the social selection and personal advancement functions of schooling.

Furthermore, these groupings of students tend to correspond to the students' socioeconomic backgrounds. Thus, whether legiti-mately or not, the social selection is loaded in favor of certain seg-ments of the population. Two questions arise concerning this selec-tion function: Is it legitimate, that is, does it select according to fair

and functional criteria? Even if it is legitimate, does it still result
in outcomes which are dysfunctional or unfair? These are critical
questions, the full answers to which require a study of far broader
scope than this one. Still, the findings contained in this work strongly
suggest negative responses to both questions.

In the first place, the descriptive lessons learned by different
groups in the schooling structure suggest a learning dynamic whereby
schools teach these lessons through the selection process. Because
this process begins with the earliest schooling encounters, empirical
documentation is not available in this study of high school learning.
Still, a learning dynamic applicable to elementary schools can be
elicited from the empirical material in this work.

In the first place, students from various backgrounds, with various backgrounds, with various school-related inclinations, encounter
a relatively monolithic evaluation system tied to social selection. Although in one sense teachers feel they should be attentive to the learning needs of each student, they are under a number of pressures to
streamline the learning process, fitting it to the overt inclinations of
dominant student types. To oversimplify, problem children require
discipline, advanced children can move ahead quickly, and pluggers
largely can be left alone. Despite good intentions on a teacher's part,
there are powerful structural inducements to separate these learner
types into groups, each of which starts to encounter a distinctive
learning environment. At least informally, tracking begins in the
very first year of schooling; it becomes overt during adolescence,
at a time when students begin to be conscious of their future adult
roles.

Within the school, this effort to tailor learning experiences to
fit types of students is functionally legitimate. Yet it can be called
unfair in two ways, and it is ultimately dysfunctional in terms of democratic citizenship norms. On the one hand, this "fitting" process is
unfair because it reinforces and rigidifies class differences in society
at the same time that the schooling process is supposed to provide all
with an equal opportunity. Schools quickly reinforce the orientations
of incoming students by providing them with learning experiences that
accentuate existing traits.

Seeing less prepared students as problems, schools shape the
learning experience to appeal to the need for immediate gratification;
factual learning becomes the norm. Yet these children come to see
that learning is fundamentally directionless and, accordingly, meaningless; they become alienated from the institution of schooling and
thus have to be more overtly controlled; being more overtly controlled for no meaningful reason, they become more alienated—and so
the vicious cycle goes. All this time, these students are going to
school to improve their chances for advancement in society.

Middle- and upper-level students encounter a similar dynamic whereby schooling rigidifies existing tendencies by fitting learning environments to the tendencies of these students; schools reinforce tendencies of dependent acquiescence and independent acquiescence. Such an environment clearly works to the advantage of those who come with upper-level tendencies. In this sense, equal opportunity is denied.

Furthermore, there is evidence that schools not only reinforce and rigidify these unequal lessons but that they actively teach them. A number of works suggest that the early fitting process is not purely a function of school-related criteria, but that doors are closed to meritocratic achievement by various forms of bias ranging from culturally biased achievement tests to measurable teacher expectations.[15]

This study also suggests that the active teaching impact of schools continues through the high school years. We have seen that student involvement is the variable that best distinguishes the three types of schooling experience and the three unequal lessons of schooling. Each level of students is involved in school and classrooms in different degrees and a different manner. It is not difficult to see how the involvement inclination that students bring with them to a classroom affects how a teacher teaches the class. As we shall see in Chapter 5, however, the way the teacher teaches the class also has an independent impact on the nature and degree of student involvement in learning. Because students in lower levels are much more likely to encounter teaching styles that discourage involvement throughout their schooling experience, we can infer that schooling not only reinforces existing inclinations but teaches these. The schools, in other words, play a significant role in shaping the citizenship orientations of different groups. And they do so largely by fulfilling a function demanded of them by society.

Finally, we can criticize the unequal outcomes of schooling as democratically dysfunctional insofar as a fully open opportunity for political participation is desirable. If our objective is a closed society geared to a status quo, schooling outcomes are functional. If, however, we truly value the perspectives of all citizens, if we seek to maximize the opportunity for all citizens to shape the common good, and if we value an element of interdependence among social groups, then we must criticize schooling for its role in undermining these objectives.

This is not to argue that the kinds of diverse social orientations outlined in this chapter are necessarily undesirable in themselves, but that individuals ought to be effectively free to choose a style of participation. Since schools are at least one of the critical environmental forces that tend to close off these choices, they perform an essentially antidemocratic socializing function.

NOTES

1. Seymour B. Sarason, The Culture of the School and the Problem of Change (Boston: Allyn Bacon, 1969), p. 69.

2. Robert D. Hess and Judith V. Torney, The Development of Political Attitudes in Children (New York: Anchor Books, 1967).

3. Robert Dreeben, On What Is Learned in School (Reading, Mass.: Addison-Wesley, 1968), p. 66.

4. David Riesman, Individualism Reconsidered, cited in Autocracy and Democracy—An Experimental Inquiry, Ralph K. White and Ronald Lippitt (New York: Harper, 1960), p. 254.

5. Willard Waller, The Sociology of Teaching (New York: Wiley, 1932), p. 196.

6. See, for example, Sidney Verba and Norman H. Nie, Participation in America: Political Democracy and Social Equality (New York: Harper & Row, 1972); and Gabriel A. Almond and Sidney Verba, The Civic Culture (Boston: Little, Brown, 1965).

7. See, for example, A. B. Hollingshead and F. C. Redlich, Social Class and Mental Illness (New York: Wiley, 1958).

8. Edward Banfield, The Unheavenly City Revisited (Boston: Little, Brown, 1974).

9. However, there is disagreement over precisely where and to what degree these behavioral patterns exist, and particularly, why they exist. See William Ryan, Blaming the Victim (New York: Vintage Books, 1971).

10. See, for example, Basil Bernstein, "Social Class and Linguistic Development: A Theory of Social Learning," in Education, Economy, and Society, ed. A. H. Halsey, Jean Floud, and C. Arnold Anderson (New York: Free Press, 1961), pp. 288–315.

11. Estelle Fuchs, "How Teachers Learn to Help Children Fail," Trans-Action 5, no. 9 (September 1969): 45–49; see also, Ray C. Rist, The Urban School: A Factory for Failure (Cambridge, Mass.: MIT Press, 1973).

12. Kenneth Keniston, "You Have to Grow Up in Scarsdale to Know How Bad Things Really Are," New York Times Magazine, April 27, 1969, pp. 27ff.

13. Bernstein, op. cit.

14. Everett Reimer, School Is Dead—Alternatives in Education (New York: Doubleday, 1971), p. 29.

15. See Robert Rosenthal and Lenore Jacobson, Pygmalion in the Classroom: Teacher Expectations and Pupils' Intellectual Development (New York: Holt, Rinehart and Winston, 1968); R. C. Rist, "Student Social Class and Teacher Expectations: The Self-fulfilling Prophecy in Ghetto Education," Harvard Educational Review 40, no. 3 (August 1970): 411-51.

5

EFFECTIVE
TEACHING

As noted in the introduction, recent social science has contributed to the view that "schools don't make any difference," at least in
terms of redistributing social outcomes. Whether or not it is intended, this view takes on distinctly conservative connotations. Because
school outcomes are largely "determined" by socioeconomic background, some are able to say that students are getting a fair shake,
that they are doing about as well as can be expected given certain abilities and traits deeply rooted in their upbringing and biological makeup. Those inclined toward this view have at their disposal a rationale
for rejecting public educational programs designed to counter early
disadvantages.

These perceptions are overtly political and arise despite the
warnings of the social scientists involved. For example, Jencks and
associates note that their findings do not suggest that schools make
no difference in a qualitative or additive sense, just that schools do
not significantly affect income and occupational inequality in society.[1]

There is still plenty of room for the view that schools have a
significant impact on the lives of students, both in experiential and
outcome terms.[2] The previous chapter strongly supports the intuitive
view that different groups of students learn behavioral and attitudinal
lessons that handicap or advantage them in later social, occupational,
and political pursuits—particularly as these lessons are reinforced in
subsequent encounters in the workplace, the community, and the government.

Obviously, students bring to their classroom encounters a variety of abilities and school orientations. And teachers clearly adapt
their teaching objectives for a given class to their perceptions of stu-

dent characteristics. Possibly the most critical stage in the teaching
process is that of "reading" student needs, interests, and ability
levels.

Nonetheless, it is highly improbable that student characteristics
alone determine the outcome of classroom interaction. One can argue
that different teaching approaches, whatever their sources, are likely
to affect similar groups of students in different ways. If this is the
case, and some students tend to encounter one type of teacher throughout their schooling career, while others encounter other types, it
would follow that schooling has a distinct cumulative impact on each
of these student groups.

This chapter examines the starting point in this causal chain:
the issue of independent teacher impact on classroom interaction.
The empirical evidence, however, focuses on the high school experience. At this point in the schooling process, it is less likely that we
would find teachers having an independent impact on classroom outcomes when students already have encountered years of cumulative
teacher input.

Despite these qualifications, the data bear out the existence of
an independent teaching impact. Although teachers consciously tailored their objectives and expectations to their perceptions of students,
the variation in teaching approaches had a modest, yet significant impact on student involvement and associated democratic learning traits.

Consideration of teaching impact takes two approaches. The
first is comparative. It asks: How much impact do teachers have,
independent of characteristics that students bring with them to class?
Regression analysis of available teacher and student variables underscores the primary significance of student track level—the single
largest, independent determinant of involvement. Tracking and the
instrumental functions it performs thereby become critical reform
concerns, considered in Chapter 6. At the same time, however, teaching approach has a significant impact on student involvement, independent of such student traits as track level, socioeconomic status,
or grade average. Most significantly, student perceptions of the teacher as unilaterally controlling through the grade function are negatively
related to involvement.

Once we establish the existence of a teaching impact, we need
to examine more carefully the critical teacher traits that affect student involvement. From the comparative data, we can see that these
traits are related to student perceptions of control. The second part
of the chapter approaches the question of teacher impact descriptively.
This section examines the dynamics of student involvement by taking
an in-depth look at classes where student involvement increases sharply, compared to classes where it declines. Analysis of the change in
student involvement attributable to classroom interaction points to

variations in teacher activism and curricular constraint as the critical factors.

Because upper-level students are more likely to encounter effective teachers, we can perceive an additional reason why tracking
and related functions loom as the critical determinants of inequality
in schooling. On the other hand, the analysis of classroom dynamics
suggests policy approaches relevant to democratizing school learning
within existing school structures. These reform implications also
will be discussed in Chapter 6.

STUDENT TRAITS AND TEACHER CONTROL

In order to determine the relative impact of student traits and
teacher input on student involvement, a series of measures was used.
The main focus for examining involvement is the statement "The best
thing about this class is the bell at the end," the measure that exhibited
the widest variation among individual students, classes, and track levels. Additional insight can be gained from the "pay attention" and "sit
still" measures and the checklist item "interesting." Since these
measures revealed less overall variation, however, they exhibit less
of a relationship with student and teacher traits. Two questions are
important for present purposes: What are the most significant determinants of student involvement among measurable and available variables? and does a measurable characteristic of teaching approach have
a significant and independent impact on student involvement?

Before turning to the empirical data, it is important to bear in
mind that statistical consideration of these questions is imperfect. A
thorough examination of teacher impact would require a study aimed
specifically at this end, incorporating a wider range of measures than
are used in this work. Nonetheless, this study has uncovered significant variation in student involvement, a variation that is closely associated with a range of democratic variables. The limited data available for this pursuit are subjected to rigorous statistical methods, resulting in a finding of significant teacher impact.

Three measures of student traits are used—all self-reported in
the questionnaire—student socioeconomic status (a three-level classification of father's occupation, following census categories), student
track assignment, and student grade average in school. As can be
seen in Table 5.1, all three are significantly correlated with each
other, and thus overlap in their impact on other variables (see also
Table A.3). As a consequence, the effort to distinguish among these
variables and their impact is not as conclusive as might be desired.
At the same time, the overlap reinforces concerns about inequality in
schooling.

TABLE 5.1

Student Traits: Correlations

	Track	Grade Average
Socioeconomic status	0.38	0.25
Track	—	0.42

Source: Compiled by the author.

A picture of these associations can be seen by breaking down the respective populations. For example, 61 percent of all general track students are from lower-working-class families as opposed to 31 percent of all college track and only 7 percent of all honors track students. On the other hand, 72 percent of the honors students are from upper-middle-class families as opposed to 34 percent of the college and 18 percent of the general students. Track populations, then, tend to be distinguishable by a dominant socioeconomic status, although the more "mixed" college track is made up of roughly equal populations from all three SES levels.

Grade-average patterns are comparable. Fifty-five percent of all A students are from upper-middle-class families; B students are fairly evenly divided among three SES levels; and 50 percent of all C or below students are from lower-working-class families. In general, we can say that students from lower-status families tend to be assigned to lower tracks and also tend to get lower grades; at the same time, lower-track students are likely to receive lower grades regardless of socioeconomic status.

Three measures of teacher input are used to examine the variation in student involvement. In focusing on the variation in individual involvement, the questionnaire statement "You have to do things the way the teacher wants if you want to get a good grade" has been used. This measure tests the association between a student's perception of the teacher as extrinsically controlling and the student's feeling of involvement. In addition, two "objective" measures of teacher input are used to focus on the variation in involvement among classes. In the first measure, teachers are categorized according to the teacher-domination ratio in their class. Seven teachers (Hawkins, Perez, Crampton, O'Reilly, Ryan, Baker, and Kopek) are classified as low domination; five are in a middle-level group (Casey, James, Schilling, Ferris, and Mitchell), while three (Gianelli, Pellagrini, and Backman) are high-domination teachers.

The second interclass measure of teacher input is based on "class-induced" involvement. Each teacher or class is categorized according to the differences among the students' collective responses to the school wide involvement statement "When I'm in school, all I can think of is other places I'd rather be" and the class-specific involvement measure "The best thing about this class is the bell at the end." Classes where students show the greatest gain in class involvement are categorized as positive-impact classes; they include Hawkins, Ferris, Baker, and Kopek. Classes where students register the greatest loss in involvement are the negative-impact classes; these also include four teachers: James, Pellagrini, O'Reilly, and Mitchell. The remaining seven teachers, whose students exhibited little change in involvement, are grouped in the middle.

When the three student-trait measures and the perceived control measure are joined as independent variables and subjected to unordered multiple regression, student track level emerges as the most significant determinant of student involvement, as can be seen in Table 5.2. Twelve percent of the individual variation in student involvement is explained by a student's track assignment (all computations were statistically significant, with an F significance of 0.000). Student socioeconomic status does not independently explain any significant variation in involvement, once track is considered. The impact of SES, in other words, is channeled through the student's track level; SES is related to track assignment, but the latter is a more significant determinant of involvement.

Student perceptions of classroom control have the second most important input into student involvement of all characteristics measured. In other words, once the impact of track is accounted for, the degree of unilateral control the student perceives concentrated in the

TABLE 5.2

The Impact of Student Traits and Teacher Control
on the Variation in Student Involvement

Independent Variables	Percent of Variation Explained (R Squared)
Student track	11.9
Perceived control	5.8
Student grade average	3.5
Total variation explained	21.2

Source: Compiled by the author.

teacher determines almost 6 percent of the variation in their feelings of involvement. The more controlling they perceive the teacher, the less they feel involved.

The third most significant cause of the variation in student involvement is student ability as measured by grade average. Once track level and perceived teacher control are accounted for, the student's grade average explains 3.5 percent of the variation. Together the three variables explain 21.2 percent of all the variation in student involvement. (One can readily imagine several other factors playing an important role in student involvement, including subject interest, class size, peer interaction, and the time of day; these, however, did not vary widely enough or were not measured in this particular study.)

When the other measures of teacher input are used as independent variables, student grade average emerges as the second most significant determinant of involvement and teacher or class input slips to third. When teacher-domination categories are included in the regression, student track explains 11.9 percent of the variation in involvement, grade average explains 4.3 percent of the remaining variation, and teacher domination explains 3.4 percent, for a total of 19.6 percent of all variation. SES is again absorbed by the track factor. When teachers are classified according to a class-inducement factor, track again explains 11.9 percent of the variation in involvement, grade average explains 4.3 percent, and the class-inducement factor explains 2.8 percent, for a total of 19.0 percent of all variation.

Thus, when we consider a measure of student involvement that taps feelings of alienation, student track level is consistently the most significant determinant of that factor. The student's socioeconomic status is absorbed by the track impact, reflecting the kind of interaction between SES types and the selection function of schooling. By the time students are in high school, their track assignment is likely to be the best predictor of their alienation level.

At the same time, the teacher's control has a significant impact on involvement, even when the track-SES factor is accounted for. By implication, if we can affect the quality of teacher control in the classroom, we are likely to have some significant impact on student involvement and alienation regardless of track level. Other characteristics of the classroom, represented by the teacher-domination ratio and the class-inducement factor, are also related to involvement.

Finally, a student's grade average is also likely to explain a degree of his or her alienation. Here, again, we encounter a function-related control in the schooling process, one that is more immediate than track level but is also tied to the social selection function. Implied by this relationship is the possibility of affecting student involvement by changing the reward system of schooling.

When other measures of involvement are examined, some variations in the basic pattern of relationships emerge. For example, student perception of teacher control has the largest independent effect
on student feelings of confinement ("sit still"). Perceived control explains 7 percent of the variation in confinement, while student grade
average explains 3.8 percent and SES explains 1.9 percent. Student
track level has an insignificant independent effect on the confinement
measure. A total of 12.6 percent of the variation is explained by the
three significant variables.

On the other hand, student track is most significantly related
to student perceptions of class as "interesting," explaining 6.6 percent of the variation. Teacher traits are nearly as significant; perceived control explains 5.4 percent of the variation, while the class-
inducement factor independently explains only 0.9 percent. Student
SES explains a miniscule 0.6 percent of the variation, independent of
track. A total of 12.6 percent of the variation in "interest" is explained by the measures studied.

Finally, when the variation in student attentiveness ("pay attention") is assessed, only two measures demonstrate any significant independent impact: student track (6.1 percent) and student grade average (5.4 percent). SES and teacher control have negligible effects.

While these findings do not add up to a conclusive explanation of
student involvement in classroom learning, they do confirm two characteristics of classroom interaction discussed at the beginning of this
chapter. The use of the more exact regression technique has demonstrated that both student traits and teacher input factors have significant independent effects on the level of student involvement, and, by
inference, the relative democratic quality of classroom learning; and
that of the two types of variables, student traits, in particular, student track level, are the more significant determinants of the variation in student involvement.

Closer examination of the two teacher-control measures adds
to our understanding of student involvement. In terms of the variation
in interstudent involvement, the perception of tight, extrinsic grading
control has a negative impact on nearly all involvement measures.
The more a student felt he or she had to "do things the way the teacher
wants in order to get a good grade," the less that student felt involved
in class (see Table A.4). Conversely, the more a student felt involved,
the less likely it is that he or she felt controlled by the teacher. In
other words, where students are conscious of tight, extrinsic controls,
they are less likely to be controlled by the intrinsic merits of classroom learning; where they feel involved in classroom learning, they
are less likely to feel extrinsically controlled.

This pattern holds up consistently on nearly all participation
measures. Students who felt tightly controlled also felt more confined,

more bored, and they paid less attention in class. These students
also perceived fewer chances to learn interesting things, were less
likely to feel that the "teacher cares about what I think," felt it was
less important to listen to the teacher, and were less likely to feel
they learned a lot in class. The students who felt most involved, who
had the most democratic experiences, were those who were neutral
or who disagreed with the control statement. (The small number of
those who disagreed strongly recorded less democratic perceptions.)

Similar patterns occurred in the interclass involvement break-
downs. When teachers were grouped according to both teacher-domination and convergent-question ratios, high-domination (and narrow-
question) teachers were associated consistently with less democratic
responses. On the other hand, students who had low-domination teachers recorded more democratic perceptions on every measure except
the deviant efficacy statement. Students of high-domination teachers
also felt more constricted by teacher grading controls (71 percent
agreed with the control statement as opposed to 51 percent in low-
domination classes).

In other words, classes where teachers asked more interpretive, discussion-oriented questions and where students initiated a
greater proportion of classroom comments tended to be those classes
where students were least conscious of tight grading control. Classes
marked by high teacher domination and a high proportion of factual
questions tended to make students more aware of the teacher's control and the grading function.

To some degree, these classroom traits reflect the way a given
teacher approaches his or her teaching job, while to some degree
they are a product of the interaction with a particular student type.
We can summarize the findings to this point by citing two types of
classroom variables that are related to student involvement and hence
to democratic learning:

1. Learning and behavior characteristics that students bring
with them to a given class, particularly as these are sorted and reinforced by the tracking process.

2. The way teachers control student learning, in particular,
the degree to which they dominate classroom interaction and stress
a narrow, factual focus. The critical distinction between high- and
low-involvement classes thus seems to be the degree to which the
teacher emphasizes a tight, grade-oriented reason for learning as
opposed to an intrinsic subject-and-process reason that engages the
student in purposeful learning.

Both findings have implications for the democratic reform of
schools. The impact of student traits, such as track level, SES, and
grade average, points to the potential effectiveness of reforms that

address these directly. On the other hand, the impact of teacher ap-proaches suggests that changes in student involvement can result from reforms directed at the way teachers teach. Before discussing reform issues, we need to distinguish effective teaching approaches in greater detail.

THE DYNAMICS OF TEACHER IMPACT

In order to gain a more precise picture of the teacher-input side of student involvement, we now turn to a descriptive examination of individual classes. By investigating the dynamics of classroom in-teraction, we gain a sense of specific teaching approaches that in-crease (or decrease) the involvement of a variety of student types.

To elicit a picture of teacher effects, classes are grouped ac-cording to the class-inducement factor used in the statistical analysis. By comparing student involvement scores on the schoolwide and class-specific measures, we can distinguish classes in which student in-volvement rises or falls substantially. Having made these distinc-tions, we can then examine classroom interaction within these class-es; since each group includes a variety of student types, this descrip-tive examination suggests approaches that are applicable to a variety of student groups within the existing school structure.

As was the case in the previous section, the two measures used for this operation are the two that appear most closely related on the surface: the schoolwide statement "When I'm in school, all I can think of is other places I'd rather be" and the class-specific statement "The best thing about this class is the bell at the end. " Both are heavily critical of the schooling experience (and thus are scored the same way); both tap student feelings of alienation from the particular envi-ronment in question. Both elicit a desire to be somewhere else out-side the class or outside the school. And student responses to the two measures are highly correlated (0.45).

When the 15 classes are compared on the basis of class-induced involvement, four classes emerge that are distinguished by a signifi-cant positive effect on involvement and four reveal a significant nega-tive effect. As can be seen in Table 5.3, a group of seven exhibits negligible impact on student involvement. Because we are concerned with classroom impact here, these seven do not figure prominently in our discussion.

Each group contains an interesting mix of classes. The positive-impact classes (large increase in involvement) include one general track class in Northdale High, one college track class in Central High, and two Middletown classes, one of which is an honors unit. Interest-

TABLE 5.3

Class-Induced Involvement

Rank	Class	School Score	Class Score	Class Effect* (Adjusted)
Positive impact				
1	Kopek (Mid/Coll)	3.19	2.52	−53
2	Hawkins (Cen/Coll)	3.24	2.65	−45
3	Baker (Mid/Hon)	2.32	1.74	−44
4	Ferris (Nor/Gen)	3.77	3.31	−32
Minimal class impact				
5	Backman (Mid/Coll)	3.17	2.88	−15
6	Schilling (Nor/Coll)	2.83	2.58	−11
7	Crampton (Nor/Hon)	2.36	2.18	− 4
8	Ryan (Mid/Coll)	2.67	2.54	+ 1
9	Gianelli (Cen/Coll)	3.38	3.29	+ 5
10	Perez (Nor/Coll)	3.06	3.00	+ 8
11	Casey (Cen/Gen)	3.28	3.24	+10
Negative impact				
12	Mitchell (Mid/Gen)	3.63	3.79	+30
13	James (Cen/Gen)	2.55	2.91	+50
14	O'Reilly (Nor/Coll)	2.50	2.91	+55
15	Pellagrini (Cen/Gen)	3.00	3.76	+90

*The overall student mean on the class-specific "bell-best" measure is 0.14 lower (2.87 to 3.01) than the mean on the "other places" measure. This difference is taken into account when subtracting the scores of individual classes. A negative sign indicates an increase in class-specific involvement.

Source: Compiled by the author.

ingly, Crampton's highly involved honors class is not among the positive-impact classes, essentially because the students in that class were already so highly involved in school that Crampton added little to their feeling of involvement in class. Student traits, in other words, largely determined the involvement in that class (although a different type of teacher might have had a different effect).

The four negative-impact classes (large decline in involvement) include at least one from each school (two from Central) and three general track classes. The one college track class, O'Reilly's, was distinguished by a group of bright, articulate students (concerned about college admissions) and a distinctively laissez-faire teacher. Interestingly, Gianelli's authoritarian class is not among the significant negative-impact group. In essence, his students were already relatively alienated from school. Because of his distinctive teaching approach, however, Gianelli's class is included in the analysis of teacher impact.

Additional characteristics of specific classes should be noted. The general track students in Ferris's positive-impact class were the most alienated from school of any of the 15 sections; 54 percent of the students in the class agreed with the schoolwide statement "When I'm in school all I can think of is other places I'd rather be" as opposed to an overall mean of 33 percent. Only 8 percent (or 2 of the 26 students) in the class disagreed with the schoolwide alienation measure. Forty-six percent remained alienated from class, while 35 percent, or 9 students, became involved.

Thus, Ferris encountered a largely alienated group of students and increased their feelings of involvement in his class. Mitchell, on the other hand, encountered students who were nearly as alienated from school, but the net result of his class was increased alienation. The schoolwide alienation score of 3.63 rose to 3.79 in Mitchell's class, despite the overall trend for class-specific scores to be lower.

Teaching techniques and classroom factors associated with a positive impact on student involvement are revealed by descriptions of the four positive-impact teachers. Before describing each class, we may note that three of the four (Kopek, Hawkins, and Baker) were categorized as active-open teachers and one (Ferris) was in the active-flexible category.

Positive-Impact Teachers

Kopek

Like other Middletown students in college and honors classes, the students in Kopek's class were generally neatly dressed and orderly. Kopek described her students as "very sociable, bright, fairly homogeneous, very tolerant and amenable to new projects, a little seductive and some a little too talky." With 22 students in regular attendance, the class was average in size for Middletown. The group included a number of visible cliques, but these were "flexible enough to absorb individuals in group work"—more so than in Kopek's other classes where students were reluctant to team up. Kopek also mentioned a "loose identification" among students with the class as a whole.

Kopek's classroom, like others in Middletown High, was clean and brightly lit. Student collages covered most of the bulletin boards; one ostentatiously focusing on current antiestablishment themes. Individual student desks were frequently drawn into a large circle for discussions or into small clusters for group projects, or they were left in rows for lectures, films, or tests.

In teaching her senior psychology class, Kopek blended a unique mixture of informal and formal traits. An amiable and outspoken young teacher, Kopek combined an awareness of current pedagogical thinking and a mixture of techniques with a highly structured, teacher-directed classroom. In her overall classroom manner, Kopek was business-like and somewhat aloof; at the same time, she frequently exchanged friendly banter with individual students.

Because of the ability level and sociability of the class, Kopek reported that she was more prone to let the students lead their own discussions. "I give an introductory lecture and sum up, and let them handle things in between." This objective is supported by the low teacher-domination ratio of Kopek's class (1.1:1, the third lowest overall). The most common classroom activity was the directed discussion, supplemented by some lectures and open-ended discussions, as well as group games and projects. Isolated individual work was confined to time outside of class. Kopek's main objectives with the class were to "broaden students' minds and create new interests," with skill development a "distant second." During the period of observation, the class studied behavioral psychology, existentialism, and interracial marriage. Compared to Baker's honors section, Kopek's class concentrated more rigorously on external subject material. Eighty-one percent of the students felt "listening to the teacher is important because she knows what she's talking about" (mean = 56 percent).

Curricular direction was effected by mimeos used to focus discussions, the blackboard to record important terms during lectures, and the teacher's general domination of discussions by lengthy commentary (despite disclaimers). The tightness of control was tempered by a large percentage of interpretive questions that required students to bring their personal perspectives to bear on class themes, by group projects, and by an emphasis on essay questions in tests and homework. Kopek's class registered the second lowest proportion of convergent questions (27 percent). All class activities, however, were unmistakably under the teacher's direction; typically, the beginning of each class period was marked by administrative announcements and directives for the day's work.

Student participation in class discussions was mixed. Much of the actual discussion time was dominated by extended teacher explanations of topic material. At the same time, however, student initiation of questions was very high; most of these were addressed to the teacher for purposes of clarification. Verbal participation, however, was largely dominated by a handful of students, while about half the class slouched back in their seats or rested with their heads in their hands, watching passively or gazing out the window. An average of 12.5 students (57 percent) made no verbal contributions to the class, while 14.5 (66 percent) made fewer than two comments.

By contrast, the student group projects I observed were very lively. Guided by mimeographed questions, four groups of five or six students worked in clusters, talking busily with each other. In one observed project, student groups were asked to devise behavior-modification strategies for recalcitrant or antisocial individuals in different settings familiar to students. Only two male students were consistently withdrawn throughout the period; one apparently did not enjoy the female domination of his small group, while the other was more disaffected with the whole class. The largest proportion of students selected discussion as the most interesting class activity and reading and taking notes as the least, views that reflected, but exaggerated, general tendencies in the survey.

Kopek described her approach to classroom discipline as "subtle, not very overt." She added, "I think they understand when I sit at my desk and stare that I'm angry and they better be quiet. I tend to use personal control and the control of the subject matter." (Seventy-six percent of the students agreed that they had "to do things the way the teacher wants . . . " as opposed to 58 percent overall.) In some ways students appeared to have wide latitude in their personal behavior. A number of girls knit or crocheted during class discussions, and occasionally a student dozed on her desk. Kopek readily granted permission to leave the room to get material from lockers, disdaining the red-tape pass procedures. At the same time, she repeatedly enforced restrictions on the noise level and disruptive behavior. More frequently than the other observed Middletown teachers, Kopek interrupted discussions with a stern "Ssssh," or she would spur student work with a sharp, "Okay, that's enough. Let's get started." Half the students characterized discipline in the class as "relaxed" and 44 percent as "strict, but fair" (more strict than the norm).

Grading in Kopek's class was adjusted to the general level of the students. Among the criteria for good grades were effort, the ability to follow instructions, initiative, creative expression, and understanding the material, in that order. In some cases, exceptions were made to encourage students who had shown some improvement. More students than the norm felt "hard work" was the trait the teacher "liked most in her students." According to the teacher, cheating was very rare, made more difficult by the use of essay tests. On the other hand, students demonstrated a normal concern about their grades, and there was considerable competition for the teacher's attention during discussions, particularly among a large group of girls. Eighty-one percent of the students found the class "interesting" (mean = 64 percent), 52 percent "pressured" (mean = 14 percent), and 57 percent felt they learned a lot in the class (mean = 47 percent).

Hawkins

Hawkins's senior social psychology class in Central High differed from Kopek's class in many ways. In the first place, there were only three other groups of students more alienated from school; Hawkins reported that his class was typical of those at Central High, that is, very heterogeneous in ability and motivation and with a number of students who had "tremendous reading problems." According to Hawkins, most students had come up through the city's school system, where they had "learned by rote, and were rewarded for passivity and nonparticipation." Most were enrolled in the college program whether or not they would eventually attend college and regardless of their comparative standing against their peers in other schools.

Of the 25 enrolled in the class, an average of 18 to 20 attended class each day. Slightly more than half the students were black (64 percent) and male (52 percent). According to Hawkins, there were two distinct groups of students in the class, crossing racial lines: one verbal and cooperative and the other nonverbal and passively withdrawn. In terms of overall activity, students tended to be attentive but restrained.

Among the four active-open teachers, Hawkins was the most behaviorally active and most curricularly open. Although student activity was variable at best, curricular involvement tended to be the highest of any Central group. Hawkins, himself, was one of the most dynamic teachers encountered in the study—a young but experienced teacher of considerable vitality who put a great deal of energy into activating members of the class. On a typical day, he would stride into the class and greet the students with a loud "Good morning, everyone." While directing the class, he talked quickly, moving in nervous bursts around the room, and he gestured with great animation while explaining topics. During the observed classes, Hawkins seemed constantly aware of all activity in the room, including my presence, which drew frequent glances after a noteworthy student comment or a provocative question.

In the curricular sphere, Hawkins actively directed all student work. Each class exercise was preselected by the teacher and announced at the beginning of each day. During class discussions, Hawkins fired rapid questions at students, yet these tended to be personally interpretive and required students to follow through on their incomplete thoughts. (Hawkins had the third highest teacher-domination ratio, 9:1, in the survey, but simultaneously, the third lowest convergent-question percentage, 28 percent.) While students worked on their own or in small groups, Hawkins circulated around the room, checking on progress and making suggestions when students seemed to bog down.

Both the course content and learning procedures accentuated personal interaction between students and subject. Hawkins drew on student illustrations of personal experiences, such as moral dilemmas involved in theft, cheating, and a father-son struggle over money, to draw students toward group generalizations and then into an external social psychology field. In terms of content, an understanding of psychological theories or generalizations about adolescence was the learning objective, approached "inductively" by the students.

Hawkins himself played a critical role in drawing students toward this engagement with the subject, particularly in directing a flow of questions to each individual student in the class. Teacher-directed discussions, cooperative work projects, and individual reading and writing exercises were the most prominent class activities. Noting that most students were "intensely subjective" and had difficulty working in groups, Hawkins's primary aim was to "give students a perspective with which to look at themselves, and ways of tackling problems and rationally interpreting the behavior of others." He stressed group work far more than most teachers, using a short film or a simulation performed by students as a takeoff point. Students were arranged by the teacher into small, cross-racial discussion groups, each of which polled the ideas and perspectives of its members on a given theme and then contributed as a group to the whole-class discussion.

Teacher input was significant in eliciting student participation in group activities. At the outset, students were reluctant to form groups and to interact with their group mates. Once underway, however, and prodded by Hawkins's questions and suggestions, the groups became engaged in lively discussions. When confronted by reluctant participants in class discussions, Hawkins rephrased questions in a nonthreatening manner, as if he and all others in the class sometimes felt reluctant to become involved.

Despite periodically high involvement, a number of students exhibited many of the characteristics of passivity and dependence alluded to by Hawkins. Active student initiative was rare. Students tended to wander slowly into class and wait passively for the teacher's official opening. In one class, the day before a test, Hawkins organized a student-administered review. Students protested, "You should head it," and Hawkins had to plead with students before a volunteer came forward to question her peers. During the discussion, Hawkins repeatedly prodded, "Does anyone have a question for him?" or "Could you speak a little more loudly please, so everyone can hear?" After the class, Hawkins commented to me:

> This was the first time I tried a student review like this. My fourth period class ran away with it; a few kids were enthusiastic, and that spilled over to others after a while. In this class, some students who have come along are the more gregarious personalities. Some are a lot more passive. Their passivity seems related to poor performance and poor attendance. A few faked involvement, which may be a first step. I think in the future I will distribute a specific mimeo sheet of points to cover.

In comparison to most other classes, overall student participation in curricular activities was high and widely distributed. Two or three black males tended to withdraw during much of class time, although they were occasionally drawn in by teacher questions. One noticeable "dropout" was selected by Hawkins to play a role in a mother-son dramatization, and was praised for his entertaining style by the teacher and students. On the average, 2.7 students (17 percent) made no verbal contributions to class discussions, while 3.7 (21 percent) made fewer than two comments. Voluntary student-initiated comments were fairly evenly distributed among two thirds of the class.

Hawkins's approach also seemed to have a significant positive impact on students who felt generally uninvolved in school. As can be seen in Table 5.4, fewer students than the norm felt bored and more felt the class was "interesting," "relaxed," "a challenge," and that "you learn a lot in it." These scores were even more significant when compared to the norm in all Central High classes. Furthermore, students were more inclined to feel the teacher was interested in students "coming up with their own ideas," and only one student dissented from the view that "I have plenty of chances in this class to learn about things I am really interested in."

Very little behavioral control was evident in Hawkins's class. Uninvolved students tended to be passive; most "discipline" emanated from class activities. Student seating was voluntary except for small-group activities, and students were required to get a pass to leave the room. Hawkins also commented on the need to define limits for class behavior, thus a "severe emotional problem" would be grounds for exclusion from class.

When interviewed, Hawkins stressed his effort to make the grading system as precise as possible so as to demonstrate to students their shortcomings and strengths. Beyond a minimal effort,

TABLE 5.4

Student Involvement in Hawkins's Class

	Percent Agreeing In Hawkins's Class	All Classes	All Central Classes
Boring	12	23	32
Interesting	76	64	53
Relaxed	53	48	28
A challenge	53	33	21
Learn a lot	53	47	34

Source: Compiled by the author.

Hawkins emphasized "understanding the concepts and being able to apply them in class discussion" as an important grading criterion. Points were awarded for attendance, notebooks, class participation, assignments, and tests, and test grades were curved according to the class's ability level. The students seemed somewhat grade conscious, occasionally asking or arguing about specific grades. Hawkins reported few instances of cheating and attributed these to reluctance to ask the teacher for clarification.

Hawkins's students seemed far more at ease with each other than those in any other observed class in Central High. There were more frequent instances of cross-racial conversation and kidding among the students. Although students were reticent in the early stages of small-group work, they rapidly became more at ease; conversations grew animated and students laughed and conversed freely with each other. While these incidents of affective community may appear minor, they were not at all evident in other Central High classes.

Baker

The students in Baker's honors level American history section present a sharp contrast to Hawkins's inner-city group. With almost no exceptions, students were alert and attentive throughout the class period, and student-teacher or student-student interchange was constantly the central focus of attention. Interest was high throughout class discussions. The most distinguishing feature of Baker's class was the teacher's use of humor. An easygoing, personable man in his late twenties, Baker was a highly entertaining and popular teacher in all his classes (attested to by other teachers and student comments).

Baker ranked among the less dominant teachers (sixth lowest ratio of 2.3:1), yet his recorded classroom questions were among the most factual (82 percent were convergent). These measures, however, represent only one side of the daily class activities. Except for occasional student projects, like panel discussions, the vast bulk of class time revolved around the teacher and his commentary. On the other hand, the teacher brought subject material close to the students' interests in a way which heightened student input.

Attention throughout discussions was focused on Baker, who spoke in a sharp commanding voice. In part, Baker played the role of entertainer. He spiced up descriptions of historical figures and events with comic one-liners, to the delight of the responsive students. In one case, for example, he described characters of the Old West, while showing the class pictures from a book; he commented, "This is William Corbett. He looks like someone I kicked out of the boy's room C period." Other times he launched into exaggerated dialects to make characters more real and humorous. In essence, Baker combined a witty, tongue-in-cheek style with a treatment of history that emphasized the personal, anecdotal side of historical material. Baker observed of his approach:

> I sense a real problem of boredom in history classes. I remember teachers I liked in high school in terms of how they taught. The technique they developed was almost entertaining to a certain degree, then sticking very serious things within that, so that they create the interest and at the same time spur the students on to greater research on their own. I think my style evolves from my personality.

Baker's dominance in class was more related to his style and active direction of learning than to a rapid-fire question approach. Students overtly looked to Baker for behavioral and personal cues of approval, especially to see if information should be taken seriously or laughed at and enjoyed. The teacher's sense of humor had the clear effect of enhancing student interest and attentiveness during class. Students consistently sat forward in their seats listening intently to Baker, taking notes on emphasized information, and smiling or laughing at his jokes. During student presentations, attention declined somewhat, and several students slouched back in their seats. Attention was also captured by colorful, graphic statements ("Justice was as near as the nearest tree") or by citing parallels to historical material in the daily lives of students.

During the period of observation, Baker's class studied the American frontier—Old West criminals, Indian culture, and the "buffalo economy." Weekly current events and panel discussions interrupted the historical focus. Baker cited lecture-discussions as the most common type of activity, and he emphasized concepts rather than facts ("which can be found in their texts"). Individual reading was never done in class but was assigned as homework. Group projects, like the weekly panels, were included to "improve public speaking and clarity of presentation," as well as to enhance student involvement.

Once Baker began the class with administrative announcements, students stopped informal conversations and sat quietly. At the end of class, most jumped out of their seats and left class in a hurry (with 3 minutes until the next session). Although the students were highly attentive, active involvement in class discussions was dominated by a handful of students. On the average, nine students (47 percent) made no verbal contributions to discussions, while fifteen (80 percent) made fewer than two remarks. (These figures were fairly typical of classes in Middletown, which was marked by far less verbal activity than the other two schools.) In part, this low distribution of discussion involvement reflects the low level of teacher questioning, a common method of dispersing participation.

Baker's teaching appeared to have a significant impact on affective qualities of the classroom. Although he reported a number of loners in the class, Baker felt that students identified strongly with the group as a whole. In part, the observable, relaxed group feeling seemed to stem from the teacher's open and humorous references to the ethnic differences among the students, in effect, removing these differences from the field of concerns that students took seriously or personally. In a fairly typical case, Baker commented on one student's hesitation in answering a question, "Michael is our only Greek hillbilly in Middletown." (Both Michael and the class laughed freely.) Or, in commenting on grading procedures, he declared, "Leave it to me. The essay is a subjective kind of question. When I read it, I'll think of (pause) your nationality (laughter) . . . and the money in those plain manilla envelopes" (more laughter). Baker advocated expressing his opinions in class as a means of getting students to think and of making class "more livable for some."

In his own words, Baker ran what he termed a "guided democracy," a class that was at the same time "free and easy" and "demanding." He observed, "I believe that good order is a necessary function in teaching, but I don't think good order means silence or feet planted on the floor. These kids need guidance, but it's relaxed." Overly rambunctious students were spoken to directly; only a "high" or "extremely withdrawn" student required the attention of school officials.

As in other areas of the class, Baker lightened the effect of disciplinary constraints with humorous remarks. On one occasion, he quieted the class with an anguished face and the remark, "Sssh! I don't like getting my tongue stepped on." In another case, he directed the class to move their seats into a semicircle, "like a little UN," prompting one student to remove his shoe and bang it on the desk. As the students laughed, Baker stopped in midsentence, paused with a look of surprise, then commented, "Usually I try to reason with people, but . . . ," and he slapped the student on top of his head with exaggerated brutality. The class responded with a chorus of boos and cheers.

Baker reported that he graded according to criteria adapted to the general class's ability level but applied without exception to all students. Conceptual knowledge and effectiveness of presentation were cited as the most important criteria, although factual information was also stressed because "some enjoy it." Baker described the students in his class as "very competitive," and noted that cheating was a "natural instinct on the part of some who are trying to achieve."

Student opinion in Baker's class reflected observed behavioral patterns. Alienation was nonexistent (no student agreed with the "best-bell" statement). Eighty percent of the students felt discipline was relaxed; all students felt the teacher gave everyone a chance to speak, and all felt they "got out" of the class what they "put in." Baker's class was the only one in which no students checked the term "boring" and where all the students checked "interesting." Sixty-eight percent felt the class was a challenge and 90 percent felt they "learned a lot," yet none felt the class was "pressured."

Ferris

The fourth high-impact class is the only one in Northdale High and the only general track class. It was also taught by the most experienced teacher in the study, and the students were the most alienated from school of any class. In contrast to the students in Hawkins's class, however, they were more active and disruptive in class.

With an enrollment of 29 students, Ferris's American history class was unusually large for Northdale High and the largest in the survey. Furthermore, the class size was made noticeable by the small classroom; student desks were arranged in six tightly packed rows, making student sociability easier and teacher circulation among students more difficult. Like most other Northdale classes, the facilities were in good condition, with a scattering of posters, photographs, artwork, and student notices.

In addition to its crowded feeling, the most prominent characteristic of the class was the students' low ability and motivation level.

According to Ferris, most students were able to express themselves verbally, but few were able to read or write well or to "deal with abstractions." He noted that, contrary to the norm in the college track, students in the low-level group attended most classes together over a long period of time, and thus became "readily identifiable" in their own eyes. As a result, their social interaction in class was high; they played off each other. In the observed class, two students in particular were major distractions to others in the room, though, Ferris noted, "not maliciously" so. Females outnumbered males by more than 2 to 1; a number of males dressed as leather-jacketed "toughs," while most of the females were dressed in sweaters and slacks or skirts.

Ferris, a large, middle-aged man with thinning gray hair, also served as a unit chairman in one of the eight decentralized units in Northdale High. He had a deep-voiced, commanding air one frequently finds among those charged with disciplinary responsibilities, although he was an amiable, relaxed person, able to tease and chat with his students (a trait more visible in his college-level classes). Ferris was businesslike in his general track class, prodding students to work and restraining student chatter. Although based on a small sample of class time, Ferris's convergent-question percentage (78 percent) reflected the factual focus of much student work. His teacher-domination ratio (4:1) places him in the middle of the group studied.

Ferris adapted his style of teaching to the low academic level of the class. He commented that he "lectured differently," concentrating on "words and their contextual meanings." He was more directive of student work, aiming to "steer them to particular things I like them to work from . . . , to give them the tools, and get them in a participatory position." Because of diverse student abilities, Ferris used a great deal of silent, individual work in class. Most frequently, he used detailed mimeographed question sheets on sections of reading.

During the period of observation, the class focused on the Lincoln presidency, with particular concentration on the life and background of the president. Much of class time was spent reading Bishop's The Day Lincoln Was Shot. The mimeographed worksheets included three pages of summary outline and twenty pages of specific, factual or narrowly interpretive questions, three or four per chapter. While students worked on their reading and question-answering, Ferris sat at his desk in the front of the room correcting completed worksheets and answering student questions. From time to time, he would leave the room to check on students who were working on subsequent assignments or extra-credit work in another classroom.

Classwork was also tightly directed by the teacher. The mimeographed worksheets narrowed student attention to particular items in short sections of reading, and questions were uniform for all students.

During directed discussions, Ferris read aloud or lectured in a loud,
domineering voice from the front of the room. Student note-taking
was cued by terms written on the board, and teacher questions focused
student attention on the understanding of definitions and factual material. At the same time, however, during the bulk of class time, students worked at their own pace on the worksheets, and those who finished early could proceed to more diversified projects, like chart- or
map-making. In addition, the course content gave the raw material
of historical information a personalized perspective, grounded in the
lives of major American presidents.

From his position at the front of the class, Ferris oversaw all
student activity and maintained an ordered classroom. His basic behavioral requirements were attendance, punctuality, and "doing the
work." As he remarked, "I don't believe in fun and games, or situations where you're there to entertain. Your attitude towards the work
rubs off on them. They'll know if you're interested in them." Students
were allowed to sit in seats of their choice, but were expected to be
working. Because of frequent student chatter and occasional fooling
and flirting, Ferris continually "kept the lid on" the noise level by
eyeing noisy students and commanding, "Let's get going, people," or
"Straighten up, Bob," or "Mary, I'm not going to speak to you again."

As a rule, students responded immediately to disciplinary comments by earnestly burying their heads in their books. Frequently,
after a few minutes, they would start chatting again. On one occasion,
Ferris warned, "Okay! Let's get with it. I'm going to talk to you once,
then throw you out one at a time." Minutes later he ordered one girl
to go to his office. The student picked up her books and left, smiling
furtively at one or two friends while the teacher continued his paper-
work. After the teacher went and spoke with her, she returned, smiling again at her friends, sat down and worked the rest of the period.
In general, whenever Ferris left the room, student chatting increased,
then subsided when he returned and prodded them to work.

Student participation during class varied widely. Generally, during individual work sessions, a third of the students worked steadily,
another third worked off and on while occasionally chatting, and a third
talked most of the time. When the two troublemakers were absent one
day, a far greater percentage of the students worked, and the teacher
made far fewer disciplinary comments. Although whole-group discussions were rare, an estimated average of 12.7 students (49 percent)
did not contribute verbally, while 13.3 (51 percent) made fewer than
two comments.

Nonparticipation generally took the form of chatting and teasing
rather than the withdrawn passivity seen in Hawkins's class. Students
would talk and joke quietly among themselves, glancing up occasionally
to see if the teacher was noticing, or they would whisper behind their

books, engaging in cat-and-mouse game with the teacher. The students also were frequently distracted by noises in the parking lot—a revved-up car engine would draw the glances of six or eight girls anxious to see who was driving. In general, student participation contrasted sharply with Ferris's college-level group observed during an earlier period. In that class, all but two or three followed attentively as he moved around the more spacious room, explaining material or exchanging comments with individual students.

In grading his general level class, Ferris used a less formalized system of grading than with higher-level students. Growth or progress, interest in work, and the degree to which students would discipline themselves were important criteria for successful grades. Ferris observed, "As long as a student tries, I try to give them a break." Cooperative work structures were essentially nonexistent, although Ferris encouraged students to "consult with each other" in their worksheet assignments. Cheating was disciplined by a grade of zero, and Ferris held all completed worksheets until all students had finished a particular assignment. Students displayed little competitiveness in class, particularly as compared to their Northdale peers.

Students in the class tended to cite "getting work done on time" and "hard work, effort," as the two traits Ferris "liked most in his students." In general, students scored more undemocratically than the norm on involvement measures, and near the norm on most others— one exception being the tendency to agree more than usual with the view that the "teacher really cares about what I think." Half the students found the class interesting, while a quarter were bored and felt it "meant nothing" to them. Half also felt the class was relaxed and one fewer than half felt they learned a lot.

Summary

In sum, one can say of the four positive-impact teachers that all played an active leadership role in structuring and directing classroom activities. All four pushed students into an involvement with the subject material, yet they did so in different ways: Kopek, by a high degree of overt prodding and the use of subject material conducive to personalized discussion; Hawkins, by an insistent questioning of all students about personal thoughts or reactions to class topics that were relevant to adolescents; Baker, by the entertaining, yet controlling, direction of discussions and the use of anecdotal, everyday referents for subject treatment; and Ferris, by a concretely focused yet individually paced approach to personal and narrative aspects of history.

Each teacher obviously directed his or her efforts to the perceived needs and abilities of the students, and thus profound differences existed among each of the classes. Furthermore, teacher personality

shaped the peculiar traits of each class. Yet all four teachers
can be described as activists. Three of the four teachers employed relatively open curricular structures, while the fourth was
flexible in his curricular constraint. To the observer, activity in all
four classes was distinctly purposeful, especially in contrast to classes in the low-involvement group. It was evident that there was an intellectual and group meaning to the various activities in which students
engaged. In all four cases, this purposeful quality reflected students'
views that what they learned and how they learned it was personally
meaningful.

In sum, we can say that the combination of teacher activism and
curricular openness or diversity draws students into active involvement in the learning process, resulting in more democratic learning.
The teaching traits of the four positive-impact teachers suggest two
types of reform consideration. The characteristics shared in common,
particularly active-open teaching, suggest aspects of schooling that
should be universal in the education of all students. At the same time,
the approaches taken by specific teachers in dealing with identifiable
types of students suggest reforms applicable to variations in learning
patterns. These considerations will be discussed in Chapter 6.

Negative-Impact Teachers

Significant democratic reforms for school learning become more
distinct when we consider classes where student involvement declined
more profoundly. The four negative-impact teachers stand out in contrast to the positive-impact teachers in their teaching approaches and
in the dynamics of class interaction. A fifth, Gianelli, also had a
slight negative impact on student involvement, and his unique active-
closed teaching style poses an additional, revealing contrast to the
positive-impact teachers.

One of the four low-involvement teachers—James, in Central
High—provides an unreliable model for unsuccessful teaching for a
number of reasons. James was a young practice teacher in his first
encounter with classroom teaching (he took over one of Pellagrini's
classes). His class was very small (13) and very subdued. Although
categorized as an active-flexible teacher, James was the most passive
of this group, partly because of his low-key manner and partly because
he was hesitantly trying out his teaching ideas.

At the same time, the students in James's general track class
were very passive, although largely attentive. They seemed unsure
of how to "psych out" the new teacher, and a number were themselves
new to the school. At the beginning of each period, students entered
the class and sat quietly, waiting while the teacher took attendance.

During discussions, teacher questions were usually followed by a long pause, until James answered his own questions or a student raised a hand. One or two students were usually resting their heads on their desks or gazing at the floor or out the window. Most were consistently attentive, watching the teacher or showing occasional signs of interest in topics. Yet, for the most part, activity seemed to drift without a sense of comprehensible purpose. James appeared somewhat flustered at his inability to draw knowledgeable responses from the students.

Although James clearly controlled the flow of curricular activities, he conducted all classes in a low-key manner. In a class distinguished by its passivity, small size, and low ability level, James exhibited a higher than average convergent-question percentage (60 percent) and the fifth highest teacher-domination ratio (5.5:1). Over the period of observation, he seemed to gain confidence as he became more familiar with the students. Most class activities were teacher-led discussions aimed at familiarizing students with basic historical information, including, for example, discussions of slavery and the Civil War, the constitutional structure of government, and a simulation of the Andersonville Trial. The latter occurred late in the observation period and was the first hard evidence of active student involvement in the class.

Although the determinants of student involvement in James's class are not as clear as in other classes, parallels exist with the other three low-involvement sections. Two of the three, Mitchell in Middletown and Pellagrini in Central, were also general track classes; both teachers took a fairly passive, resigned approach to their difficult sections. O'Reilly's college track in Northdale was made up of articulate, motivated students, but was distinguished by the teacher's laissez-faire classroom direction. All four classes exhibited a quality of teacher passivity not found in the four high-involvement units.

Pellagrini and Mitchell were the two teachers in the study classified as passive-closed. Both seemed resigned toward the observed class, confiding that it was their "worst" and most difficult to manage. Both sections were made up of general track students who exhibited typical symptoms of restless alienation. Of the two, Pellagrini was somewhat more active in directing class exercises, although he had to counter greater disruptiveness on the part of his students than did Mitchell. Except for peculiarities arising out of interaction with this particular class, Pellagrini would probably have been more accurately labeled an active-flexible teacher.

Mitchell, on the other hand, took a less active stance in classroom activities and tended consciously to employ a more closed curricular structure. Of all teachers studied, Mitchell asked the highest proportion of convergent questions (94 percent were right-answer), while Pellagrini ranked sixth with 72 percent factual questions. On

the other hand, Pellagrini was the second most dominant teacher during lecture discussions (ratio = 9. 8:1), while Mitchell fell into the
middle range (ratio = 4. 2:1).

Pellagrini's American history class was informal, noisy, and
frequently chaotic. A slight, wiry man in his tenth year of teaching,
Pellagrini's classroom manner was the most relaxed of the five Central High teachers. At the same time, he gave indications of being a
conscientious teacher worn down by years of teaching in the city
schools. On more than one observed occasion, he and a colleague sat
in the small teachers' room and laughed hysterically at episodes of
bizarre student behavior they had encountered in their classes. On
the other hand, Pellagrini displayed a genuine, personal interest in
his students before, during, and after classes, frequently teasing
them or chatting informally.

Pellagrini described his history class as "my most difficult of
five," with large gaps in IQ level, reading ability, behavior, and motivation. Also, a number of "special education" students were in the
class. Three or four students frequently interrupted the flow of class
by talking loudly among themselves. On one occasion, when all four
were absent, the class was far more orderly and responsive to the
teacher's questions. Males and females were divided evenly in the
class, while black students outnumbered whites by almost 3 to 1. During the observation period, the class focused on pre-Civil War America and current events, notably the Watergate scandal. By his own
account, Pellagrini tried to "teach people to think for themselves and
to realize what's going on around them." Yet he noted, "Most of these
kids have come up through the kind of system where there's an answer
for everything, usually a 'who' or a 'what' answer." Most of his own
questions were factual; some definition questions were used to facilitate explanations. Key terms were written on the board, and students
transcribed them into their notebooks. During class, Pellagrini directed question-and-answer discussions while circulating around the
room. He frequently interrupted himself or a responding student by
asking loud students to be quiet. As often as not, isolated outbursts,
for example, a boy hollering out the window to a friend, would be ignored and Pellagrini would continue the lesson.

In his Middletown class, Mitchell was somewhat less active and
more closed than Pellagrini. A young, easygoing instructor, Mitchell
focused mainly on the dissemination of factual information and basic
skill development. Although his troublemakers were more restrained
than those of Pellagrini, the two classes were very similar in several
ways. Mitchell described his students as:

> . . . my most limited group. Their reading ability is in-
> ordinately low. Their attention span is shorter, and they're

> less disciplined. Actually, they're almost in a way too
> disciplined; in the junior high they were very policed
> and given very little responsibility. . . . I'm not too
> pleased with this class.

As a consequence, Mitchell stressed the basics in the class: note-
taking, preparatory vocabulary, repetition of information, frequent
everyday examples. The class was more "story oriented," including
more current events than higher-level classes (and frequent discussions of local sports events). Class activities included factual question-and-answer sessions, individual note-taking, and occasional
films. During the period of observation, the class studied the Cru-
sades, a map of Europe, current events, and included a test-review
session and a factual exam.

Mitchell described his approach to classroom discipline as
"easygoing" and observed that he did not make the effort to put the
class through "the usual period of conditioning that I went through in
the past." Student seating was assigned, and noisy students were occasionally moved by the teacher. Mitchell's manner of controlling
the class, however, seemed to be largely reactive rather than active
and in charge.

On the other hand, curricular activities were tightly controlled
by the pervasive factual orientation of all work. Lecture-discussions
followed a mimeographed set of questions handed out to students.
Mitchell's instruction included such comments as: "You just have to
write down what I put on the board" or "Under 'climate,' put 'it varies.'" Test reviews were made up of factual questions ("Geography
is the study of what?"), corrected student responses, and the explanation of terms. Mitchell emphasized factual tests because "they're
good at it; they've been geared towards them."

Questionnaire responses in the two classes reveal the students'
perceptions of teacher characteristics. The largest proportion of students in Mitchell's class (39 percent, also the largest in any class)
felt the teacher was most concerned about students "being quiet," and
Mitchell's students were least likely to feel "free to be themselves."
They also were least likely to feel the teacher "gave everyone a chance
to speak." Students in both classes were the most likely to feel the
bell at the end was the best thing about the class (59 percent in Pellagrini's class and 58 percent in Mitchell's) and that sitting still was a
"big problem" in the class (71 percent in Pellagrini's and 74 percent
in Mitchell's). Despite both teachers' resigned approach to class, a
sizable majority of students felt they had to "do things the way the
teacher wants" in order to get a good grade (71 percent in Pellagrini's
class and 58 percent in Mitchell's).

Forty-one percent of Pellagrini's students found the class "boring" as opposed to 21 percent of Mitchell's; less than 11 percent (two students) in each class found the class a "challenge." Roughly one third of Mitchell's students characterized the class as "a zoo" and "it means nothing to me"; on the other hand, 42 percent felt they learned a lot (as opposed to 18 percent in Pellagrini's section). In general, Mitchell's class seemed to include both a greater number of involved and severely alienated students than Pellagrini's class, whereas general boredom was more prevalent in the latter. At the same time, despite pronounced alienation, students in Pellagrini's class were likely to view the teacher as caring personally about them (77 percent felt the "teacher respects me as a person" regardless of performance, a proportion exceeded in only two other classes).

In large part, the low involvement in both classes seemed to derive from an encounter between built-in student alienation and both curricular constraint and teacher passivity. Because of the largely closed, external subject approach, students found little of interest in the learning material itself. Because of teacher passivity, existing alienation was not overcome, and disruptive students were more successful in depriving the subject material of meaningful continuity.

An interesting contrast to the Mitchell and Pellagrini classes is presented by Gianelli's active-closed (authoritarian) section. Although his curricular focus closely paralleled the factual-drill emphasis found in Mitchell's class, Gianelli was clearly a different type of teacher. He dominated all class discussions with a loud voice and rapid-fire questioning. (He had the highest teacher-domination ratio, 10:1.) Furthermore, he was a very strict disciplinarian, not allowing even the slightest deviation from classroom rules.

Gianelli had only a small negative impact on preexisting (low) student involvement. However, his students were more attentive than Mitchell's or Pellagrini's and more able to follow a continuous flow of activity. Yet Gianelli's brand of activism for the most part succeeded only in preventing disruptions of academic work, not in engaging students in intrinsically interesting learning. Students sat passively in class and exhibited few behavioral or attitudinal signs of heightened interest in learning, and their overall alienation remained essentially untouched. Activism alone seems to be successful only as a deterrent to total uninvolvement; without an open, engaging subject focus, learning remains a rigid, uniform, and external process.

On the other hand, O'Reilly's passive-open class demonstrates what happens in the absence of teacher control. O'Reilly's class was a unique example of laissez-faire classroom management in both behavioral and academic areas. It was also composed of students largely involved in school who became largely uninvolved in this particular class.

O'Reilly's senior political science class was one of two in the survey in which student-initiated comments outnumbered those initiated by the teacher (Crampton's honors section was the other). Roughly half of the recorded teacher questions were factual, but this figure is based on a peculiar type of classroom activity where teacher questions were relatively insignificant. On a typical day, students wandered into class late, left occasionally to get material from lockers, or engaged in strategy sessions for classroom games. Usually some official classroom activity was in process, sometimes carried over from the previous day or growing out of a 20-minute discussion between students and the teacher. During these activities some students talked in small groups about such disparate topics as college admissions or a recent football game, while other students sat on the radiators along the edge of the room and read or gazed out the window. As the teacher chatted with one or two students in their seats, others engaged in whatever activity interested them—talking, resting, reading newspapers, or, in several instances, playing cards.

A large, nervous woman in her midthirties, O'Reilly was given to quick bursts of enthusiasm or opinion (On one class, "They're a riot." On teaching, "It's fun. It's a barrel of laughs. I think kids are neat."). Much of her activity in class centered around private conversations and laughter shared with small groups of students. O'Reilly joined in the students' laughter and their competitive banter. She described her students as "energetic, lively, verbal, funny, and very bright."

Curricular activity in the class was far less directed than in any of the others. Once during the spring term, O'Reilly asked a class, "What's your pleasure today, shall we goof off or work?" Two or three students laughed; another said with sarcasm, "Let's have a heavy rap." The teacher suggested getting coffee and doughnuts at a nearby stand and the students chorused their agreement. While waiting for the arrival of food, students pursued individual conversations, read their own books, or played cards.

The unique qualities of O'Reilly's class reflect the teacher's stated intention of running the class as a "lab in which students look at themselves and their power relationships. I want them to develop a social science attitude, being participant-observers in their lives, and I want them to enjoy social studies and go on with it." Classroom discussions, insofar as these existed, included frequent arguments over student domination and gamelike simulations such as a Middle East negotiation and a mock trial involving a "stolen" grade book. Student behavior was relatively free from restraint, except for occasions when the teacher interrupted student arguments or rivalries to quiet them or to calm student animosities ("Okay! This is a social studies class, not character assassination!") or to control physical horseplay.

The absence of teacher direction in the class was most universally apparent in the overall impression of disconnected activities and scattered student participation. A film was shown, discussed for 1 or 2 minutes, then dropped as the class splintered into small-group discussions and nonparticipatory activities that had been "interrupted" by the film. Similarly, games like the classroom trial appeared to be activities unto themselves, largely unrelated to forces beyond the classroom or other classroom activities. As a consequence, classroom learning frequently seemed to lack a definable purpose, regardless of who suggested the learning activity.

Student questionnaire responses bear out these impressions. As might be expected, students did not perceive "sitting still in one place the whole time" to be a "big problem" with the class (91 percent disagreed with the statement as opposed to an overall mean of 40 percent). O'Reilly's students were also least likely to feel they had to "do things the way the teacher wants" in order to get a good grade, and they characterized classroom discipline as the most lenient in the survey (opinion was divided between "relaxed" and "too easy"). Additionally, 73 percent felt "free to be themselves" in class (compared to an overall average of 64 percent), 73 percent characterized the class as "relaxed," while none chose the term "pressured." Finally, 64 percent of the class also selected the phrase "a zoo" as one that "best described" the class (compared to 13 percent of all students choosing this term).

Students in O'Reilly's class also revealed low involvement sentiments. They were least attentive (paying attention an average of 48 percent of class time) and most likely to find it "hard to stay awake." Despite the "freedom" in the class, they were least likely to feel they had "chances to learn plenty of things I'm really interested in." Forty-one percent felt the class was boring, while 77 percent described it as interesting (some apparently felt it was both). Yet only 9 percent (two students) felt the class was "a challenge" or that they "learned a lot in it." Not surprisingly, given these responses, O'Reilly's students were least likely to feel it was "important to listen to the teacher because she knows what she's talking about."

Although O'Reilly's students were close to the norm in their perceptions of the teacher's caring about their thoughts and respecting them as persons, they tended to view the class as less fair than any other group. They were least likely to feel the teacher gave everyone a chance to speak in class, felt grading procedures were less impartial (than all but one class), and were least likely to feel they "get out of class what you put in." They cited "personal interest in students" as the characteristic they liked most about their teacher and "too

lenient" and "tries to be one of the students" as the traits they liked
least. O'Reilly's unique class type, in short, suggests several insights into the dynamics of democratic teaching. Most fundamentally,
it demonstrates how democratic concepts of learning are not grounded
in the absence of control but in certain qualities of control.

DEMOCRATIC TEACHING

Discussion of the four "successful" teachers has underscored
the positive impact of active-open teaching approaches adapted to the
aims and personality of a particular teacher and existing traits of
particular students. In essence, we have seen how teachers who combine active direction of curricular activities with a relatively open or
diversified curriculum have increased their students' feelings of involvement in meaningful learning, even at the relatively late high
school level. The four classes suggest generalizations about the various teaching and classroom ingredients that are related to democratic involvement.

In addition, discussion of various teaching styles related to diminished student involvement has clarified the effects of different
teaching ingredients. By comparing active-closed to passive-closed
teachers, we can see that teacher activism by itself performs certain
important functions in the classroom. Perhaps the most significant
function is preventive in nature. Individual student domination of classes is prevented by teachers who limit the activity of all students. Furthermore, total withdrawal is prevented as students are forced to be
at least somewhat attentive in class. Finally, teacher activism, by
itself, provides a limited sense of direction to a class.

Combined with a closed, or external, focus, however, teacher
activism achieves at best a passive kind of involvement, an attentiveness unkindled by individual interest. The direction provided by this
control provides meaning for class activities, but becomes meaningless beyond its own existence, since the classroom activities are not
related to any significant forces outside the class. Without a subject
focus that students can become engaged in, teacher control comes to
mean control for its own sake, just as the subject is studied for its
own sake or facts are learned for their own sake. Factual learning
that does not extend beyond itself becomes meaningless. If it is solely
directed at the acquisition of good grades, it is undemocratic.

The successful teachers, on the other hand, engage the students
in the subject—in part by active teacher direction but also in significant part by opening up the learning structure to accommodate more
diverse subject and process interests. Students become engaged
through the subject, not simply because they have to be engaged in

what the class is doing. In the process, involvement becomes meaningful to the individual student; control takes on meaning, as do facts. As a result, insofar as these traits are maximized, the intrinsic qualities of school control are maximized.

At the same time, inactive teaching or laissez-faire direction of classroom learning undermines the benefits of an open curricular focus. Although students are, in a sense, "free" to get involved in what they are interested in, they feel they have fewer chances to learn things that interest them. In part, the student peer-group controls learning when the teacher abdicates; some students will become more involved (and have more "fun"), but others become less involved. Also, to some degree, the students react against the normal controls they experience in the schooling process, and they are more inclined to waste time. In the process, they feel they are accomplishing and learning less, and they gain little intrinsic satisfaction from their learning encounter.

The benefits of active teacher direction combined with a relatively open curriculum suggest the ingredients of more democratic classroom learning and, by implication, types of reform objectives relevant to existing classrooms. Having sketched out the dynamics of student involvement, we may return briefly to the first question examined in this chapter: How much difference do positive-impact teachers make in student involvement? Given the obstacles of tracking and associated student traits, can we expect teachers to have a sizable impact on student involvement?

This question can be approached in two ways. First, we can ask how sizable an impact a teacher can have on his or her class. In the case of the positive-impact teachers, 22 of 83 students (27 percent) in these classes became more involved (that is, they moved from agreement to neutral or from neutral to disagreement on the alienation question). On the other hand, 13 of 69 students (19 percent) in the negative-impact classes became less involved. Given the overall tendency for students to show higher involvement in class than in school, the most accurate estimate of teacher impact would draw on both of these groups. In all, a total of 35 of 152 students (23 percent) experienced a change in involvement.

These are, admittedly, limited figures. However, if a teacher can affect the established involvement inclinations of about one fourth of his or her students, we might ask what impact this might have on the overall schooling picture. This question poses far more difficult problems, and an accurate answer requires far more data than are available in this study. Still, we can consider two speculative points. If the teacher sample in this study is at all representative, we can conclude that the effective teachers are a relatively small minority of all teachers that students are likely to encounter. Thus, without any changes in teaching activities, we would not expect the positive teacher impact in any given class to carry over very much to other school experiences.

On the other hand, if all classes were suddenly taught by active-open teachers, we might expect a profound change in student learning patterns, particularly if these models were adapted to elementary school classrooms. The benefits of active teacher direction combined with a relatively open curriculum suggest the ingredients of more democratic classroom learning and, by implication, types of reform objectives relevant to existing classrooms.

At the same time, however, the systematic implementation of active-open teaching is likely to be extremely difficult to accomplish, for it poses a fairly radical alternative to the prevailing structure of school learning. Most fundamentally, the type of democratic control implicit in active-open teaching confronts structural obstacles in existing schools and, ultimately, the instrumental functions of schooling. These various obstacles to democratic learning suggest a number of sticky policy issues and the need to reevaluate priorities. We now address these questions.

NOTES

1. See Christopher Jencks, and Marshall Smith, Henry Acland, Mary Jo Bane, David Cohen, Herbert Gintis, Barbara Heyns, Stephan Michelson, Inequality: A Reassessment of the Effect of Family and Schooling in America (New York: Basic Books, 1972), Ch. 1.

2. See, for example, the systematic study by James W. Guthrie, George B. Kleindorfer, Henry M. Levin, and Robert T. Stout, Schools and Inequality (Cambridge, Mass.: MIT Press, 1971); and the more personal study by Jonathan Kozol, Death at an Early Age (New York: Bantam Books, 1967).

6

EQUALITY AND DEMOCRATIC REFORM

This work has undertaken an empirical examination of the process of school learning as an experiential foundation for adult democratic citizenship. Essentially, secondary school learning has been investigated from the perspective of three democratic norms: the importance of individual personality and intellectual independence, the importance of a capacity for active social and political participation, and the universal applicability of both of these. Approached from this perspective, much of everyday life in schools and classrooms appears to embody the antithesis of these traits. Most school control (at least in the sample) appears to conform to the principles of fairness and impartiality, yet this control only reinforces qualities of learning that violate prescriptions for the development of individual autonomy and a participatory capacity.

Much of the control in school learning draws on extrinsic incentives rooted in the instrumental functions of public schooling. Instead of drawing on intellectual and social controls that are intrinsically a part of learning, the schooling process relies on the future rewards of school success, backed up where necessary by autocratic controls, to engage its student clients. Instead of teaching self-definition and active participation in an intellectual and social environment, schooling teaches students to define their needs and interests according to instutional definitions that "fit" the social selection function.

Both the democratic norms and the empirical findings contained in this work suggest an approach to equality in education that is the antithesis of traditional equal opportunity concerns. Indeed, the effort to make the social selection function work more equitably and effectively for all students only promises to reinforce antidemocratic sociali-

zation. Furthermore, as seen in Chapters 3 and 4, the institutional
pursuit of effective social selection only results in unequal political
lessons that rigidify existing social class inequities. In terms of its
impact, schooling is clearly more democratic for some students and
less democratic for others.

Taken as a whole, these findings constitute a powerful indictment
of the institution of public schooling. At the same time, however, they
do not support a simplistic condemnation of schools or school officials.
Instead, they suggest that much of the antidemocratic quality of schooling derives from the fact that schools and school officials are trying
to perform functions that society expects them to perform. Furthermore, these instrumental functions can be seen as legitimate in themselves. Yet the degree to which they shape the learning environment
is counterproductive to the aims of effective learning and of an open,
democratic society.

These findings speak directly to the issue of educational reform.
In short, the empirical study of high school learning points to needed
classroom reforms. At the same time, because classroom learning
reflects the larger context of schooling, and secondary schools reflect
other institutions which educate, socialize, and select the young, we
need to consider the broader sweep of reform. The discussion which
follows is necessarily speculative, since it is not based on the empirical study of reform, per se. However, the purpose of this chapter is
to suggest feasible means of accomplishing much-needed ends. Essentially, what follows is an analysis of the relationship between democratic learning and the ongoing reform debate.

To begin, the empirical evidence of effective teaching provides
an outline of democratic learning objectives. The basic thrust of this
chapter will be to answer the question: What are those learning variables most clearly related to democratic experiences and how might
they be universalized? The normative reform agenda that emerges
is based on an effort to universalize a learning experience that is far
more diversified, is built upon active teacher direction, and incorporates processes that teach the lesson of social interdependence.

The consideration of these objectives leads to a discussion of
appropriate reform targets. It seems natural, at this point, to begin
the discussion of specific reforms with a look at existing classrooms.
However, to maximize democratic learning, we need to examine the
broader context of schooling. In short, we need to consider reforms
which will make it more likely that teachers can teach democratically.
As a consequence, we must move beyond classroom reform to consider
the need to restructure the secondary schools. These efforts, in turn,
require attention to the overall system of public schooling, in particular, a redefinition of the respective functions of secondary and ele-

mentary education. Finally, we will conclude with a discussion of related social and economic reforms in society at large.

The following pages will be concerned primarily with the maximization of democratic learning objectives, in particular, the development of individual personality, a capacity for active participation
in public life, and a social interdependence among disparate groups
in society. It is the author's view that each of these objectives is vitally important in and of itself, and that society needs all three. At
the same time, however, these objectives will be discussed with an
eye toward their effects on other social and educational concerns.

As noted in the introduction, we face a series of policy trade-
offs. It has been argued, however, that we currently enjoy the worst
of two worlds. The self-fulfillment and participatory capacity of many
of the young are suppressed by the institutionalization of equal opportunity functions. Yet, at the same time, private advantages and disadvantages are rigidified and legitimized by the schooling experience.
To correct this condition, a basic shift in our policy priorities seems
imperative. What follows is a proposal for rebalancing our schooling
priorities in keeping with democratic principles.

A REFORM AGENDA: DEMOCRATIC OBJECTIVES

Drawing on the normative democratic principles and the empirical findings described in earlier chapters, it is possible to construct
an ideology or agenda for the democratic reform of school learning.
The intention here is to outline basic reform objectives against which
specific reforms can be weighed. In short, the aim is to avoid what
Charles Silberman has called the "mindlessness" of educational reform. [1] Such an agenda is not internally consistent, for conflicts
among competing principles cannot be finally resolved. Instead, what
follows is a statement of reform objectives, none of which provides
an answer in and of itself, yet all of which together call for a radical
restructuring of our schooling priorities.

Each of the three norms of democratic citizenship outlined at
the beginning of this work suggests a basic element of democratic reform. All three stem from one common denominator: that schools (at
least at the secondary level) should consider their students as their
primary clientele—not as is currently the case, parents, colleges, or
future employers, important as these may be. At the same time, however, this reform thrust is justified on the grounds that it best serves
the interests of a democratic society. In short, the needs of all students as future democratic citizens should stand at the center of
schooling concerns.

The norms of democratic citizenship would require a dramatic change in the existing schooling process. An individualist or libertarian concern requires considerable diversification of school learning in order to reflect the needs and inputs of individual students. A social or communitarian concern requires that learning provide an experiential basis for students to engage in social and political interaction, that the learning process itself should incorporate cooperative enterprise. Finally, a concern for equality requires the universalization of both of these characteristics. In short, the needs and inputs of all students should be reflected in the learning process, and all groups should be drawn into cooperative interaction.

The universalization of democratic learning draws on a very different conception of equality from traditional equal opportunity concerns. In considering reform objectives, then, the first step is to redefine the principle of equality as it applies to education.

Redefining Educational Equality

At the outset, a redefinition of equality in education incorporates two types of reform objectives. On the one hand, we must weigh the merits of the traditional input-outcome concern for equal opportunity. On the other, we must focus on the intrinsic quality of the schooling experience. Although documentation is not conclusive, the evidence considered in this work suggests that the two are interrelated. Essentially, one can argue that the democratization of school learning enhances efforts to achieve equal opportunity in society. At the same time, the pursuit of traditional income-outcome objectives as ends in themselves furthers the objectives of democratized learning. The critical shift in egalitarian concerns entails a focus on each objective as important in itself.

The first type of egalitarian concern arises out of traditional equal opportunity issues. Most critically, these are:

1. A guarantee of an equitable distribution of educational resources so that no children are subjected to an inferior education
2. A guarantee that the outcome of the educational process will not deprive a person of basic human dignity or open access to full membership in society

The first of these objectives concentrates on "preeducational" concerns, while the latter focuses on those that are posteducational.

Traditionally, both objectives have been tied to the instrumental functions of education. We have been concerned about educational re-

sources because these are seen as instrumental in enhancing educational achievement and ultimately in realizing a just distribution of
social and economic rewards. (If anything, studies like the Coleman
Report, which draw these assumptions into question, have only made
us look harder for evidence of these instrumental relationships.)

The findings of this work suggest that these instrumental ties
should be reduced, that egalitarian objectives should be pursued as
ends in themselves. No child should be subjected to an educational
experience that rests on demonstrably inferior resources (however
these are defined). Why is this norm important? Because such a condition violates the principle of equality in a democratic society, not
simply because these resources are purported to be critical in determining educational and social outcomes.

One problem with the instrumental approach to educational equality is that it has the effect of undermining efforts to achieve equitable
educational resources. Although state school finance programs have
been moving in the direction of resource equalization in recent years,
these efforts have been hampered by the inability of social science to
demonstrate convincingly that monetary resources aid educational outcomes. Instead of justifying equal educational resources on the grounds
of educational achievement, we should view their equitable distribution
as a legitimate, independent principle. Although the Supreme Court
has not yet seen arbitrarily unequal school resources as a violation
of Fourteenth Amendment rights, such a ruling would be one component of a revised egalitarian perspective. As a consequence, the burden
of justification would shift to those who maintain unequal resources.

At the same time, we might consider learning as an end in itself, not solely as all instrumental means to external ends. Traditionally, we have considered educational outcomes to be unfair if the
school testing ground discriminates against identifiable social groups,
or if the testing ground fails to give all young persons the training that
will free them to pursue social and occupational goals to the best of
their abilities. For the most part, we do not ask if the outcomes themselves are both functional and humane; nor do we ask if other significant outcomes need to be evaluated. Except for the voices of recent
social critics, our tendency has been to see the functional ends of education as justified as long as the means to those ends are fair. This
study suggests that perfection of impartiality and fairness in schooling,
if this is possible, will not result in just or democratic outcomes. In
the schools, at least, the opposite may be the case.

In turning to the principle of equality as it applies to the self-
contained educational experience, we can draw on both normative and
empirical characteristics of democratic learning. In brief, two basic
principles for evaluating educational equality are proposed:

1. Equal involvement in a quality educational experience on the part of all the young
2. Individual participation in an inclusively interdependent learning experience

The terms "equal involvement" and "inclusively interdependent" are the principal guideposts of these objectives. If the criteria for equality were involvement and participation instead of productivity—as they could be if the instrumental constraints on learning were diminished—we might take a long step toward democratized learning for all of our young. Let us examine the implications of these principles.

Most fundamentally, the equal involvement principle requires that we evaluate the quality of the learning experience at least in part by the degree to which it engages the learner's interest and active participation. As a universal objective, it requires that all learners should be and feel involved in purposeful learning. This does not mean that all learning has to be fun. It does, however, require a fundamental shift away from the current meaning of equal involvement in education, namely, equal exposure to uniform learning experiences. As will be described below, this shift requires far more diversity to be built into the schooling process, in combination with active teacher direction.

The objective of equal involvement is also based upon a more democratic concept of educational quality. Rather than considering quality solely in terms of dollar inputs or teaching certification, or simply in terms of measurable test scores, our attention shifts to a more intrinsic view of the learning process itself. Most fundamentally, the evaluation of educational quality would involve the incorporation of some implicit or explicit student voice. Because this study focuses on high school students, it suggests ways in which a student voice might become a part of the evaluation process at the secondary level. We might, for example, test for student feelings of involvement, alienation, interest, and confinement, in addition to traditional evaluation criteria.

On the surface, the principle of equal involvement raises two related concerns. In the first place, must we forget about the educating function of schooling and concentrate solely on whatever activities engage students and make them feel involved? Most definitely not. It is only suggested that student involvement be one measure of educational quality. The student voice would be one of several heard in the evaluation process. Yet, this objective involves a fundamental shift away from the current pattern of school evaluation.

Additionally, the evidence gathered in this study suggests that student involvement is positively associated with student learning. Although cognitive outcome measures were not available, students who scored high on involvement measures also tended to feel that they were learning "a lot" in class, in contrast to low-involvement students. Furthermore, the examination of teacher traits associated with high student involvement points to characteristics that at least intuitively correspond to our perceptions of good teaching. O'Reilly's laissez-faire section, which appeared to be the most fun, was marked by low student involvement.

The equal involvement principle also results in a learning environment that is far more conducive to the individualistic meaning of equal opportunity. By incorporating an element of student input, the learning experience is better tailored to maximize the opportunity for development of individual abilities.

Nonetheless, one can legitimately ask whether a total pursuit of equal involvement might not leave other social objectives unfulfilled. In short, we need to include a second component of educational equality: the need to pass on to all students those traditions and learning objectives that we as a society consider worthwhile. In cognitive terms, these would include a proficiency in those skills—such as reading, writing, and computation—that would free the young person to pursue his or her own ends effectively.

From the perspective of citizenship socialization, however, this objective would seem to require more than just cognitive aims. It is important that students learn how our political system works; in fact, there is probably room for considerable improvement and an injection of twentieth-century reality in most citizenship education programs. [2] However, it is also important to pass on to the young the political values that form the normative basis of our culture and political system, values such as tolerance for a diversity of views and subcultures, respect for the individual personality, and the importance of political participation and social interdependence.

Instead of merely teaching these values as a series of platitudes, it would seem that the most effective and most legitimate way to teach them would be through an educational process that itself incorporated these values. This study found that most teachers espoused values such as these at one point or another in their teaching—some verbally, others in their behavior. Still, the overall learning experience is one that submerges the individual personality and requires at best very little social interdependence. An important egalitarian objective would be to incorporate these qualities in the schooling process and include all elements of society in interdependent learning.

In sum, a redefinition of educational equality is proposed that incorporates a concern for democratic socialization. Both equal involvement in quality educational experiences and inclusive social interdependence are basic ingredients of universal democratic learning.

At the same time, two egalitarian concerns traditionally associated with educational quality should be considered as legitimate ends in themselves, namely, equal resources for educational needs and more equal social outcomes. Collectively, these four prescriptions change the focus of egalitarianism from the instrumentality of schooling to the quality of learning itself.

By distinguishing each of these four prescriptions as an end in itself, we theoretically increase the likelihood that both democratic socialization and equal opportunity can be achieved. Most fundamentally, this shift in emphasis would reduce the grip that instrumental functions have on schools. By making schooling outcomes more just and equal, we would reduce the costs and rewards of the schooling race. Although a selection function and extrinsic incentives would remain, their impact on school learning would be diminished. In particular, extrinsic controls could be supplanted more easily by intrinsic incentives; learning could be diversified more easily and could draw more freely on cooperative interaction. The need to measure individual student performances in uniform activities would be reduced, as would the need to track students.

Conversely, the effort to construct a universally democratic learning experience would enhance the chances of all future citizens for full membership in society—subject, of course, to the existence of equal opportunities in society. If all students encountered learning environments that reflected their needs and interests, the lesson of active participation would not be confined to those at the top of the schooling ladder. If learning involved an element of cooperative interaction, students might experience firsthand the payoffs as well as the frustrations of social interdependence. Finally, if all student groups were involved in interdependent learning, schools might reduce rather than reinforce class-based barriers in society.

Before turning to specific reform targets mandated by the pursuit of educational equality, we need to consider the two basic objectives of democratic reform in greater depth.

Diversifying School Learning

A fundamental need for democratizing school learning, perhaps the most urgent need of all, is that of individualizing and diversifying the learning structure. According to the findings of this study, the most effective way for schooling to become more democratic would be for student interest, involvement, and initiative (the "three I's") to be encouraged, and meaningful student choice and efficacy to be increased, by diversifying much of student work.

Specific policies toward this end could take any number of forms, including structuring student input in classroom decision making, allowing wide-ranging student selection of study topics based on personal interests, and supporting student mobility in pursuing learning interests outside school walls. For those needing more direction and skill development, basic learning processes, such as reading, writing, reporting, and analysis, could be adapted to particular subjects of interest to individual students. In essence, diversification would mean that there could be more than one path to educational fulfillment and school success. It would address the lament of more than one teacher in this study that "there are no real alternatives."

Regardless of the particular form diversification might take, the aim would be to increase the meaningful nature of the learning experience for each student and thus enhance the intrinsic importance of schooling. Student motivation might more aptly be called accomplishment motivation, rather than achievement motivation, since a work structure tailored to individual needs and interests would undermine the pervasiveness of uniform, competitive learning. Motivation to learn would be enhanced by confidence gained from successful task performance.

Such a learning structure obviously requires interaction between an individual student and an instructor. A student who is "left alone" may accomplish tasks that are important to him or her, but, to have any social meaning, those tasks also must reflect an element of social significance. In a more democratic structure, performance evaluation could be based on completion of tasks that the students have evolved in counsel with an informed instructor. Task importance would be established not on the extrinsic basis of having a good record as an end in itself but on the intrinsic meaning to the student, the encouragement of the teacher, and on noncompetitive comparability to the work of other students.

In a study of motivation and morale in instructional groups, D. H. Jenkins has observed that a supportive environment is one that includes a sense of positive direction and accepted goals and purposes for activities; a sense of mutual support, based on others sharing in the purpose; a sense of contribution or of usefulness and relevance to the task; a sense of progress, whereby one's work seems to move toward the goal; and a sense of challenge, that the task is big enough to warrant striving for its completion. [3]

These characteristics reflect traits observed in classes marked by an increase in student involvement, yet, for the most part, they contrast sharply with the vast majority of observed classroom time. Although some teachers emphasized motivating forces intrinsic to the learning process and subject material, these efforts were countered by built-in student resistance to classroom effort (as was the case in

Hawkins's class) or the overall effects of extrinsic, competitive objectives (particularly pronounced in Crampton's honors class).

In addition, these motivational characteristics require active teaching authority, at least if schools are to serve any extrinsic or social ends. O'Reilly's laissez-faire class exhibited more aimless activity than any class in the study, and students felt less involved than in most classes. Examination of high-involvement classes bears out this need for instructional direction. Active teacher direction of classroom work combined with a relatively open or diversified curriculum was associated with significantly higher levels of student involvement, interest, and attentiveness, regardless of previous student inclinations.

Thus, a teacher like Hawkins was successful in engaging students in their learning environment by combining highly active instructional direction with a subject orientation that touched the world of student concerns. Comparably, Ferris increased the involvement in learning of his low-level students by a concrete examination of the lives of historical figures—an approach that enhanced interest and made learning more manageable and purposeful. Students in these and other positive-impact classes were more likely to feel they were learning a lot in class than their peers in other sections.

Classes that lacked teacher direction or that reinforced the uniform, closed curricular constraints of learning exhibited significantly lower student involvement. O'Reilly's laissez-faire section was marked by student drift. Gianelli's tightly controlled students, on the other hand, were passively acquiescent, showing little interest or active involvement in learning. The classes of Pellagrini and Mitchell, reflecting passive leadership and a closed curriculum, exhibited the highest level of alienation in this study. As a consequence, we can say with some confidence that student interest, involvement, and initiative are served by a learning structure that combines considerable subject and process diversity with active teacher leadership. Both elements are related to the enhancement of intrinsic student involvement, even in a system that is largely oriented to extrinsic incentives. Students felt least involved in classes where they viewed the teacher as a unilateral classroom regulator, especially where they viewed success in terms of "doing what the teacher wants." Diversification of learning not only requires teacher leadership but the removal or reduction of those structural constraints on teachers and students that reinforce extrinsic control and motivation.

Cooperative, Communitarian Learning

The objective of diversity in school learning is tied to two aspects of democratic citizenship: respect for individual autonomy and encouragement of an active stance toward learning participation. By itself, however, diversification contains forces that work against the social side of citizenship objectives, namely, the interdependence of all elements of the community. Insofar as diversity means individualizing learning pursuits, it separates learners either into isolated learning projects or activities shared with a socially homogeneous group.

In part, this conflict is inevitable, and it compels us to select between two conflicting objectives in specific circumstances (as will be discussed in the latter portion of this chapter). Yet, at the same time, diversified learning, freed from the constraints of uniformity and comparative measurement, can be more truly communitarian than existing schooling. Relying on a form of individualism that stresses the interests and uniqueness of each person, rather than the isolated productivity of each, such a learning structure can encompass far greater cooperative participation.

In a cooperative learning structure, group work is based on the collective contributions of separate individuals to a common end. Each participant contributes to group objectives according to his or her abilities and each learns according to his or her interests. Evaluation is based on group accomplishment rather than individual achievement, and rewards are allocated on a group basis. Such a combination of individual efforts and competing interests within the framework of common objectives clearly would provide experiential background for such traits of democratic participation as discussion of competing interests, compromise and coalition formation in the pursuit of common objectives, public spiritedness, and tolerance for views and interests other than one's own.

Empirical evidence supporting these arguments for cooperative learning must come largely from sources other than this study, for the simple reason that such a learning structure is so alien to the basic achievement orientations of schooling that examples are few and far between. In part, teachers did not pursue group work because of the resulting difficulty in distinguishing individual performance. Still, those teachers associated with increased student involvement (especially Hawkins and Kopek) tended to include greater social interaction and more group projects in their classes. In observed cases of group projects, student interest, participation, and interaction all increased markedly over normal classroom levels.

Most of the findings on cooperative interaction are derived from experimental research. In their study of socialization, Paul Breer and Edwin Locke argue that cooperative socialization has a marked impact on learning:

To the extent, for example, that a given task can be performed most effectively when the individuals present co-
operate closely with each other, it is to be expected that
in the course of working on the task members will 1) become cognitively aware that cooperation is instrumental
to task success, 2) behave in a cooperative fashion, 3) develop a cathectic interest in cooperating with each other,
and 4) establish norms defining cooperation as a legitimate and expected form of behavior. [4]

As noted earlier, other researchers have found that cooperative
learning projects are associated with a number of "lessons" that fit
the democratic concept of participatory interaction. Morton Deutsch
has demonstrated that cooperative groups tend to develop a greater
"we-feeling," fewer communication difficulties, higher productivity,
and friendlier relations than competitive group structures. [5] In his
study of adolescents, James Coleman has argued for interscholastic
competition in the academic realm as an inducement for cooperative
academic efforts and an alternative to interpersonal competition. [6]
Seymour Spilerman suggests that cooperative learning structures within the classroom would be more productive and might enhance learning
involvement on the part of "slow learners. "[7]

The democratic implications of cooperative learning are borne
out also by the sentiments expressed by teachers and students in this
study. Students cited small-group projects as the second most interesting form of classroom activity, and their behavior in the few observed cases supports this view. Additionally, an alarmingly large
proportion of all students agreed with the view that "school is most
interesting as a place to see friends. " Learning that involves interaction with friends (and an expanding circle of friends) might tap this
natural student inclination far better than the existing pattern of classrooms, wherein many students come to see class time as an infringe-
ment on the pursuit of friendships in the halls.

Teachers also responded favorably to the concept of group work.
Those who had experimented with group projects found it easier to
play leader and resource roles in the classroom, rather than regulator and feeder roles. Most cited increased student interest and initiative and the potential for learning constructively from peers as the
greatest advantages of group work. On the other hand, the most frequently cited disadvantage was the work created for the teacher. As
in the case of a diversified learning format, group projects require
careful planning, active oversight, and necessary limits on the kind
of spontaneous hyperactivity that can arise in adolescent groups.

These concerns become important in considering cooperative learning
as a policy objective.

More significantly, however, learning that involves cooperative
group reward systems implies a radical departure from present practices. In terms of the implications for such democratic lessons as
cooperative enterprise, strengthened human relations, and public spiritedness, cooperative learning would seem to be a vital ingredient—
and one that is sorely lacking—in a young person's education. Norma-
tively, it is limited by our concern that students also learn the value
of individual enterprise and responsibility. In other words, we must
still be concerned with individual as well as collective evaluations.
Structurally, cooperative learning is limited by the degree to which
school learning is extrinsically controlled, uniform, and competitive.
And these constraints, growing out of the instrumental functions of
schooling, again point to the need for systemic reform.

REFORM TARGETS

Thus far, we have examined the basic objectives for universal,
democratic education. We now turn to a discussion of the relationship
between these objectives and specific reform targets relevant to the
public debate on educational policy. Although this study has focused
on secondary schooling, we have seen how the high school learning
process reflects forces that range well beyond the reach of high school
personnel. Most fundamentally, these emanate from the instrumental
functions of equalized opportunity and social selection. These functions, in turn, reflect both normative and political characteristics of
the American economic and occupational structure.

In a sense, we can say that high school learning is sandwiched
between, and therefore shaped by, the early elementary school encounters of its students and the functional demands of society. To be
systematically effective, then, efforts to achieve democratic learning
objectives would have to go forward at several levels. The institution
of public schooling in its broadest meaning would be the major target
of democratic reform.

At the same time, however, we have considered evidence that
some teaching practices in secondary school classrooms are associated with democratic learning outcomes. Consequently, in considering
reform targets, we can draw on these findings to examine their specific implications for the various levels of reform. In effect, we can
follow the path of reform requirements from the high school classroom, to the structure of secondary schools, to the overall functions
of elementary and secondary schooling, to root causes in society at
large. Essentially, what follows is an analytic rather than an empirical

consideration of school reform. In the discussion of specific reforms, the objective is to examine how they fit into the agenda mandated by both normative principles and empirical evidence contained in this work.

Teacher Input: The High School Classroom

One of the major findings of the empirical study was that individual high school teachers were able to affect the level of student involvement in their classes, regardless of their students' socioeconomic status, track level, or grade average. This impact is significant from the perspective of democratic socialization because high involvement is associated with such democratic learning traits as high student interest, a relaxed learning atmosphere, and a perception of teacher fairness and respect for students. Additionally, teachers of high-involvement classes focused greater attention on individual student needs and interests in a variety of ways. Finally, highly involved students also felt they learned a lot in their classes. Low-involvement students had learning experiences that tended in the opposite direction.

The examination of teaching approaches that affect student involvement resulted in the isolation of two significant variables: teacher activism and curricular openness. Active-open teachers enjoyed the greatest success in their classes, regardless of student characteristics. In brief, teachers who took an active hand in directing the class, who reached out to involve individual students in class activities and structured curricular exercises for individuals or small groups, were associated with purposeful student involvement and a high level of interest in learning activities. Additionally, when asked which classroom activities they found most interesting, all but a tiny minority of students singled out discussions, student group projects, and lecture-discussions; while the latter was characterized as the type of activity in which students felt they learned the most. Lectures and reading and note-taking were cited as least interesting.

Specific characteristics of teacher activism were critical to student involvement. In curricular terms, all positive-impact teaching focused on ways of relating learning to student interests and orientations. Thus, Hawkins concentrated on subject material close to the concerns of young adults, and drew inductively on student experiences and observations in analyzing social, moral, and psychological phenomena. Ferris focused the attention of his general track students on concrete tasks that drew on the personal side of presidential history. Both teachers included an element of detective work in student learning, leading students from close-to-home observations to generalizable lessons. Other teachers of low-level students attempted to include elements of this learning focus with less success, either because they failed to provide a continuity or direction to learning exercises or they felt confined by such environmental forces as student alienation and the necessity of acting as custodians or classroom police.

Successful teachers of high-level classes, on the other hand, also drew on student interests and orientations but on a more sophisticated intellectual plane. Thus, Kopek held group discussions on philosophical issues that could be brought to the level of adolescents' concerns. She also included some small-group cooperative projects, such as designing group strategies for dealing with different social or psychological problems in children. Baker brought the study of American history down to earth by accenting humorous, daily-life anecdotes, discussing a historical period as if students confronted it in their current lives, and structuring some small-group panel discussions on topics of current interest. Student involvement in Crampton's honors class was a unique phenomenon, tied to the high academic ability of his students, their concern for their academic futures, and his hard-driving emphasis on exact (and exacting) work.

While teacher activism and curricular openness were necessary ingredients of democratic classes, neither was sufficient by itself. Student alienation tended to increase in classes where one or both of these ingredients was absent. Teachers of low-involvement classes either took an essentially passive teaching stance or they dominated classroom learning with an imposed, tightly constricted subject orientation. Involvement in O'Reilly's passive-open class was sporadically intense, but lacked direction. Students felt alienated, bored, and discontented, as if there were not much purpose to the class. On the other hand, Gianelli's tightly directed, teacher-dominated class was distinguished by student passivity. Students exhibited some interest and attentiveness, but also revealed strong group feelings of alienation and confinement. Their learning experience was almost entirely imposed from without. Finally, classes marked by the greatest increase in student alienation were taught by teachers who combined a closed curricular focus with a generally passive stance toward classroom leadership. Pellagrini's and Mitchell's classes were the most chaotic and meaningless in the eyes of the students.

What do these classroom traits tell us about school reform? In the first place, by distinguishing the impact of specific teaching traits, we can establish criteria for teacher training. As noted above, teaching activism by itself has a largely preventive effect. Most significantly, it prevents interruptions in the flow of classroom learning, it prevents classroom domination by one or two students, and it prevents existing student alienation from "taking over" the classroom. The absence of teacher activism opens the way for intrusions on purposeful group learning.

The findings on teacher activism counteract what has rightly or wrongly been seen as educational libertarianism. Currently, the educational policy debate is dominated by the theme of back to the basics. In many ways, libertarian reforms have borne the brunt of the blame for declining academic achievement and the breakdown of school discipline. To a significant extent, this criticism is unfair, since these patterns coincide with such general social trends as increasing public alienation and the pervasive influence of television. All told, the decline in educational achievement is a phenomenon so complex that we cannot legitimately blame it on educational innovations.

On the other hand, the findings on teacher activism suggest that criticism is properly directed at school reforms that aim simply at the removal of authority in education. Laissez-faire teaching in this study was associated with the absence of purposeful learning and a decline in democratic socialization. At the same time, however, teacher activism by itself is also counterproductive, unless accompanied by an increase in curricular diversity. Some elements of the back-to-the-basics movement are essentially progressive in that they reject a return to rigid uniformity. [8] The alternative to excessive libertarianism in classrooms is not necessarily excessive authoritarianism, as evidence in this work illustrates. Instead of choosing between passive-open and active-closed teaching, we need to stress active-open teaching. In other words, the second ingredient of democratic reform, and the one that poses the more fundamental challenge to existing schools, is that of curricular openness or diversity.

Within the classroom, the need for curricular diversity suggests two basic shifts in dominant educational practices. In the first place, a democratic learning format would require that we deemphasize the function of teacher-as-feeder and examine and emphasize the function of teacher-as-resource or facilitator. Such a shift would be geared to the intrinsic controls of learning. It would focus on an effort to encourage accomplishment motivation rather than the externally mandated achievement orientation. A main function of the teacher-as-facilitator would be to work with individual students in establishing learning objectives that emanate from the student's experience and interests. In such a learning process, the teacher's main task would be to construct learning activities to enable the student to accomplish the mutually acceptable task; the teacher would provide feedback in the form of evaluation.

The shift to teacher-as-facilitator would require active teacher direction of learning experiences, and would sustain the teacher's role as judge or evaluator. Additionally, the teacher would have to regulate behavior in order to maximize the opportunities for individual learning. Yet this learning process would be far more diversified since it must reflect individual student interests.

Simultaneously, teachers would have an important role in making individual student activities socially meaningful by drawing students into a group process. As a rule, the combination of individual and group learning, which is critically related to educational success, requires that students work in isolation on uniform assignments, turn these in for evaluation, and move on to subsequent tasks.

Hawkins's teaching methods suggest an alternative, inductive approach. Students in his class studied external phenomena in a way that made learning both individually and socially meaningful. They began by exploring their own field of experience for evidence related to a common theme; individual experiences were then pooled in small-group interaction aimed at distinguishing between shared and unique perceptions. Finally, the whole class pooled the small-group reports and tied the results to an external subject matter. Throughout the experience, Hawkins operated as the facilitator of student learning—making suggestions, asking leading questions, encouraging hesitant students, and directing the class discussion.

The emphasis on teacher-as-facilitator supports the relevance of reforms that reduce external demands on the teacher's time and energy. For one, the use of paraprofessionals fully acquainted with the teacher's objectives and working with individual, needy students would advance this end. The use of resources outside the school building is also suggested. As we will see below, however, these objectives are systematically constrained by forces inherent in the schooling process.

Coinciding with the shift to teacher-as-facilitator is a curricular shift to more open, diversified subject focus and learning process. In many ways, this objective touches the same learning traits as the shift in teaching emphasis, namely, the need to incorporate diverse student interests, experiences, and abilities. It also suggests that we ought to incorporate in our curricula a socially interdependent form of learning. At the risk of oversimplification, we can say that a group of learners must at some point touch base with a common experience—a common language and a common set of facts. These may be gained from teacher input, individual reading, or inductive group research. The meaning and interpretation of this common experience are derived from social interdependence in the learning process, aided and directed by the teacher. At one level, this learning objective simply suggests that classroom experiences should include more diverse learning activities and a significant element of cooperative learning among small groups. In the area of social studies, it suggests that students could learn about society in a way that makes society—its history, institutions, and mores—experientially meaningful.

These classroom reforms raise a number of difficult issues. For one, they underscore the need for teaching excellence. In many

ways, it is possible that truly excellent teachers possess rare personal talents. On the other hand, in examining the active-open teachers, we can perceive a variety of personalities and approaches working effectively with a variety of student types. Some inroads on current classroom practices might result from policies designed to train
or retrain the "less talented" prospective teachers in the kinds of
learning dynamics involved in democratic classrooms, and attract
more talented teachers by making the teaching job better geared to
their talents.

These considerations raise a basic shortcoming in the effort to
change classroom practices directly, namely, that democratic practices are constrained and undermined by structural and functional
forces inherent in public schooling. For example, teachers in the
study complained about the heterogeneity of their classes. Yet this
complaint arises mainly because the teacher's task is essentially one
of fitting students to a common learning mold. Teachers and students
feel the pressures of social selection—teachers because they know
they must constantly distinguish among students according to a dominant mode of educational success and students because they feel the
pervasive constraints of grades and postschool outcomes. At the same
time that they complained about the heterogeneity of their students,
teachers bemoaned the lack of real alternatives.

In such a learning environment, it is hardly surprising to find
that truly successful and democratic classes are largely the result of
exceptional teaching efforts. It is also not surprising to find most
teachers complaining about obstacles to effective teaching, such as
course load, class size, lack of administrative support, and the pervasive pressures of grading.

Educational policy makers must ask: Is it right that truly effective teaching and democratic learning in our schools are primarily
the product of exceptional circumstances or persons? If we do not
believe that the basic constraints and reinforcements that shape school
learning should be antidemocratic, much less antieducational, we
must include these targets in our policy considerations. In the remainder of this section, these institutional constraints on democratic
learning will be considered.

Restructuring the High School

Essentially, the democratization of classroom learning includes
three basic elements: active teacher input combined with a diversified
learning focus and socially interdependent processes. It is not difficult to see how each of these elements encounters stiff obstacles in
secondary schools as we now know them. As illustrated in Figure 6.1,

FIGURE 6.1

Structural Obstacles to Democratic Learning

Democratic Classroom Variables	(encounter)	Structural Traits	(and are translated into)	Classroom Dynamics
1. Active teacher direction	——	Student resistance (general: extrinsic motivations; particular: alienation)	——	Teacher domination
		Bureaucratic scheduling	——	Discontinuous involvement
2. Curricular diversity	——	Need for uniform subject and process as a "scale" for distinguishing between students	——	Individuals working on their own; tracking
3. Cooperative learning interaction	——	Need to distinguish among individual student performances and achievement	——	Homogeneous grouping of students; uniformity in processes; tracking

Source: Prepared by the author.

the requisites of democratic learning are confronted by autocratic and bureaucratic characteristics of the school structure.

In the first place, active teacher direction encounters built-in student resistance to learning involvement. Overall, this resistance reflects the fact that students are geared to extrinsic rather than intrinsic learning incentives. The pervasiveness of extrinsic school compulsion and imposed control are forces that teachers have to overcome if they are to engage students intrinsically in the learning process. In addition, teachers have to counteract bureaucratic efficiency that compartmentalizes student involvement and subverts continuity and purposefulness in learning.

With some students, however, teacher activism encounters a more difficult obstacle. Among students who have been tracked into low-level learning environments, alienation and withdrawal are so pervasive that teacher activism all too easily becomes teacher domination. In large part, the teacher performs a custodial function. The teacher's task is easiest when he or she gears the learning experience to minimal involvement on the part of these students, thus perpetuating the students' alienation from purposeful learning. Like the encounter with extrinsically motivated students, interaction with alienated students reflects the way schools are organized to pursue instrumental functions, in particular, the function of tracking.

Whereas teacher activism encounters function-related student traits, the objectives of curricular diversity and cooperative learning directly encounter the instrumental functions themselves. The effort to diversity learning, to open up the curriculum, is confronted by the need for uniform subject material and learning procedures that facilitate the measurement of student performance level. Comparably, the effort to establish cooperative work tasks, to build group rapport and a sense of social interdependence, are confronted by the competitive work and grade structure required by the need to distinguish among individual abilities.

Despite the best intentions of secondary school personnel, the objectives of democratic learning are tightly constrained by the very nature of secondary schooling as we now know it. If anything, the social selection function becomes most overt and pervasive during the high school years. Tracking becomes an overt part of the schooling structure, and guidance departments are established to give advice and counseling about careers and future schooling. Students are faced with the prospect of adult life and adult expectations on completion of high school, if these are not postponed by further schooling. In an immediate sense, one can argue that secondary schools reflect the political priorities of their communities. Yet community political input into secondary schooling frequently is aimed at making the schools perform instrumental functions more effectively.

In contrast to these kinds of institutional (and political) pressures, it seems particularly appropriate that secondary schools be sensitive to their socialization impact on adolescents and their role in the larger socialization context. Most fundamentally, this means that students should encounter learning environments that teach democratic lessons—stressing participatory behavior, individual initiative, cooperative interaction, and meaningful responsible involvement in one's environment. These aims require a fundamental diversification of the secondary school experience.

Although this reform suggests a radical restructuring of high schools, it does not mean that we must abandon social selection functions; in fact, it might allow room for more occupationally relevant learning. While the format for democratized secondary schooling might take many forms, essentially it would aim at diversification of learning options. Students would have increased mobility and flexibility

in structuring learning experiences of interest to them, with a varying blend of intellectual, social, and occupational elements. Student
choice, for example, could be effected by some form of student vouch-
er plan, whereby students could choose from learning options within
existing classes and schools, in alternative learning centers, or in
community agencies and businesses.

Two factors are critical to the legitimacy and success of school
diversification: all students must have equal access to engaging learning environments and student choices are effectively free only when
they are not tied prohibitively to future costs and rewards, as they
now are. The latter requirement strikes at the school compulsion that
is rooted in the instrumental functions of schooling. Before addressing
this larger context of schooling directly, we may consider some rami-
fications of a diversified secondary school structure.

The effort to diversify school learning at the secondary level
raises one of the dilemmas of democratic reform: how to pursue both
diversity or localism, on the one hand, and universalism, on the
other. The latter concern underscores the importance of traditional
egalitarian objectives. In particular, it points to the continuing need
for educational controls—in the form of required attendance and active
teacher input—and for inclusive group learning. Attendance and learning controls would assist efforts to bring students into contact with a
wider range of experiences than might be the case in a laissez-faire
structure and to aid in seeing experiences through. Cooperative learning is desirable from the perspective of broadening students' perceptions of social interdependence to include, rather than exclude, disparate social groups. One fact of classroom life that stood out in all
three observed schools was that the classroom provides a unique opportunity for students of varying backgrounds to mix. Left to their
own devices, however, most students could be observed staying with
"their own." These forms of racial and social segregation occur not
only between and within schools but within classes in the absence of
external intervention.

On balance, there seem to be sufficient democratic grounds for
maintaining an organized school structure, in order to take advantage
of the leadership that good teaching can provide and opportunities for
broadened educational experiences. The primary objectives of universalism at the secondary level would be to protect equal access to
quality educational experiences and to provide all students with an inclusive, experiential familiarity with democratic norms and procedures. The latter is particularly critical at a time when many are
concerned about the breakdown of authority or the dissolution of a core
of common beliefs and principles. However, all the evidence in this
work suggests that the restoration of authority or community norms
does not result from an increase in institutional uniformity. Instead,

if students encountered a more intrinsically meaningful authority in their learning experiences, we might begin to revive some of the lost virtues of community.

On balance, then, the most critical need of secondary schooling is the need for greater diversification, for a profound opening up of learning options to meet the needs and interests of diverse students. In short, secondary schools need to move away from rather than toward educational uniformity. In terms of educational equality, we need to strive for a concept of equal involvement in personally meaningful learning, not in increasingly identical learning experiences. At the same time, the distribution of educational opportunities and resources also must be guided by the norm of universalism.

These reform objectives suggest a substantially altered institutional experience at the secondary level. A large proportion of a student's high school experience would be devoted to the exploration of various learning projects. In essence, students would have an opportunity to explore and receive feedback on their developing intellectual, social, and occupational interests. To be effective, such a learning format would require active teacher guidance and evaluation of student accomplishments.

This format, in turn, would require considerable redirection of teacher energies and teacher training. Successful teaching would require the effective utilization of diverse educational resources and effective teacher-student interaction within an accomplishment-motivation format. It would also require far greater educational planning at the communitywide level, concentrating on the exploration and development of community learning resources.

At the same time, the secondary school itself would serve a different purpose. Instead of being a largely custodial institution for many of its students, the high school would be the focal point for four types of concerns. In brief, it would serve as:

1. The major resource and communication center for the network of community learning opportunities
2. The primary center for learning options not likely to be found in the community; these might include specialized classes in science, math, or languages, or courses on the ethnic heritage of community groups
3. The central location for learning interaction between various groups and levels of students, focusing on the social studies and such nonacademic pursuits as intramural and interscholastic athletics
4. A center for remedial activities, where students can receive concentrated, skill-oriented learning experiences

These school functions are suggested as a format for the diversification of high school learning. The particular blend of functions, of course, would be subject to community inputs. The main point of this reform agenda is that it calls for a change from diversification through tracking to diversification based on a balance between student development needs and norms that govern both socialization and cognitive learning concerns. Tracking and the destructive stigma attached to it would be abolished. The guiding purpose of these changes is the effort to free teachers to foster educational experiences that take on the democratic traits elicited in this study.

These reform objectives are not strikingly new. Much has been written about the need to diversify secondary schooling, and many urban school systems have attempted to incorporate community learning resources in the high school curriculum (including both Central and Northdale High Schools in this study). [9] Nonetheless, the fact is that high schools remain essentially unchanged. On a daily basis, they continue to perform the same instrumental and custodial functions, and they continue to teach and reinforce the same antidemocratic lessons.

Therefore, a basic shift in the functions of high schools is proposed, a shift that requires for its success two ingredients that have been underemphasized in many reform efforts. One ingredient is the need for compulsion, control, and planning. Students would be compelled to attend secondary schools, they would be actively directed by instructors, and they would have to meet certain learning requirements for the completion of secondary school. Thus, students might be required to cover all four of the learning areas mentioned above, depending on the educational standards that evolve through the political process. For example, students might be required to choose from a selection of specialized courses in areas like English, mathematics, or science; they would be required to engage in a social studies curriculum that could involve an element of interdependent learning and basic familiarity with national and local heritages; they would engage in a program of community learning activities, which could also provide the focus for considerable written communication to instructor-evaluators. Students lacking in basic skills could be required to undergo intensive remedial experiences.

Clearly, then, an element of compulsion is needed to make the pursuit of these functions universally effective. It is also clear that school systems would have to devote a significant effort to development and planning in order to provide and oversee student learning experiences. These objectives raise questions about political and economic feasibility. Yet they also suggest ways in which schools could save money by tapping (and contributing student input to) community resources. Furthermore, they suggest ways in which struggles between teachers and parents or between teachers and alienated students could be made less intransigent. On the one hand, parents and students might gain increased input into educational decision making. On the other hand, the teacher's job would shift from that of an imposed custodian who has to battle students to get them interested in learning to that of a facilitator of learning that reflects student (and parent) interests.

Despite the implied potential for meaningful reform, however, a more critical and pervasive obstacle looms in pre- and posthigh school concerns. In many ways, political obstacles that stymie reform efforts at the local level are based on these broader concerns. Insofar as parental pressures reflect concern about instrumental outcomes of schooling, they can be seen as antieducational by school personnel. As illustrated in Figure 6.2, the successful implementation of these reforms requires that we focus on two characteristics of secondary school students: the cognitive and socialization effects of their elementary school experience and their concerns about postsecondary school outcomes. In short, we need to draw both elementary education and the broader social context of schooling into our discussion of secondary school reform. We now address each of these reform targets in turn.

Reforming Elementary Education

Two contraints on the likely effectiveness of high school reforms are reflected in the comments of teachers involved in this study. Several teachers complained about deeply rooted student passivity and withdrawal from learning. Many also complained about "incredibly" poor reading and writing skills. Both of these concerns raise issues that strike at the core of elementary school reform. To some degree, the success of secondary school reform depends on the implementation of elementary school reform. Thus, seemingly, we have shifted the difficult burdens of reform onto the shoulders of elementary schools.

However, this need not be the case. A number of democratically legitimate proposals can be made for increasing both learning and democratic socialization at the elementary school level. It is conceivable, however, that a redefinition of the functions of elementary and secondary education, together with the implementation of function-related reforms at each level, can result in the democratization of public schooling. At the same time, both elementary and secondary school reforms ultimately depend for their effectiveness of revisions in the instrumental functions all levels of schooling are called upon to perform.

FIGURE 6.2

Secondary School Reform and Beyond

Functions of the High School	Secondary School Reforms (encounter)	Elementary Education Issues (met by)	Elementary School Reforms (and both encounter)	Extrinsic Functions (which reflect)	Social, Political, and Economic Context
A. Center for network of community opportunities	1. Diversification of learning, with active teacher direction	1a. Inadequate skill preparation 1b. Passive learning habits			
B. Center for specialized (academic) learning options	2. Cooperative learning tasks	(student separatism)	Mastery learning and integration	Social selection function: Parent concerns	Economic inequality (disadvantages passed on to the next generation)
C. Center for communal learning interaction: "socialization in common," integration	3. Abolition of tracking	(informal tracking)		and Student incentives	and Social status
D. Center for remedial learning activities					

Source: Prepared by the author.

From both social and individualist perspectives, the principle of equality requires that all children should learn basic skills and capacities that will enable them to enjoy full membership in society. On this basis, we might follow prevalent views of cognitive and moral development[10] to make a conceptual distinction between elementary and secondary education. Elementary education can be defined as the full development of basic cognitive skills and capacities, while secondary education can be defined as the full development of socially relevant skills and capacities. Such a distinction between the two levels of schooling might have profound implications for the pursuit of democratic education. Simultaneously, it provides a way to balance efforts to maximize universality and diversity in education.

Given their primary task of cognitive skill development, elementary schools and school personnel would be accountable for precisely this end. Although a number of reforms could be suggested to advance this aim, the most basic reform would be a shift to the concept of "mastery learning" or teaching.[11] Under such a shift, most teaching practices, the organization of classroom interaction, and learning schedules all would aim at universal student mastery of basic skills. Most fundamentally, this approach, which has been used at various levels of schooling, reverses the normal method of giving all students the same exposure to the same material with the intention of measuring differences in the thoroughness with which they learn it. Instead, skill development is broken down into incremental units, and the class advances only when all members have mastered a given step.

Such an approach incorporates the basic concept of elementary education suggested here. It also has implications for democratic education. In the first place, when a class completes a learning unit, the students are tested to see whether they have mastered the material. Those who have not are then given special corrective assignments and are retested until they achieve mastery. This supplementary stage provides critical insights into the changes entailed by this approach to learning. During the catch-up stage, teachers can provide a variety of learning tools, including audiovisual resources or workbooks, to diversify the format of learning. They also can require those students who have learned the material to aid the teaching process. In such a system, heterogeneity no longer becomes a drawback, and social interdependence can be enhanced.

We do not yet know enough about mastery learning to shift all elementary education to a specific format. Yet, those who have employed this approach argue that the overall efficiency of classroom learning is greatly enhanced, behavioral problems are reduced, and the initial retardation of fast learners virtually disappears.[12] Most fundamentally, the mastery concept supports the egalitarian view that everyone (except perhaps those who have severely retarded or disturbed mental capacities) can achieve significant mastery of basic learning skills.

Further data on the impact of mastery learning are needed, yet, insofar as it is successful, incorporation of this approach into the mainstream of elementary education would coincide with a basic shift toward democratic public schooling. It would satisfy the concern of parents and egalitarians for educational results, and would counter the complaints of secondary school teachers.

Furthermore, it would involve a democratically consistent socialization experience. Student alienation would be dissipated by successful accomplishment of learning tasks and social interdependence could be greatly enhanced. Ultimately, student learning would be more democratic by becoming more socially and educationally meaningful. Even if considerable teacher authority was required, it would perform an enabling function. The teacher would be the active facilitator of individual learning and social interaction, resulting in progress toward intrinsically meaningful ends.

More generally, a redefinition of elementary and secondary education would be conducive to a balance between universalism and diversity in education. Elementary education and skill mastery would be universalized and could incorporate learning interaction among diverse student types. Secondary education would become more democratic by becoming more diversified. Students could be freer to structure their own priorities, with ample opportunity for all to explore directions of their own choosing, under sufficient control to guarantee broadening of experiences and productive outcomes.

This shift might also provide a balance among conflicting forces that currently plague urban areas, in particular, the struggles over school desegregation and school decentralization. Since most within-school resistance to desegregation is located at the high school level, structural diversity would be more suitable to the secondary schools. On the other hand, desegregation and its universalistic aims could be concentrated in elementary schools. Skill-mastery classrooms could be integrated with the result that both educational achievement and social integration norms might be satisfied. The concerns of minority parents would be defused by demonstrable educational outcomes; the concerns of "advantaged" parents might be partially assuaged if their children showed little or no learning retardation. Finally, secondary school students who had previously encountered mastery teaching in integrated elementary schools might well be less resistant to the experiences in common that would form part of the high school curriculum. For instance, there might be more room in high schools for meaningful cross-cultural studies taught in an anthropological spirit.

If public schools were restructured to fit these functional distinctions, successful democratic outcomes would still depend to a significant degree on forces external to the schools themselves. In fact, the political effort to restructure the schools depends to some extent on these external forces.

In short, when we ask why these reforms would be difficult to implement, we again confront reasons that reflect the instrumental functions of public schooling. Parents of elementary school children will likely be concerned about retarded learning paces under mastery learning—even if confronted by contrary evidence—because they are critically, and understandably, concerned about their children's futures. Secondary students (and their parents) would not feel free to take advantage of learning options with prohibitive future costs and rewards hanging over their heads. When all is said and done, we cannot talk about meaningful systematic educational reform without considering the systemic constraints that are built into public schooling in our society.

Democratic Schooling: The Need for Social Reform

The empirical analysis of schools undertaken in this work has pointed to functional reasons why school reform cannot be systematically effective if pursued in a vacuum. In short, the obstacles to reform are more pervasive than such localized factors as regressive school administrations, inefficient (or overly efficient) school organization, community pressures, or ineffective teaching—despite the immediate importance of these for educational outcomes. As policy-oriented school researchers have discovered, and as the Kettering Commission on secondary school reform has observed, "The larger problems of American society are reflected in the high schools."[13] At the same time, study commissions also have noted that the past "decade of change and innovation in the schools had little or no lasting effect on the content of school programs or the quality of teaching and learning."[14]

The reasons for the failure of school reform are many, as are the "problems of American society" reflected in the schools. The empirical evidence in this work, however, points to at least one significant and systematic force that shapes the learning process and the reform debate: the instrumental functions of social selection and equalized opportunity. Most of the evidence considered in earlier chapters suggests that school learning and school reform are pervasively in the grip of these functions.

The basic thrust of this work, therefore, has been to distinguish between these extrinsic schooling forces and those that are intrinsically important, namely, the pursuit of learning and democratic socialization. Each can be considered in its own right. For reasons of principle and practicality, however, we cannot simply abandon efforts to maximize equal opportunity through schooling or efforts to select employees according to relevant performance criteria.

Where does this leave us? Contrary to this picture of a reform dilemma, one can argue that it is feasible to relax the grip of instrumental functions in order to facilitate meaningful educational reform. Thus, we could systematically reduce the antidemocratic nature of schooling by focusing on the future costs and rewards of the schooling race that make the social selection function so critically important. We might be able to change the functional relationship between schools and society by various direct policies, yet these are unlikely to prove effective in a systematic way unless we reduce the extrinsic costs of school failure and the extrinsic pull of school success. On the other hand, as this work demonstrates, the democratic alternative is not a system that is totally lacking in controls. In policy terms, we need to examine carefully the optimal balance between intrinsic and extrinsic incentives.

As illustrated in Figure 6.2, the most pervasive extrinsic motivations in schooling are those that reflect economic and social status outcomes. The impact of the socioeconomic structure on schooling functions operates in the schooling context through the drive to better oneself by means of education, in short, deriving from the characteristics of "contest mobility" attributed to American schools by Ralph Turner. [15] As a consequence, a major democratic reform priority would be to move beyond the concept of equal opportunity to focus on the achievement of equal circumstances or equal results. Many have advocated the equalization or redistribution of income and wealth. To these arguments can be added one based on the quality of school learning.

It seems probable that anxiety-producing, conformist qualities of the schooling race and intransigent reform obstacles could be diminished by economic policies aimed at the reduction of income and wealth inequality in America. At the very least, two significant factors could be affected. The bite could be removed from the schooling race by policies that established a fair and humane "floor" and "ceiling" for personal wealth, independent of any behavioral or intellectual qualities that schools select as the criteria for reward and punishment. And preschool disadvantages related to wealth inequities could be reduced.

The effort to reduce income and wealth inequality obviously raises a number of complex economic and political issues. Analysts disagree over such politically sensitive issues as work incentives and appropriate levels of income maintenance. [16] From the perspective of democratic schooling, however, greater income equality seems imperative, and the minimal level ought to be sufficient to reduce failure anxieties in schooling. However, since there is no direct substantiation of this relationship in this work, we can only speculate about the precise degree of equality that would be needed.

Overall, one can argue that a society that relies significantly on intrinsic incentives to engage its learners and its workers is a much healthier society than ours currently is. It must also, of neccessity, be more democratic.

In short, within the democratic context, we need not advocate the elimination of hierarchies in society, if, indeed, such an objective were possible. However, for hierarchies to be legitimate, they must be just and functional. One can criticize present social inequalities both for being unjust and for being dysfunctional in their impact on school learning.

The second type of extrinsic motivation, social status, is less susceptible to direct policy input. Whereas we can affect income inequality through legislation, we cannot legislate changes in social status. These are far more deeply rooted in social mores and underlying economic structures. In one sense, though, we can say that many of our beliefs about social status reflect previous socialization experiences in schools. [17]

If our young were to experience a learning environment that did not track students into separate, stigmatized groups, but instead were taught lessons of social interdependence, we might achieve a society where social status was less of an external phenomenon; we might learn to value qualities of the human personality as well as leadership traits that enhance and enrich social interdependence. However, to achieve this social end, we would have to have more democratic schools, and thus we are back where we started from. Policies directed at nonschool status reinforcers, such as television, advertising, and the commercial interests behind these, might well have an impact on status motivation. Yet, the importance of democratic learning seems to imply that educational policy makers and social reforms face a chicken and egg dilemma: Which kind of reform comes first?

THE DILEMMA OF EDUCATIONAL REFORM

Since this work has focused on the interrelatedness of schooling and society, it is only appropriate to close with a comment on the strategic question of reform. In essence, reformers are confronted by the dilemma of which comes first: educational reform or social and economic reform. In short, do we strive to change the schools in order to democratize the orientations of future adults, thus facilitating democratic reforms in society? Or do we attempt to restructure society so that school reform can become more feasible, even though existing political forces in society are less likely to be democratically inclined?

This writer would argue that our first step is simply to recognize that we confront such a dilemma. Most importantly, we need to be guided by an awareness that school learning, of necessity, reflects forces at large in society. In short, the structure of school learning reflects the functions of public schooling, which, in turn, reflect the social and economic structure of society. We need to be aware of structural impediments to democratic school reform and of the way traditional reform policies reinforce these impediments.

In essence, this means that reform should not be guided by a more-of-the-same approach. Theoretically, at least, we can speak of an either-or choice between two types of objectives. On the one hand, we can continue to strive for the perfection of equal educational opportunity as it is commonly understood. We can try to make the rules of schooling fairer in their administration. In short, we can strive to achieve an optimal meritocracy, despite the costs in terms of the kind of citizenry we produce. On the other hand, we can attempt to maximize the democratic traits of the school learning experience itself, with all the social and economic reforms implied by this objective.

In practical terms, the policy debate must be informed by an awareness of the interrelatedness of reform targets. At the very least, efforts to equalize opportunity through the instrument of schooling should be made with an eye to their impact on democratic socialization. The latter objective has long been ignored by policy makers; instead, it should be elevated to a primary status among our reform concerns. In short, we should strive for some semblance of ideological compatibility or balance in our reform efforts. One possible format has been proposed for an ideologically balanced approach to reform, a format that calls for a radical shift in the direction of our school concerns. Much in this statement adds support to the efforts of those who seek structural changes that touch the roots of our economic institutions.

At the same time, we need to be guided by political feasibility. In this respect, the empirical evidence contained in this work is less helpful since it focuses on institutional analysis of school learning, not on school reform, per se. In a sense, it seems that the antidemocratic traits of schooling are so deeply embedded in the school system, in society, and even in traditional reform concerns that there is little to be gained from considering the democratic reform of education. The systemic nature of antidemocratic learning traits might suggest to some that these are beyond our capacity for change. At best, it would seem, we are left the option of developing a utopian vision of democratic learning.

This tendency to resign ourselves to our institutional fates is reinforced by two factors. On the one hand, we have heard the words of visionary school critics who have stridently underscored the failings of our schools and have touched our intuitive sense that things should be otherwise. On the other hand, we have been baffled by a sense that "the more things change the more they stay the same," that these visions fail to lead us anywhere. Together these factors have led some to a fatalistic acceptance of our public institutions and their faults, while others have moved to a revolutionary stance that says in effect "everything must change" if our educational institutions are to change.

Although these are understandable reactions to the failure of educational reform, the empirical evidence contained in this work suggests one reason why the antidemocratic qualities of schooling are so intransigent. In short, the reform dilemma involves a trade-off between feasibility and effectiveness. On the one hand, direct, piecemeal reforms are more feasible, yet they are usually pursued without sufficient regard to the constraints inherent in the broader context of schooling. On the other hand, efforts to affect the latter require changes which are far more sweeping and difficult to achieve.

At the same time, however, this work suggests ways in which individual teachers can enhance democratic learning in existing classrooms. It also provides a blueprint for systemic reform by analyzing the relationship between democratic learning and such broader objectives as restructuring the secondary school, redefining elementary education, and redistributing income and wealth in society. In short, democratic learning requires a fundamental shift in our policy priorities.

Ultimately, it is argued, the resolution of the reform dilemma cannot be achieved philosophically, however hard some reformers may try. In effect, it depends on the situation of the reader. With an awareness of the interrelatedness of reform issues, teachers can adopt new teaching ideas and can support related external reform efforts. Comparably, educational policy makers can begin to reshape educational priorities in light of a more coherently democratic outlook. In either case, it is imperative that educational reform include those forces that systematically make school learning unequal and undemocratic.

NOTES

1. Charles E. Silberman, Crisis in the Classroom (New York: Random House, 1970).

2. See John J. Patrick, Political Socialization of American Youth: Implications for Secondary School Social Studies, Research Bulletin no. 3 (Washington, D. C. : National Council for the Social Studies, n. d.).

3. D. H. Jenkins, "Characteristics and Functions of Leadership in Instructional Groups," in Dynamics of Instructional Groups, ed. Nelson B. Henry (Chicago: University of Chicago Press, 1960), p. 13.

4. Paul E. Breer and Edwin C. Locke, Task Experience as a Source of Attitudes (Homewood, Ill. : Dorsey Press, 1965), p. 13.

5. Morton Deutsch, "The Effects of Cooperation and Competition upon Group Processes," in Group Dynamics: Research and Theory, eds. Dorwin Cartwright and Alvin Zander (Evanston, Ill. : Row, Peterson, 1953), p. 338.

6. James S. Coleman, Adolescents and the Schools (New York: Basic Books, 1965).

7. Seymour Spilerman, "Raising Academic Motivation in Lower Class Adolescents: A Convergence of Two Research Traditions," Sociology of Education 44, no. 1 (Winter 1971): 103-18.

8. See, for example, The Council for Basic Education Bulletin, Washington, D. C. , 21, no. 1 (September 1976).

9. For insights into the political issues encountered by urban school systems, see Joseph M. Cronin and Richard M. Hailer, Organizing an Urban School System for Diversity (Boston: Massachusetts Advisory Council on Education, 1970); Henry S. Resnick, Turning on the System (New York: Paneheon, 1970); and George R. LaNoue and Bruce L. R. Smith, The Politics of School Decentralization (Lexington, Mass. : Lexington Books, 1975).

10. See, for example, David Elkind, Children and Adolescents (New York: Oxford University Press, 1970); Jean Piaget, The Moral Judgment of the Child (New York: Free Press, 1965); and Lawrence Kohlberg and Alan Lockwood, "Cognitive Developmental Psychology and Political Education—Progress in the Sixties" (Cambridge, Mass. : Harvard University).

11. See, for example, James A. Block, ed. , Mastery Learning: Theory and Practice (New York: Holt, Rinehart and Winston, 1971); Benjamin S. Bloom, "Learning for Mastery," Evaluation Comment 1 (1968): 2; and Edward B. Fiske, "Mastery Teaching: Until All Are Caught Up," New York Times News of the Week in Review, August 29, 1976, p. 9.

12. Fiske, op. cit.

13. The National Commission on the Reform of Secondary Education, The Reform of Secondary Education (New York: McGraw-Hill, 1973), p. 3.

14. Ibid. , pp. 7-8; and A Foundation Goes to School (New York: Ford Foundation, 1972), p. 3.

15. Ralph Turner, "Modes of Social Ascent through Education: Sponsored and Contest Mobility," in Education, Economy, and Society, eds. A. H. Halsey, Jean Floyd, and C. Arnold Anderson (New York: Free Press, 1961), pp. 121-39.

16. See, for example, Joseph A. Pechman and P. Michael Timpane, eds. , Work Incentives and Income Guarantees (Washington, D. C. : The Brookings Institution, 1975); Christopher Green, Negative Taxes and the Poverty Problem (Washington, D. C. : The Brookings Institution, 1967); and Daniel P. Moynihan, The Politics of a Guaranteed Income (New York: Vintage Books, 1973).

17. For evidence of the status accorded those with high educational attainment, see Robert Lane, Political Ideology (New York: Free Press, 1962), pp. 68-71.

TABLE A. 1

Background Data: The Three Communities and High Schools

	Easton (Central High)	Middletown	Northdale
Percent of total adult population completed high school	41.4	55.1	83.4
Per pupil (enrollment) expenditure, systemwide (dollars)[a]	747	713	935
Median teacher salary, systemwide (dollars)[a]	12,084	11,900	13,672
Starting teacher salary, high school (dollars)	8,924	8,358	8,490
Total student population, high school	1,607	2,540	2,199
Total faculty, high school	113	169	160
Student-faculty ratio (rounded)	14:1	16:1	14:1
Percent of classes designated as "honors", high school	0.0	2.9	17.0
Percent of classes designated as "college"	41.4	69.8	64.0
Percent of classes designated as "general"	58.6	26.5	19.0
Percent of graduates attending four-year college[b]	25.0	30.5	55.0
Percent of graduates attending two-year college	35.0	30.5	15.0
Percent of graduates working	31.0	33.1	11.4

[a]1971 figures.
[b]Based on previous year's graduating class.
Source: Records provided by the three school systems.

TABLE A.2

Individual Classes

No.	Teacher's Name	Sex	Age	Years Experience	Degrees	Course Title	Grade	Track[a]	Avg. Students[b]
Central High									
1.	Casey	M	27	2	AB, MA	U.S. history	Jr.	G	25/18
2.	James	M	21	(Pract.)	—	U.S. history	Jr.	G	13/11
3.	Hawkins	M	29	5	BA, MA+	Social psychology	Sr.	C	19/17
4.	Gianelli	M	31	3	BA, MA	World civilization	Soph.	C	24/24
5.	Pellagrini	M	33	10	BA, MA+	U.S. history	Jr.	G	18/17
Middletown High									
1.	Backman	F	26	6	BA, MA	Sociology	Sr.	C	25/24
2.	Ryan	F	30	8	BA, MA	U.S. history	Jr.	C	27/27
3.	Baker	M	28	6	BA, MA	U.S. history	Jr.	H	19/19
4.	Mitchell	M	27	3	BA, MA	World history	Soph.	G	19/19
5.	Kopek	F	27	5	BA, MEd	Psychology	Sr.	C	22/21
Northdale High									
1.	Perez	M	32	6	BA, MA	American problems	Sr.	C	18/18
2.	Crampton	M	45	5	BA, MA	U.S. history	Jr.	H	22/22
3.	Schilling	M	31	8	BA, MA	Great Men and Women	Soph.	C	24/24
4.	O'Reilly	F	36	15	BA, MA	Political science	Sr.	C	22/22
5.	Ferris	M	45	19	BA, MA	U.S. history	Jr.	G	26/26

[a]Track: H = honors, C = college, G = general.
[b]Highest observed attendance/Number of students responding to questionnaire.
Source: From school records.

197

TABLE A. 3

Breakdown of Students by Track Level

	Honors	College	General	Total Percent	(N)
Percent upper-middle class	72	34	18	35	(78)
Percent middle class	21	35	21	30	(67)
Percent lower-working class	7	31	61	36	(80)
Total	100	100	100	100	(225)
Percent white	91	86	58	78	(214)
Percent nonwhite	9	14	42	22	(59)
Total	100	100	100	100	(274)
Percent attending Central High	6	21	55	29	(87)
Percent attending Middletown High	33	45	18	37	(111)
Percent attending Northdale High	67	34	27	34	(103)
Total	100	100	100	100	(301)

Source: Data self-reported.

TABLE A. 4

Teacher Control and Student Alienation

	Teacher Control ("You have to do things the way the teacher wants if you want to get a good grade")				
Alienation ("bell = best")	Agree Strongly	Agree	Neutral	Disagree	Disagree Strongly
Percent agree (alienated)	42	34	29	19	08
Percent neutral	25	29	29	27	42
Percent disagree (involved)	33	37	42	54	50
(N) =	(67)	(110)	(53)	(61)	(12)

N = 303; correlation = 0.26.
Source: Student responses.

TABLE A. 5

Teacher Control and Student Confinement

	Teacher Control ("You have to do things the way the teacher wants if you want to get a good grade")				
Confinement ("have to sit still")	Agree Strongly	Agree	Neutral	Disagree	Disagree Strongly
Percent agree (confined)	61	37	27	26	33
Percent neutral	14	23	33	23	00
Percent disagree (involved)	25	40	40	51	67
(N) =	(67)	(110)	(52)	(61)	(12)

N = 302; correlation = 0.26.
Source: Student responses.

STUDENT QUESTIONNAIRE

(Student responses are represented by percentages.)

The questions below are part of a study I am doing on schools and school life. Please answer with your honest feelings and opinions. Please do not write your name anywhere on the questionnaire. Thank you.

I. GRADES AND SCHOOL IN GENERAL: (The following apply to your school experience and high school generally.)

1. What do you think should be the most important factor in getting good grades? What should be the least?
   What is the most important in your school? Second most? Least?
   (Check only one in each column)

	should be most	should be least	is most	is second most	is least
a. being considerate of others	4.3	9.7	3.4	5.6	36.6
b. hard work	14.5	5.8	17.6	15.9	6.4
c. knowing facts	3.9	7.6	22.1	15.6	5.3
d. teacher liking me	0.7	61.7	2.1	7.9	23.4
e. careful, thorough work	13.5	0.4	18.6	17.9	3.8
f. coming up with original ideas	4.9	5.4	3.1	10.9	13.6
g. understanding the subject	36.8	1.4	18.6	11.3	1.1
h. other (write in)	3.9	1.1	1.7	1.0	2.6
(Multiple answers)	17.4	6.9	12.8	13.9	6.8
N =	304	277	290	302	265

On the next several questions, please check whether you agree or disagree with the statement, and how strongly.

2. The grades I get have a lot to do with how I feel about school.
   Agree strongly 18.8 Agree 37.7 Neutral 18.2 Disagree 20.5 Disagree strongly 4.9 (N = 308)

3. Grades are important because they have a lot to do with what kind of job you end up getting.
   Agree strongly 19.7 Agree 34.0 Neutral 18.4 Disagree 20.7 Disagree strongly 7.1 (N = 309)

4. No matter what people say about grades, you usually get what you deserve.
   Agree strongly 11.7 Agree 41.7 Neutral 16.8 Disagree 24.6 Disagree strongly 5.2 (N = 309)

5. Grades make me feel like I'm always being told I'm better or worse than somebody else.
Agree strongly 15.6 Agree 29.9 Neutral 22.4 Disagree 23.1
Disagree strongly 9.1 (N = 308)

6. If it weren't for grades, school could be really interesting.
Agree strongly 14.7 Agree 24.8 Neutral 19.5 Disagree 28.3
Disagree strongly 12.7 (N = 307)

7. When I'm in school, all I can think of is other places I'd rather be.
Agree strongly 11.7 Agree 21.7 Neutral 30.7 Disagree 27.8
Disagree strongly 8.1 (N = 309)

8. Most of my teachers are people I can talk to about things that are important to me.
Agree strongly 6.8 Agree 25.7 Neutral 20.5 Disagree 35.5
Disagree strongly 11.4 (N = 307)

9. School is most interesting as a place to see friends.
Agree strongly 19.6 Agree 36.3 Neutral 23.9 Disagree 17.3
Disagree strongly 2.9 (N = 307)

10. To get along in school, you have to do what people say.
Agree strongly 13.4 Agree 35.8 Neutral 20.5 Disagree 19.9
Disagree strongly 10.4 (N = 307)

11. Most days, I look forward to going to school.
Agree strongly 9.1 Agree 31.7 Neutral 24.3 Disagree 21.7
Disagree strongly 13.3 (N = 309)

(please answer with your own words):

12. (complete the following:) A good teacher is one who . . .

	Percent	N
understands students and their problems	33.0	102
respects students, can communicate with	18.1	56
is open, flexible; listens	12.6	39
cares about students, is friendly	15.9	49
helps students understand	26.2	81
doesn't overwork students	3.9	12
is fair, unbiased	13.3	41
makes class interesting	17.8	55
is competent, knows subject	17.8	55
enjoys his or her work	3.9	12
is lenient, relaxed	4.7	14
other	13.1	40

13. What do you feel is missing most in your school?

	Percent	N
unity	5.8	18
school spirit, enthusiasm	8.1	25
closeness, caring, warmth	6.4	20
individual help, attention	5.2	16
understanding, communication	11.0	34
trust, students given responsibilities	3.5	11
freedom	19.0	59
modernization	3.5	11
more good teachers	9.4	29
more motivated, mature students	3.2	10
more discipline, security	2.9	9
nothing, I like it	4.2	13
other	24.2	67

14. Do you feel it's very important to do well in school?
    Yes 83.4 No 3.6 Neutral 13.0 (N = 308)

15. If yes, why?   -because:
    a. it makes me feel like I've accomplished something 37.2
    b. it helps me get a good job 30.4
    c. it makes my parents happy 20.7
    d. it makes things easier all around 36.2
    e. other helps for college (10.0),   other (12.7) (N = 257)

16. (Below are some of the reasons people give for having schools
    in a society like ours. Starting with #1 as most important,
    please rank them from 1-5 as you view them.)

    Schools are important to:

	Rank	N
a. bring together people from different backgrounds to build a society common to all	3.7	287
b. give people the skills and knowledge they need for later jobs	2.55	292
c. give everyone a chance to make the most of his or her abilities	2.24	287
d. train people's minds to be able to meet future challenges	2.48	291
e. give people an understanding of how society works	3.74	289

II. SOCIAL STUDIES CLASS: (The following questions apply only to this class. I remind you that your teacher will not see individual questionnaires, so please give honest answers.)

17. How much of class time would you say you are paying close attention to the class?
0-20% 4.3   20-40% 12.8   40-60% 18.7   60-80% 35.4
80-100% 28.9   (N = 305)

18. What kind of class activity do you find most interesting? (check one)
What do you find least interesting? (check one)
In which do you learn the most?   "

	most interest	least interest	learn most
a. lectures by teacher	5.9	25.5	9.1
b. discussions	35.6	3.0	14.1
c. combined lecture-discussion	17.8	2.3	36.6
d. reading & taking notes	3.0	39.9	15.8
e. student group projects	19.1	10.1	8.4
(multiple answer)	18.5	19.1	16.1
N =	303	298	298

19. Do you feel that your teacher grades you on the same basis as everyone else in the class?
always 28.9   usually 41.5   sometimes 18.3   rarely 5.3
never 6.0   (N = 301)

20. How would you describe discipline in this class?
too harsh 4.9   strict but fair 24.9   relaxed 57.0
too easy 6.9   other 6.2   (N = 305)

21. What do you feel your teacher likes most in his or her students? (check one)
     44.8 coming up with their own ideas
     9.7 doing work on time
     4.5 being quiet
     19.2 working hard
     3.2 being considerate of others
     2.6 playing up to the teacher
     6.8 other _____
     9.1 (Multiple answer)

Now, please check whether you agree or diagree with the following:

22. In this class I am free to be myself.
Agree strongly 15.0 Agree 36.5 Neutral 23.8 Disagree 19.9
Disagree strongly 4.9 (N = 307)

23. I find it hard to stay awake in this class.
Agree strongly 4.9 Agree 10.8 Neutral 22.5 Disagree 37.9
Disagree strongly 23.9 (N = 306)

23a. I have plenty of chances in this class to learn about things I am
really interested in.
Agree strongly 18.6 Agree 38.6 Neutral 25.2 Disagree 13.7
Disagree strongly 3.9 (N = 306)

24. I don't feel the teacher cares very much about what I think.
Agree strongly 2.3 Agree 9.8 Neutral 18.6 Disagree 46.9
Disagree strongly 22.5 (N = 307)

25. This teacher gives everyone a chance to speak.
Agree strongly 31.3 Agree 53.1 Neutral 7.5 Disagree 7.8
Disagree strongly 0.3 (N = 307)

26. Listening to the teacher is important because he (she) knows
what he's (she's) talking about.
Agree strongly 24.4 Agree 41.7 Neutral 25.1 Disagree 6.8
Disagree strongly 2.0 (N = 307)

27. The best thing about this class is the bell at the end.
Agree strongly 11.7 Agree 16.0 Neutral 31.3 Disagree 30.0
Disagree strongly 11.1 (N = 307)

28. I feel I have a real influence on the way this class is run.
Agree strongly 3.3 Agree 15.7 Neutral 35.4 Disagree 32.8
Disagree strongly 12.8 (N = 305)

29. I sometimes don't speak out in class because of what other stu-
dents might think of me.
Agree strongly 7.2 Agree 20.6 Neutral 19.9 Disagree 30.4
Disagree strongly 21.9 (N = 306)

30. A big problem with class is that you have to sit still in one
place the whole time.
Agree strongly 15.9 Agree 23.2 Neutral 21.6 Disagree 30.4
Disagree strongly 9.8 (N = 306)

31. Even if I don't do well in class, I feel the teacher respects me
as a person.
Agree strongly 17.8 Agree 46.4 Neutral 23.4 Disagree 10.2
Disagree strongly 2.3 (N = 304)

32. You have to do things the way the teacher wants if you want to
get a good grade.
Agree strongly 22.1 Agree 36.3 Neutral 17.5 Disagree 20.1
Disagree strongly 4.0 (N = 303)

33. You really can't make excuses in this class, because you get
    out of it what you put in.
    Agree strongly 23.6 Agree 42.3 Neutral 21.6 Disagree 9.5
    Disagree strongly 2.6 (N = 305)

34. Check any of the following that apply to this class.   (N = 309)

    boring 23.0   interesting 64.4   relaxed 48.2   pressured 14.2
    a challenge 32.7 competitive 20.4 a zoo 12.6   a put-down 5.5
    doesn't mean anything to me 10.7   you learn a lot in it 46.9

35. I think this teacher uses grades mainly to: (check one) (N = 299)

    a. help students learn 19.1
    b. judge students' progress 59.2
    c. punish and reward 8.0
    d. compare students, for college and jobs 11.7
       (multiple answer) 1.3

36. Which of the following do you like most about your teacher?
    (check one)   (N = 299)

    a. is a good entertainer 5.0
    b. keeps good order in class 4.3
    c. shows personal interest in students 20.1
    d. makes subject interesting 33.8
    e. knows what he or she is doing 2.14
    f. other 7.7
       (multiple answer) 7.7

37. Which of the following do you dislike the most about your
    teacher? (check one) (N = 257)

    a. lets class run him (or her) 9.3
    b. not interested in the students as people 8.9
    c. tries to be "one of the students" 8.2
    d. doesn't know what he (she) is doing 4.7; (disorganized) 5.1
    e. plays favorites 6.6
    f. is too strict (behaviorally) 7.0; (academically) 11.7
    g. other (nothing) 19.1
       other 16.7
       (multiple answer) 2.3

III. FAIRNESS: ("Fairness" is a term that is hard to pin down, that
     is different for all of us. Thinking of school in general, which
     of the instances below would you call "fair" and which "unfair"?)

	Percent Fair	Percent Unfair	Percent Neutral	N
38. teacher grades you on the opinions you express	24.0	52.3	23.7	304
39. teacher gives zero to student who hands in an assignment a week late	24.0	46.7	29.3	304
40. teacher grades everyone by exactly the same standard	49.3	34.5	16.1	304
41. teacher sends late student without pass to school official	23.5	50.0	26.5	302
42. teacher downgrades a late assignment or test	40.9	36.6	22.4	303
43. teacher pays more attention to students who agree with him or her	5.6	84.8	9.6	303
44. teacher tells student who is talking to a friend to be quiet	71.4	9.9	18.8	304
45. teacher doesn't allow students to criticize him or her in class	16.2	67.7	16.2	303
46. student borrows homework assignment, copies it, and turns it in as his or her own	11.8	67.9	20.3	305
47. teacher changes a student's seat, so he or she can keep an eye on him or her	35.2	34.6	30.2	301
48. when asked why student is given detention, teacher says, "I have my reasons"	3.6	90.5	5.9	304
49. student copies answers from another student's paper while taking exam	7.2	75.7	17.1	304
50. student caught turning in copied test is suspended indefinitely from school	14.5	61.8	23.7	304

	Percent Fair	Percent Unfair	Percent Neutral	N
51. student interrupts another student who is having trouble answering a question	12. 5	63. 8	23. 7	304
52. student turns in another student who cheated on a test	10. 8	61. 0	28. 2	305

IV. BACKGROUND INFORMATION: (The last few questions are of a factual nature. Again, these are only for purposes of describing "types" of answers and groups of students. Your identity will remain entirely confidential and anonymous. (Please fill in appropriately.)

53. Age: N
       15 or under   15. 3%
       16   42. 3
       17   36. 8
       18 or over   5. 5   307

54. Sex: Male 49. 8   Female 50. 2   307

55. Race: White 79. 6   Non-white 20. 4   294

56. Religion: Protestant 31. 4
                Catholic   47. 1
                Jewish   10. 7
                Other   10. 5   280

57. Father's occupation: upper-middle   32. 9
                           middle   27. 4
                           lower-middle (working) 34. 2
                           other   7. 5   255

58. Mother's occupation: upper-middle   13. 5
                           middle   29. 3
                           working   8. 6
                           housewife   47. 7   266

59. Class in school: freshman (9th)   0
                       sophomore (10th) 24. 2
                       junior (11th)   42. 5
                       senior (12th)   33. 3   306

60. How long have you been in this school system?

                       1 year or less   13. 5
                       2-6 years   24. 9
                       7 years or more   61. 7   297

61. What is your course of study? (check <u>one</u>)

business training	25.9
college preparatory	54.8
honors college preparatory	11.0
vocational training	4.0
(other)	4.3

301

62. What are your plans after you graduate from high school?

get a job	18.5
go to four-year liberal arts college	26.4
go to four-year state university	26.1
go to technical school	4.0
go to two-year college	9.9
get a job, and go to school nights	3.3
other	8.6
(don't know)	3.3

303

63. What is your grade average in school?

A	27.9
B	46.3
C and under	24.9

294

BOOKS

Ashton-Warner, Sylvia. Teacher. New York: Simon & Schuster, 1963.

Averch, Harvey A., Carroll, Stephen J., Donaldson, Theodore S., Kiesling, Herbert J., and Pincus, John. How Effective is Schooling? A Critical Review and Synthesis of Research Findings. Prepared for President's Commission on School Finance. Santa Monica, Calif.: Rand Corporation, 1972.

Benn, S. I., and Peters, R. S. The Principles of Political Thought. New York: Free Press, 1959.

Berg, Ivar. Education and Jobs: The Great Training Robbery. Boston: Beacon Press, 1971.

Berlin, Isaiah. Four Essays on Liberty. London: Oxford University Press, 1969.

Bowles, Samuel, and Gintis, Herbert. Schooling in Capitalist America. New York: Basic Books, 1976.

Bronfenbrenner, Urie. Two Worlds of Childhood. New York: Russell Sage Foundation, 1970.

Bruner, Jerome S. The Process of Education. New York: Vintage Books, 1963.

Callahan, Raymond E. Education and the Cult of Efficiency. Chicago: University of Chicago Press, 1962.

Carnoy, Martin, and Levin, Henry M. The Limits of Educational Reform. New York: David McKay, 1976.

Cicourel, Aaron V., and Kitsuse, John I. The Educational Decision-Makers. Indianapolis: Bobbs-Merrill, 1963.

Coleman, James S. Adolescents and the Schools. New York: Basic Books, 1965.

Coleman, James S. , Campbell, E. Q. , Hobson, C. J. , McPartland, J. , Mood, A. M. , Weinfeld, F. D. , and York, R. L. Equality of Educational Opportunity. Washington D. C. : U. S. Government Printing Office, 1966.

Corwin, Ronald G. A Sociology of Education. New York: Appleton Century Crofts, 1965.

Dawson, Richard E. , and Prewitt, Kenneth. Political Socialization. Boston: Little, Brown, 1969.

Dennison, George. The Lives of Children. New York: Vintage Books, 1969.

Dewey, John. Democracy and Education. New York: Free Press, paperback edition, 1966.

Dexter, Lewis Anthony. The Tyranny of Schooling: An Inquiry into the Problem of "Stupidity." New York: Basic Books, 1964.

Dreeben, Robert. On What Is Learned in School. Reading, Mass. : Addison-Wesley, 1968.

Elkind, David. Children and Adolescents. New York: Oxford University Press, 1970.

Fein, Leonard J. The Ecology of the Public Schools: An Inquiry into Community Control. New York: Pegasus, 1971.

Friedenberg, Edgar. Coming of Age in America. New York: Vintage Books, 1965.

Goffman, Erving. Asylums. Garden City, N. Y. : Anchor Books, 1961.

Goodman, Paul. Compulsory Mis-Education and the Community of Scholars. New York: Vintage Books, 1964.

Greeley, Andrew M. , and Rossi, Peter M. The Education of Catholic Americans. Chicago: Aldine, 1966.

Guskin, Alan E. , and Guskin, Samuel L. A Social Psychology of Education. Reading, Mass. : Addison-Wesley, 1970.

Guthrie, James W. , Kleindorfer, George B. , Lenn, Henry M. , and
    Stout, Robert T. Schools and Inequality. Cambridge, Mass. :
    MIT Press, 1971.

Henry, Jules. Culture Against Man. New York: Vintage Books, 1965.

Henry, Nelson B. Dynamics of Instructional Groups: Socio-Psycho-
    logical Aspects of Teaching and Learning. The 59th Yearbook
    of the National Society for the Study of Education. Chicago:
    University of Chicago Press, 1960.

Hess, Robert D. , and Torney, Judith V. The Development of Political
    Attitudes in Children. Garden City, N. Y. : Anchor Books, 1967.

Holt, John. How Children Fail. New York: Dell, Delta Books, 1964.

Illich, Ivan. Deschooling Society. New York: Harper & Row, 1971.

Jackson, Philip W. Life in Classrooms. New York: Holt, Rinehart
    and Winston, 1968.

Jencks, Christopher, and Smith, Marshall, Acland, Henry, Bane,
    Mary Jo, Cohen, David, Gintis, Herbert, Heyns, Barbara,
    Michelson, Stephan. Inequality: A Reassessment of the Effect
    of Family and Schooling in America. New York: Basic Books,
    1972.

Jones, Richard M. Fantasy and Feeling in Education. New York:
    Colophon Books, 1968.

Katz, Michael B. Class, Bureaucracy and Schools: The Illusion of
    Educational Change in America. New York: Praeger, 1971.

_____. The Irony of Early School Reform. Boston: Beacon Press, 1968.

Kohl, Herbert. The Open Classroom. New York: Vintage Books,
    1969.

Kozol, Jonathan. Death at an Early Age. Boston: Houghton Mifflin,
    1967.

Levine, Donald M. , and Bane, Mary Jo. The "Inequality" Contro-
    versy: Schooling and Distributive Justice. New York: Basic
    Books, 1975.

Massialas, Byron G. Education and the Political System. Reading, Mass.: Addison-Wesley, 1969.

Minogue, Kenneth R. The Liberal Mind. New York: Vintage Books, 1963.

Mosteller, Frederick, and Moynihan, Daniel P. On Equal Educational Opportunity. New York: Random House, 1972.

National Commission on the Reform of Secondary Education. The Reform of Secondary Education. New York: McGraw-Hill, 1973.

Neill, A. S. Summerhill: A Radical Approach to Child Learning. New York: Hart, 1960.

Pateman, Carole. Participation and Democratic Theory. Cambridge: Cambridge University Press, 1970.

Patrick, John J. Political Socialization of American Youth: Implications for Secondary School Social Studies. Research Bulletin no. 3. Washington, D. C.: National Council for the Social Studies, n.d.

Pennock, J. Roland, and Chapman, John W., eds. Nomos IX: Equality. New York: Atherton Press, 1967.

Peters, R. S. Ethics and Education. London: Allen & Unwin, 1970.

Postman, Neil, and Weingartner, Charles. Teaching as a Subversive Activity. New York: Delacorte Press, 1969.

Reimer, Everett. School Is Dead—Alternatives in Education. New York: Doubleday, 1971.

Rich, John Martin. Education and Human Values. Reading, Mass.: Addison-Wesley, 1968.

Rist, Ray C. The Urban School: A Factory for Failure. Cambridge, Mass.: MIT Press, 1973.

Rosenthal, Robert, and Jacobson, Lenore. Pygmalion in the Classroom: Teacher Expectation and Pupils' Intellectual Development. New York: Holt, Rinehart and Winston, 1968.

Rousseau, Jean Jacques. Emile. Translated and edited by William
    Boyd. New York: Teachers College Press, 1967.

Sarason, Seymour B. The Culture of the School and the Problem of
    Change. Boston: Little, Brown, 1969.

Sartori, Giovanni. Democratic Theory. Westport, Conn.: Green-
    wood Press, 1962.

Sexton, Patricia Cayo. Education and Income: Inequalities in Our
    Public Schools. New York: Viking Press, 1961.

____. The Feminized Male. New York: Vintage Books, 1969.

Silberman, Charles E. Crisis in the Classroom. New York: Random
    House, 1970.

____, ed. The Open Classroom Reader. New York: Vintage Books,
    1973.

Snyder, Benson R. The Hidden Curriculum. New York: Knopf, 1971.

Spring, Joel. Education and the Rise of the Corporate State. Boston:
    Beacon Press, 1972.

Sykes, Gresham M. A Society of Captives: A Study of Maximum Se-
    curity Prisons. Princeton, N.J.: Princeton University Press,
    1958.

Tawney, R. H. Equality. London: Unwin Books, 1964.

Thompson, Dannis F. The Democratic Citizen. Cambridge: Cam-
    bridge University Press, 1970.

de Tocqueville, Alexis. Democracy in America. New York: Vintage
    Books, 1945.

Verba, Sidney, and Nie, Norman H. Participation in America: Po-
    litical Democracy and Social Equality. New York: Harper &
    Row, 1972.

Waller, Willard. The Sociology of Teaching. New York: Wiley, 1932.

Weissberg, Robert. Political Learning, Political Choice, and Demo-
    cratic Citizenship. Englewood Cliffs, N.J.: Prentice-Hall, 1974.

White, Ralph K., and Lippitt, Ronald. Autocracy and Democracy—
An Experimental Inquiry. New York: Harper & Bros., 1960.

Young, Michael. The Rise of the Meritocracy. Baltimore: Penguin,
1971.

ARTICLES AND REPORTS

Ashton-Warner, Sylvia. "Spearpoint." Saturday Review of Education, 40 (June 24, 1972): 33ff.

Bidwell, Charles F. "The School as a Formal Organization." In
Handbook of Organizations, edited by James G. March. Chicago: Rand McNally, 1965, pp. 972-1023.

Boocock, Sarane S. "The School as a Social Environment for Learning: Social Organization and Micro-Social Processes in Education." Sociology of Education 46 (Winter 1973): 15-50.

Conklin, Kenneth R. "Due Process in Grading: Bias and Authority."
School Review 11 (November 1972): 85-95.

Deitsch, Morton. "The Effects of Cooperation and Competition upon
Group Processes." Group Dynamics: Research and Theory,
edited by Dorwin Cartwright and Alvin Zander. Evanston, Ill.:
Row, Peterson, 1953, pp. 414-49.

Ecstein, Harry. "Authority Patterns: A Structural Basis for Political
Inquiry." American Political Science Review 67 (December
1973): 1142-61.

Flanders, Ned A. "Diagnosing and Utilizing Social Structures in
Classroom Learning." Dynamics of Instructional Groups: So-
cio-Psychological Aspects of Teaching and Learning. The 59th
Yearbook of the National Society for the Study of Education.
Chicago: University of Chicago Press, 1960, pp. 187-217.

Getzels, Jacob W., and Thelen, Herbert A. "The Classroom Group
as a Unique Social System." In Dynamics of Instructional
Groups: Socio-Psychological Aspects of Teaching and Learning,
edited by Nelson B. Henry. Chicago: University of Chicago
Press, 1960, pp. 56-83.

Gibb, Jack R. "Socio-Psychological Processes of Group Instruction."
    In Dynamics of Instructional Groups: Socio-Psychological As-
    pects of Teaching and Learning, edited by Nelson B. Henry.
    Chicago: University of Chicago Press, 1960, pp. 115-35.

Greenstein, Fred I. "A Note on the Ambiguity of 'Political Socializa-
    tion'" Definitions, Criticism, and Strategies of Inquiry."
    Journal of Politics 32 (November 1970): 969-79.

Jenkins, D. H. "Characteristics and Functions of Leadership in
    Instructional Groups." In Dynamics of Instructional Groups:
    Socio-Psychological Aspects of Teaching and Learning, edited
    by Nelson B. Henry. Chicago: University of Chicago Press,
    pp. 164-84.

Jennings, M. Kent, and Niemi, Richard G. Patterns of Political
    Learning." Harvard Educational Review 38 (Summer 1968):
    443-67.

Kohlberg, Lawrence, and Lockwood, Alan. "Cognitive-Developmen-
    tal Psychology and Political Education—Progress in the Sixties."
    Mimeographed. Cambridge, Mass.: Harvard University.

Langton, Kenneth P. "Peer Group and School and the Political So-
    cialization Process." American Political Science Review 61
    (September 1967): 751-58.

_____. and Jennings, M. Kent. "Political Socialization and the High
    School Civics Curriculum in the United States." American Po-
    litical Science Review 62 (September 1968): 852-58.

Lippitt, Ronald, and White, Ralph K. "An Experimental Study of
    Leadership and Group Life." In Readings in Social Psychology,
    edited by Guy E. Swanson, Theodore M. Newcomb, and Eugene
    L. Hartley. Rev. ed. New York: Holt, 1952, pp. 340-55.

Lipsky, Michael. "Toward a Theory of Street-Level Bureaucracy."
    Paper delivered at the annual meeting of the American Political
    Science Association. New York, September 1969.

Litt, Edgar. "Civic Education, Community Norms, and Political
    Indoctrination." American Sociological Review 28 (February
    1968): 64-75.

Medley, Donald M., and Mitzel, Harold L. "Measuring Classroom
   Behavior by Systematic Observation." In Handbook of Research
   on Teaching, edited by N. L. Gage. Chicago: Rand McNally,
   1963, pp. 247–328.

Merelman, Richard M. "The Adolescence of Political Socialization."
   Sociology of Education 45 (Spring 1970): 134–57.

National Panel on High Schools and Adolescent Education. "The Education of Adolescents: Summary, Conclusions, and Recommendations." Mimeographed. Washington, D. C. : U. S. Office of
   Education, Department of Health, Education, and Welfare.

Parsons, Talcott. "The School Class as a Social System: Some of Its
   Functions in American Society." Socialization and the Schools.
   Harvard Educational Review reprint, 1968, pp. 69–90.

"Perspectives on Inequality: A Reassessment of the Effect of Family
   and Schooling in America," Harvard Educational Review 43,
   no. 1 (1973): 37–165.

Rhea, Buford. "Institutional Paternalism in High School," Urban
   Review 2, no. 4 (February 1968): 13ff.

Schaar, John H. "Equality of Opportunity and Beyond." In Nomos
   IX: Equality, edited by Roland Pennock and John W. Chapman.
   New York: Atherton Press, 1967, pp. 228-50.

Spilerman, Seymour. "Raising Academic Motivation in Lower Class
   Adolescents: A Consequence of Two Research Traditions."
   Sociology of Education 44 (Winter 1971): 103-18.

Susskind, Edwin C. "The Role of Question-Asking in the Elementary
   School Classroom." In The Psycho-Educational Clinic—Papers
   and Research Studies, edited by Frances Kaplan and Seymour
   B. Sarason. Boston: Massachusetts Department of Mental Health
   Monograph, n. d., pp. 130-51.

Turner, Ralph H. "Modes of Social Ascent Through Education: Sponsored and Contest Mobility." In Education, Economy, and Society, edited by A. H. Halsey, Jean Floud, and C. Arnold
   Anderson. New York: Free Press, 1961, pp. 121-39.

Washburne, Chandler. "Conflicts Between Educational Theory and
   Structure." Educational Theory 3, no. 2 (April 1959): 91-94.

Zeigler, Harmon, and Peak, Wayne. "The Political Functions of the Educational System." Sociology of Education 43, no. 2 (Spring 1970): 115-43.

Ziblatt, David. "High School Extra-Curricular Activities and Political Socialization." Annals of the Academy of Political and Social Science 361 (September 1965): 20-21.

EDWARD P. MORGAN is assistant professor of government at Lehigh University, Bethlehem, Pennsylvania. Before 1976, he was assistant professor of government at Oberlin College, Oberlin, Ohio, and previously was acting executive director of the Special Commission on Unequal Educational Opportunity, Massachusetts General Court, Boston, Massachusetts.

Mr. Morgan has written in the overlapping areas of politics and education. Of relevance to this work are School Finance Reform in Massachusetts, 1975 (Interim Report, Special Commission on Unequal Educational Opportunity), "Democracy and the High School: The Political Structure of Classroom Learning" (Ph. D. dissertation, Brandeis University), and essay reviews published in Alternatives (Oberlin, Ohio).

Mr. Morgan holds a B. A. degree from Oberlin College and an M. A. and Ph. D. from Brandeis University, Waltham, Massachusetts.

CARRASCOLENDAS: Bilingual Education Through
Television

Frederick Williams and
Geraldine Van Wart

CHILDREN'S TELEVISION: An Analysis of Pro-
gramming and Advertising

F. Earle Barcus with
Rachel Wolkin

PLURALISM IN A DEMOCRATIC SOCIETY

edited by Melvin M. Tumin
and Walter Plotch

SPECIAL EDUCATION: A Sociological Study of
California Programs

Carl Milofsky